The Counselor
as Gatekeeper

SOCIAL INTERACTION IN INTERVIEWS

LANGUAGE, THOUGHT, AND CULTURE: *Advances in the*
Study of Cognition

Under the Editorship of: E. A. HAMMEL

DEPARTMENT OF ANTHROPOLOGY
UNIVERSITY OF CALIFORNIA
BERKELEY

Michael Agar, Ripping and Running: A Formal Ethnography of Urban Heroin Addicts

Brent Berlin, Dennis E. Breedlove, and Peter H. Raven, Principles of Tzeltal Plant Classification: An Introduction to the Botanical Ethnography of a Mayan-Speaking People of Highland Chiapas

Mary Sanches and Ben Blount, Sociocultural Dimensions of Language Use

Daniel G. Bobrow and Allan Collins, Representation and Understanding: Studies in Cognitive Science

Domenico Parisi and Francesco Antinucci, Essentials of Grammar

Elizabeth Bates, Language and Context: The Acquisition of Pragmatics

Ben G. Blount and Mary Sanches, Sociocultural Dimensions of Language Change

Susan Ervin-Tripp and Claudia Mitchell-Kernan (Eds.), Child Discourse

Lynn A. Friedman (Ed.), On the Other Hand: New Perspectives on American Sign Language

Eugene S. Hunn, Tzeltal Folk Zoology: The Classification of Discontinuities in Nature

Jim Schenkein (Ed.), Studies in the Organization of Conversational Interaction

David Parkin, The Cultural Definition of Political Response: Lineal Destiny Among the Luo

Stephen A. Tyler, The Said and the Unsaid: Mind, Meaning, and Culture

Susan Gal, Language Shift: Social Determinants of Linguistic Change in Bilingual Austria

Ronald Scollon and Suzanne B. K. Scollon, Linguistic Convergence: An Ethnography of Speaking at Fort Chipewyan, Alberta

Elizabeth Bates, The Emergence of Symbols: Cognition and Communication in Infancy

Mary LeCron Foster and Stanley H. Brandes (Eds.), Symbol as Sense: New Approaches to the Analysis of Meaning

Willett Kempton, The Folk Classification of Ceramics: A Study of Cognitive Prototypes

Charles Goodwin, Conversational Organization: Interaction between Speakers and Hearers

P. L. F. Heelas and A. J. Lock (Eds.), Indigenous Psychologies: The Anthropology of the Self

Frederick Erickson and Jeffrey Shultz, The Counselor as Gatekeeper: Social Interaction in Interviews

In preparation
Louise Cherry Wilkinson (Ed.), Communicating in the Classroom

The Counselor as Gatekeeper

SOCIAL INTERACTION IN INTERVIEWS

Frederick Erickson

College of Education
Michigan State University
East Lansing, Michigan

Jeffrey Shultz

Department of Educational Leadership
College of Education
University of Cincinnati
Cincinnati, Ohio

ACADEMIC PRESS
A Subsidiary of Harcourt Brace Jovanovich, Publishers
New York   London
Paris   San Diego   San Francisco   São Paulo
Sydney   Tokyo   Toronto

ACADEMIC PRESS, INC.
111 Fifth Avenue, New York, New York 10003

United Kingdom Edition published by
ACADEMIC PRESS, INC. (LONDON) LTD.
24/28 Oval Road, London NW1 7DX

Library of Congress Cataloging in Publication Data

Erickson, Frederick.
    The counselor as gatekeeper: Social interaction in interviews

    (Language, thought, and culture)
    Bibliography: p.
    Includes index.
    1. Student counselors. 2. Interviews. 3. Personnel
service in education. I. Shultz, Jeffrey J. II. Title.
III. Series.
LB1027.5.E68   371.4   81-19043
ISBN 0-12-240580-3   AACR2

PRINTED IN THE UNITED STATES OF AMERICA

82 83 84 85   9 8 7 6 5 4 3 2 1

Contents

8
Some Implications for Practice and for Research

Appendix A
Scoring Comembership Levels for the Interviews

Appendix B
Equipment and Its Use in Filming and Recording

Appendix C
Examples of Summary Tables and Corresponding Examples of Transcripts

Appendix D
Descriptions of "Uncomfortable Moments" and "Asymmetry Segments" Coding and Procedures

References

Subject Index

Foreword

The immediate subject of this book is college counseling, but it raises broader theoretical issues concerning verbal interaction and the role of sociocultural and language difference in public affairs, which are in many ways basic to modern social theory. The work has its intellectual antecedents in the writings of Sapir and Whorf, who were the first to discuss the communicative implications of language and culture in systematic terms. However, Erickson and Shultz depart from the conventional anthropological practice of comparing our own society with lesser-known tribal groups to focus on an urban research site that reflects in microcosm many of the comparative issues of ethnic and social diversity.

A city junior college counselor's office would at first glance hardly seem a natural candidate for research on the communicative consequences of ethnicity. Although both interviewers and interviewees come from a variety of different backgrounds, their interactions within the counseling context are for the most part routine and have few of the characteristics we commonly associate with intergroup tensions. Erickson and Shultz demonstrate that underneath the surface of what, to the outsider, seem quite unremarkable ordinary encounters, subconscious, taken-for-granted sociocultural conventions are at work which, when they are not shared, significantly affect what is achieved in the encounter.

The methodology employed to reveal the workings of these factors can best be compared to that of the naturalist microphotographer who relies on special lenses to reveal the unfolding of processual detail, thereby enabling us to see features of the interaction that would otherwise escape attention and to understand the part that these features play in making up the larger phenomenon. The theoretical perspective and the analytical techniques illustrated in the book are timely. Many of us who have been involved in sociolinguistic research since its inception realize that we have reached a crossroads where anthropologists' microethnographic studies of interactive behavior, sociologists' conversational analyses, and linguists' studies of discourse coherence are beginning to come together to provide for new interpretive approaches to sociolinguistic phenomena. The methods that Erickson and Shultz employ are situated at this crossroads.

The work is more than a mere exercise in analysis. Counseling is charactistic of the selection processes of modern industrialized society that channel access to education and occupational opportunity and mediate individuals' relations to public institutions. We tend to think of these procedures as basically instrumental ways of evaluating ability and performance. Since they rely on empirically verifiable, quantified measures and are governed by set, publicly available rules of conduct, it is assumed that they avoid the bias inherent in other informal means of assessment where personal opinion, social background, and the access it provides to face networks often count for more than technical ability. But with the growth of social mobility and the increase in diversity of the populations that the new evaluative procedures are intended to serve, their impartiality has once more been placed in doubt. Despite official efforts to equalize opportunity, educational institutions and places of employment continue to be stratified along class and ethnic lines, and selection mechanisms are singled out as a major factor in perpetuating these inequities. Attempts to explain the problem have so far focused primarily on overt content or on outcomes, as if bias were exclusively a matter of cultural stereotype or personal intent. The analysis of counseling as a verbal process shows that additional hitherto unnoticed responses to interactive cues are involved.

Such cues are essential to interpretation in conversational exchanges of all kinds; but given the social definitions of counseling in our society, they can materially affect both the quality of the encounter and the nature of the information conveyed. By calling attention to automatic conversational processes that may ultimately constrain career placement, this study points the way toward a type of sociolinguistic analysis that is theoretically innovative, novel, and socially relevant.

JOHN J. GUMPERZ
University of California, Berkeley

Preface

This book deals with what happens in counseling interviews in which academic advising is done. More generally, it is a study of *institutional gatekeeping*—that is, brief encounters in which two persons meet, usually as strangers, with one of them having authority to make decisions that affect the other's future. Institutional gatekeeping is ubiquitous in modern societies. Gatekeeping situations occur not only in educational settings at all levels but also in business, medicine, law, social work, and in other "human services" settings. Throughout the life cycle one finds oneself from time to time in circumstances of talking to "The Man"—the person in authority.

Gatekeeping encounters are done through first-hand talk. Because of this, the main topic of this book is face-to-face communication—the social organization and cultural patterning of speech and nonverbal action and the processes of inference and coordination through which meaning is assigned and cooperation is maintained in communicative action. Talking face-to-face in ways that are both intelligible and appropriate involves an intimate interpersonal partnership. This study considers some of the terms of that partnership and some of the ways in which difficulties occur when the partnership is not complete.

The book is addressed to diverse audiences. What is "figure" for one reader may be "ground" for another. Practitioners and teachers of academic counseling and therapeutic counseling may be most interested in implications of this study for improving communication in counseling, while linguists and those who study nonverbal communication may be more interested in details of the analysis of discourse, body motion, and interpersonal distance. Policymakers may be most interested in what the book has to say about issues of ethnic, racial, and social class equity in gatekeeping interviewing, and about implications for the hiring and training of interviewers and counselors. Sociolinguists may be interested in gatekeeping encounters as scenes in which speech style and interactional style become grounds for social evaluation. Anthropologists and sociologists will probably focus on discussions of cultural patterns of communication and its social organization, with interest in how a close look at face-to-face relations inside the gatekeeping encounter illuminates our understanding of patterns and forces that can also be studied at the societal level. Issues such as maintenance or change in cultural boundaries and ethnic, racial, and social class stratification can be seen through our analysis as in part interactionally produced, "from the bottom up," as well as societally reproduced, "from the top down."

We have tried to accommodate multiple audiences in two ways: first, by avoiding technical terms as much as possible and by not adopting any one special field's terminology and theoretical presuppositions exclusively; and second, by organizing the book so that it can be read in various ways, depending on the reader's main interests.

Nonspecialists may still find the book too technical, whereas specialists may find that it ignores important fine distinctions made in their particular fields of study. This is due in part to what we have set out to do: a *microethnographic* study of face-to-face interaction. That approach is still in its infancy. We believe it should be deliberately eclectic. It is necessary to account adequately on the one hand for the situation of the communication event—that is, its social and cultural context—and on the other hand to pay very close attention to the organization of verbal and nonverbal action within the event, displaying in detail the behavioral evidence on which the analytic claims rest. This requires a commitment both to scope and to specificity, bringing together levels and kinds of analysis usually held separate by linguists, anthropologists, sociologists, and social psychologists. The tensions inherent in this eclecticism are necessary in a unified, holistic study of communication face-to-face.

Given their different interests, readers can cover the chapters of the book in different sequences. The first two chapters introduce the issues to be considered. They prefigure evidence and conclusions reported later. The last two chapters broadly summarize evidence, conclusions, and implications of the research. The middle chapters and the appendices are much more detailed. They discuss research design and procedures, and they report evidence of the social and cultural organization of communication in face-to-face interaction.

Readers with general and "applied" interests might read the initial and final pairs of chapters first, and then read selectively in the middle chapters. Specialists in academic disciplines will find their main interests most fully discussed in particular sections within the middle chapters, but it is suggested that the intitial two chapters be read first, since they provide necessary framing for what follows.

This is primarily a research report. It is not a manual of procedures to prevent cross-cultural miscommunication, or to prevent miscommunication resulting from any of the myriad other reasons that people come to "miss" each other interactionally. The book may be of use to those who are concerned with the improvement of communication in academic advising, or in more therapeutic kinds of counseling and interviewing, or in supervisory interaction in schools, workplaces, social service agencies, and governmental settings. If the book proves useful it will not be because it prescribes specific remedies, but because it provides relatively new ways of thinking about the nature of conversation face-to-face—about its tremendous complexity and the delicate interactional balancing required in its performance.

ACKNOWLEDGMENTS

Many people have influenced this work, directly and indirectly. Special thanks are due to Edward T. Hall, whose creative teaching and generous support inspired the work and enabled its beginning. Adam Kendon, William Condon, and Paul Byers provided advice, as did colleagues at the Harvard Graduate School of Education: Beatrice Whiting, Victoria Steinitz, Karen Watson-Gegeo, and especially Courtney Cazden. Invaluable guidance and encouragement came from John and Jenny Gumperz and also from Hugh Mehan, Ray McDermott, and Susan Philips. Readers will notice our intellectual debt to Gregory Bateson, Eliot Chapple, Ray Birdwhistell, Albert Scheflen, Erving Goffman, and Dell Hymes.

Principal grants for the study came during 1970–1973 from the National Institute of Mental Health through its Center for Studies of Metropolitan Problems (Projects MH 18230 and MH 21460). We thank the Center's first director, Steven Baratz, for supporting what was then a new kind of research. Additional support came from the Ford Foundation through the generosity of Basil Whiting.

Carolyn Leonard-Dolan collaborated in the early stages of the research and helped develop procedures for coding nonverbal behavior. Patrice Williamson-Baker, Jacqueline Reed, and Jack McFadden provided administrative and logistical support. Assistance in filming and videotaping came from Gerald Temaner and James Morisette of the Office of Institutional Resources, University of Illinois at Chicago Circle. Veronica Maleckar and Judith Rumler typed a difficult manuscript carefully and with forbearance.

Our informants and their institutions deserve much gratitude. It must be offered anonymously here. The counselors we studied were decent and competent people who worked in conditions that were often difficult. We have tried to portray them as such in our research.

To all, many thanks.

Gatekeeping in Counseling: Processes of Social Selection in Face-to-Face Interaction

AN INTERVIEW

On a day during spring semester in a junior college, a student walks down the hall on the way to the counselor's office. The hall is long and is lined on both sides with lockers. It reminds one of a high school corridor in a school built in the 1920s. On the right side of the hall is the door to the counseling department. The student enters and checks in at the counter where the receptionist sits. Then he takes a chair in the waiting area, which is in the front part of one large room.

After a while his name is called. He goes behind the counter into a section of the room honeycombed with counselors' offices. They are cubicles, really, about 15 of them, separated by frosted glass partitions that do not reach to the ceiling. Each office has an open doorway, and from all the cubicles comes a constant buzzing of voices.

The counselor gets up from his chair and greets the student as he enters the office.

"How ya doin', Jim?"

"OK."

"Good...have a seat." They both sit. "Do you plan on returning next semester?"

"Yes."

The counselor hands the student a registration card and asks him to fill it out. There is a period of silence as he does so, hunched over the card. The student sits up and looks across at the counselor, who leans forward and asks some questions.

"OK, let's have some grades from last semester...English 101... what did you get for a grade?"

"A."

"How about Math 95?"

"C."

As the student answers, the counselor writes the grades in the student's cumulative record folder which is open before him on the desk. They finish up the grades from last semester, and then the counselor asks about the current semester, looking down at the student's program card in the cumulative folder:

"This semester...English 102?"

"You mean, uh..." The student shifts in his chair as the counselor looks up and changes seating position.

"No, no... these are the courses you're taking. English 102."

"Yes."

"Math 96."

"No, I dropped that." The student leans forward and the counselor looks up.

"How come?"

"Well, 'cause it...the only time they had was at 6 to 7:15 and it was kinda late 'cause I start at 8 every morning." The counselor looks down again at the program card.

"Mech Tech 205?"

"Yeah."

The counselor goes on checking the rest of the courses the student is taking this semester. Then the counselor asks about the future.

"You're gonna stay in the Mech Tech program?"

"Yeah."

The counselor checks the requirements for this major in the school catalog and then he and the student pick the courses for next fall semester. After that the counselor asks, "Where do you intend to go from here, Jim?... as far as college or school?"

"Maybe State Tech...for a while."

"Have you been checking any other catalogs up in our library?"

"No." The counselor leans back in his chair.

"What you should start doing now is..." The counselor gives advice about how to check to make sure the courses the student has taken will transfer to the 4-year school the student plans to go to next. Then he gives some advice about what to do about registering next fall—get a fall catalog in the late summer, check on the times the requisite courses will be offered, and make up a course program before going to register on the assigned day so that "When you stand in line you know exactly what you're looking for."

"Mhm."

"Otherwise you wait till that day and you'll be pushed around quite a bit."

"Yeah."

"Trying to see what classes are open and so on."

"Mhm." The counselor leans forward.

"OK. Any questions?"

"No." The counselor and the student rise from their chairs together.

"All set?"

"Yup."

"Let's do well this semester, now."

"OK." The student leaves.

This is a quite perfunctory conversation. The counselor has many students to see each day, and about 10 minutes to spend with each one. The school requires each student to see a counselor before registering for the next semester, so the main purpose of the interview is to plan the student's academic program. After he has seen hundreds of students, the planning process becomes routine for the counselor.

There is an invarying sequence of topics in the interview. Across this sequence the planning of the student's program gets done. First the counselor asks what the student has been doing in the current semester and in the previous one—what courses have been taken, what grades have been received. Then the counselor asks what the student's future plans are. On the basis of the student's replies, the counselor gives advice about what to do in the coming semester—what courses to take, what information to seek about future schooling or employment. After giving this advice the counselor says good-bye and waits for the next student. Most interviews last 10 to 12 minutes.

THE INTERVIEW AS A SOCIAL OCCASION

Though such a conversation seems very ordinary and straightforward, in some ways it is quite unlike other conversations that occur in everyday life. It is not a casual chat among acquaintances face-to-face or on the telephone. Nor is it the kind of conversation that occurs as a background accompaniment to another social activity, as in the talk people engage in while doing work together. In the counseling interview, communication is in the foreground of attention.

Typically the interview is an encounter among strangers who are unequal in authority and in familiarity with the conversational routines of the interview. It is an essential task of the senior person in the encounter to inquire into, and then officially ratify, *who the junior person is*—who the student is now, and who the student wants to be in the future. It is also practically important that the student find out who the counselor is in order to know how to talk to the counselor, but that importance is unofficial. Officially, it is absolutely essential that the counselor make some determination of who the student is, in order to be able to give advice that makes sense and to help the student pick a reasonable set of courses for the next semester. The counselor is accustomed to a set of usual conversational ways of finding out who the student is and then giving advice. The student may not be familiar with those patterns of interaction.

In this sort of interview the counselor acts as an *institutional gatekeeper*. He or she[1] has the responsibility and the authority to make decisions about the social mobility of the student within the organization—to allow the student to transfer from one course sequence to another, or from the "technical track" to the "academic track"—from preparation for immediate employment after 2 years in a job of relatively low social rank, or to preparation for further study in a 4-year college and subsequent employment in a job of higher rank. In a sense the counselor is tending the gates and channels of mobility not only within the junior college but within the larger society as well.

It could be argued, as it has been by social critics, that these gatekeeping decisions are not real choices, in that the school experience and achievement of students actually has little effect on their future life chances. Recent correlational studies suggest that schools do make a difference in student's later social mobility.[2] If that is in fact the case, then

---

[1] Because virtually all the counselors reported on here were male, as were all but one of the students on whom data are reported here, we will use male personal pronouns throughout most of our discussion, for simplicity's sake.

[2] While earlier studies (Jenks and Brown, 1975; Bowles and Gintis, 1976) suggested that schools have little influence on social mobility, a recent restudy by Jenks *et al.* (1979) suggests that schooling does have an effect on students' life chances. The issue is not clearly resolved either way by correlational studies. What is clear, however, is that, whatever the aggregated effects of schooling, at the level of specific encounters between specific individuals in schools it is possible to see interaction that succeeds or fails at the manifest purpose of the encounter at hand. In this sense, at least, schools clearly do make a difference in individuals' lives.

gatekeeping encounters of the sort we are considering here may be social occasions that have special importance in the social selection process.

Whatever the distribution of access routes and probabilities of mobility in the society as a whole, all the counselors and students we studied said of their own interviews that they assumed the gatekeeping decisions that were made involved genuine choices with actual consequence for the student's future. Whether this is "false consciousness" or not, *from the point of view of the counselors and students* their choices were real and the interview was an important social occasion. A personal future was at stake, contingent at least in part on the decisions being made at that moment. The counselor, as institutionally authorized gatekeeper, had the final and official say.

The Interview as Socially and Culturally Organized Improvisation

On the surface it would seem that so standardized an interview ought to be simple to conduct. It does not seem to be the sort of speech situation that would be of much interest to anyone. Yet the very ordinariness of the occasion and the constraints imposed on it by the press of time, by organizational rules, and by general cultural standards of appropriateness in its conduct make this kind of occasion interesting for the study of communication face-to-face. Despite the overall standardization there are subtly different ways available to play the scene.

Each particular interview is distinctive in subtle ways. In one interview a student may feel affirmed. He may come away thinking that he was given trustable and clear advice. In another a student may feel insulted and confused. He may come away thinking that the counselor was unreasonable and arrogant. A counselor may see the first student of the day as enthusiastic and articulate and the next student who walks through his doorway as disinterested or unable to define clear and realistic goals.

The overall differences among interviews in their character and outcomes are the result of differences in specific communicative choices, made for the most part outside conscious awareness, by the counselor and the student. Of central interest here are the specifics of choice and organization of the communicative means the counselor and student employ. They are choosing from among optional ways of acting together, verbally and nonverbally, in speaking and listening. They have available different ways of asking a question, of answering it, of showing attention while the other person is speaking, of saying to each other in implicit ways, verbally and nonverbally, such interactional *steering messages* as, "The next thing I'm about to say is the most important thing I've said so far," or "That does it! From now on I'm not going to trust anything more you say."

Extremes of communicative choice were avoided in the interviews we studied. No one shouted, or broke into tears, or sang, or switched to a language other than English, or slapped the other person in the face, or, usually, even shook hands. The literal *referential meaning* of what was said explicitly was very similar in each interview: the literal meaning of talk about course numbers, programs of courses, future jobs, and choices in these areas. What differed was the metaphoric *social meaning*[3] implicit in what was said and done, that is, ways of talking about the referential content that implied approval or disapproval of the student's plans and hopes.

Given the limited range of options of verbal and nonverbal means of communicating, each choice made carried relatively great social meaning. The economy of available communicative means together with the starkly routinized sequence of topics in this sort of counseling interview makes it especially appropriate for study by those interested in (*a*) the ways by which everyday discourse comes to have distinctive shading in its subtleties of social meaning; and (*b*) the processes of social and cultural organization of communicative behavior and interpretive strategies by which people are able to carry out interaction face-to-face.

Conversation is *socially organized* in that the actions taken by a speaker and a listener together are actions taken in account of what the other is doing then.[4] The social organization of interaction takes place in, in fact is constituted by, the succession of moments in real time. At any moment one party has just done something and is about to do the next thing. The other party or parties take action in account of that immediate past and immediate future. Also, at any moment each party is doing something right then. The other party or parties take action in terms of what the others are doing at that very time.

In the counseling interview this social organization in and across moments of real time is reflexive; who the student is able to be depends in part on how the counselor acts, and who the counselor is able to be is influenced by how the student acts. The ways in which each talks and listens from moment to moment becomes an environment for the other

---

[3] The distinction between referential and social meaning is a crucial one in the fields of sociolinguistics and linguistic pragmatics. For seminal discussions of this distinction, see Austin, 1962; Hymes, 1964; Blom and Gumperz, 1972.

[4] This follows Weber's definition of the social: "A social relationship may be said to exist when several people reciprocally adjust their behavior to each other with respect to the meaning which they give to it, and when this reciprocal adjustment determines the form which it takes [Weber, 1978 (1922): 30]."

party.[5] They are continuously part of one another's immediate social ecology.

Conversation is *culturally organized* in that the options people choose in their ways of acting communicatively and interpreting the communicative actions of others are options learned from and shared with others outside the social occasion in which the communicative knowledge is being practically employed. Cultural conventions or norms provide definitions of what is appropriate and intelligible in communicative action. Knowledge of these conventions involves differing substantive areas, and different patterns of sharing where different kinds of social groups are involved. One substantive area of shared knowledge is that of "language." Talk by persons who speak different languages is not mutually intelligible. In the case of language, the substantive knowledge involved can be said to be shared knowledge of a grammar and a sound system.[6]

Another level of shared knowledge involves that of speech style and other aspects of *ways of speaking* within a given language.[7] Here many different kinds of elements of style in speaking can affect the referential and social meaning of what is said—vocabulary, pronunciation, pitch and tempo, relative elaboration in speech, direction and indirection—and this list is not at all exhaustive. Shared knowledge of principles of appropriateness and strategic stylistic preference in ways of speaking is necessary if persons are to understand the subtleties of what is meant by what is said. Knowledge of grammar and sound system by itself is not enough, as can be attested by the experience of anyone who learns a new language or dialect and tries to use it appropriately and effectively among native speakers. Moreover, given the continuous presence to one another of partners in face-to-face interaction, knowledge of culturally stylistic ways of *speaking* is not even enough by itself, without accompanying knowledge of culturally stylistic *ways of listening.*[8] Shared knowledge of style in such things as posture, gesture, eye contact, and the amount and kinds of talk one should do while listening, is necessary if two people are able to communicate effectively face to face.

---

[5] The point is aptly made in terms of the organization of nonverbal behavior by McDermott: "By their behavior members embody our ideas about what a particular context should look like and they accordingly keep us informed as to what they are doing. We are environments for each other [McDermott, 1976: 27]." See also Scheflen, 1973.

[6] On the distinction between knowledge of linguistic code (grammar and sound system) and knowledge of speech style and speech use, see the critique of Chomsky in Hymes, 1974: 145–178 and, in contrast, see Chomsky, 1965.

[7] See Hymes, 1964, 1974: 29–66.

[8] See Erickson, 1979. Our research on listening behavior and the research of others will be extensively discussed in Chapters 4 and 5.

The complete knowledge needed has been called *communicative competence.*[9] It involves not only knowledge of a particular language system, but knowledge of everything else about ways of speaking and ways of listening that one person needs in order to cooperate in the conduct of a conversation with another person who has similar knowledge. Such knowledge is shared in *speech communities.*[10] Within a single linguistic community (a set of people who share knowledge of a grammar and sound system) there may be differing speech communities—subsets of the linguistic community within which people share differing sets of knowledge of ways of speaking.

Diversity of speech communities within the same linguistic community is characteristic of many large-scale multiethnic societies around the world, including the United States.[11] Institutional settings such as schools are places in which strangers who meet to talk together may come from different speech communities even though they are members of the same linguistic community. Because of cultural differences in their knowledge of ways of speaking and ways of listening, they may be unable to cooperate conversationally—each take communicative action in account of the other—as well as they would be if they were members of the same speech community. In this sense, the normative cultural organization of conversation is related to its immediate and emergent social organization. Cultural differences in ways of acting and of interpreting the actions of others can lead to face-to-face interaction which is not adequately *social,* in the sense in which the term is used here.

LOCAL PRODUCTION AS IMPROVISATION

We have said that the social organization and the cultural organization of communication are jointly involved in the conduct of face-to-face interaction. This interaction can be said to be *locally produced* in the taking of practical action of the moment by the particular people who encounter each other in an immediately local face-to-face situation.[12] It is through this *local* production that distinctive *local* nuances of meaning and impression arise.

The production is orderly and institutionalized, yet also creative and spontaneous. We assume here that people apply cultural principles in

[9] See Hymes, 1974: 29–66.
[10] See Gumperz, 1962, 1968.
[11] See the discussions by Hymes in Cazden, Hymes, and John, 1972: xxiv–xxix; by Gumperz and Cook-Gumperz, 1980; by Scollon and Scollon, 1980.
[12] The notion of "local" production of interaction and its meanings for participants is a key concept in the approach taken by "ethnomethodologists" in sociology. See Garfinkel, 1967; Cicourel, 1973; Mehan and Wood, 1975.

their social operating face-to-face, but that the practical application of these normative standards is not done by people in mechanical ways. That is why, although we are now able to program computers to talk, we are unable to build them to act as engaging conversationalists. People can do that, we argue, because they are able to make sense in the immediate circumstances of the local scene from moment to moment in real time.

It is necessary to assume that the normative prescriptions for how to act in practical circumstances are inherently incomplete.[13] They do not provide conversational partners with the specific knowledge that is necessary to accomplish conversation successfully. If one thinks of a conversation as role-playing, it is as if the conversationalists must fill in what is left unspecified on their role cards. If one thinks of conversation as if it were musical performance, it is necessary for the conversationalists to play together by ear.[14] It is useful to draw on analogies from improvisation in the fine arts, and two examples come quickly to mind from drama and music: commedia dell'arte and playing jazz.

In commedia dell'arte, the improvised drama of Renaissance Italy that was performed by troupes of traveling players, there were conventionally fixed characters and plots. One of these characters, Arlecchino (the prototype of Harlequin in the Comédie Française), always languishes in unrequited love. Another character, the aging husband married to a young wife, is inveterately lecherous and continually cuckolded. Another character, the Spanish Captain (the model for Shakespeare's "Ancient Pistol"), always swaggers and curses. But when a plot was actually acted out at a village fair or saint's day festival, the story emerged in performance a bit differently each time. The players, who had traveled together for years, had come to share expectations for each other's ways of adapting together in producing specific spoken lines, gestures, and pratfalls. They were a little speech community in terms of the local production of comedies. There was order in each of their performances, but it was emergent in the doing of the action as well as institutionalized in the culturally shared conventions governing the doing.

Improvisation is also a hallmark of the performance of jazz; such music is played by ear. In jazz performance the institutionalized and emergent aspects of the organization of social action are combined. There is a melody line and a series of chord changes with an inner logic of sequential relationship between successive chords and among successive sets of chords. These define shape and direction in the music. Common under-

[13] See Garfinkel and Sacks, 1970; McDermott, 1976; Gumperz, 1977.
[14] See Meyer, 1956; Sudnow, 1978, 1980.

standings of this are culturally shared among the musicians. But within the constraints of a conventionally agreed-upon musical syntax, improvisation occurs. The constraints provide relatively stable, constitutive turning points around and within which the leeway of choice by each musician becomes possible. As realized in actual performance, the outline of the underlying, agreed-upon musical form is filled in by the combination of the relatively prestructured elements together with the choices made from ranges of options as they become available from moment to moment. What results (except in atonal improvisation) is not apparent chaos and discord, but melody and harmony. These are combinations of sounds that make musical sense as heard simultaneously and in succession. Their organization as coherently hearable musical forms results from cooperative social decision making and action across the real time of the playing.

As it was for the actors and the musicians engaged with others in improvisatory performance, so the counselor's and the student's problem of how to act in the actual performance of their interview is a practical problem of the moment. Such a problem of specific action cannot be solved simply by the application of general guidelines; things must be specified in terms of the circumstances of local production. At the same time, cultural norms provide the general, repeatable guidelines within which improvisation can take place—the themes upon which the variations are done.

A SOCIAL AND CULTURAL ECOLOGY OF
COMMUNICATION, EMPATHY, AND RAPPORT

This book may be of use to those who are concerned with the improvement of communication in academic advising, in more therapeutic kinds of counseling and interviewing, or in supervisory interaction in schools, work places, social service agencies, and governmental settings. If the book proves useful it will not be because it prescribes specific remedies, but because of the perspective it takes toward the nature of communication face to face, and thus to the nature of problems of miscommunication and other interactional troubles.

One thing that is distinctive in this perspective is the view taken toward what is often called *empathy* and *rapport* in the literature on counseling. We do not consider empathy and rapport to be entities residing simply or primarily inside the individuals—residing in "temperament" or "motivation," or "feeling-states" as the individual interacts with others. In our analysis, empathy and rapport are seen as part of an interactional ecosystem—as residing within the structure and process of communication face-to-face, as well as inside the individual engaged in communicating.

This ecological view of the social and cultural organization of relationships of empathy and rapport leads one to pay special attention to the actual behaviors of communication, verbal and nonverbal. Sometimes the attention paid is very close, focusing on detailed aspects of the organization of communicative action. Through detailed analysis and reflection, some of the previously "transparent" principles of order in the action become visible.

Sometimes the attention paid to the organization of behavior is quite general and global. This is equally appropriate for the study of communication, because it seems to be at the global and general level of behavioral gestalts that people form overall impressions of one another during interaction face-to-face. But whether at a specific or at a general level of attention, it is communicative action as socially and culturally organized cooperation—the mutuality and interdependence involved in what the counselor and student are doing together—that is focused on here much more centrally than is usual in the literature of counseling and interviewing. Through that emphasis comes ways of thinking about empathy and rapport which, while they are by no means unique to this book, may seem new to many practitioners and teachers of counseling and interviewing practices.

CONCLUSION

> It is obvious that for the building up of society, its units and subdivisions, and the understandings which prevail among its members some processes of communication are needed. While we often speak of society as though it were a static structure defined by tradition, it is, in the intimate sense, nothing of the kind, but a highly intricate network of partial or complete understandings between the members of organizational units of every degree of size and complexity.... It is only apparently a static sum of social institutions; actually it is being reanimated or creatively reaffirmed from day to day by particular acts of a communicative nature which obtain among individuals participating in it [Sapir 1931: 78].

Sapir points to the reality and importance of the local production of interactional events, and also to the connections between the processes of that production and the wider cultural and social-structural patterns of life in society considered as a whole—patterns he says are being creatively reanimated and reaffirmed in the particular communicative acts of individuals face-to-face. To look at the organization of local production in a gatekeeping interview entirely apart from its wider sociocultural context would be misleading. But equally misleading would be an attempt to consider the *outcomes* of gatekeeping interviews entirely apart from the interactional dynamics of local production by which outcomes are produced. A correlational approach would be especially inappropriate, by itself. Simply to total up the counselor's final gatekeeping decisions, or to summarize student opinions of counselors, and then to correlate these outcome indices with other supposedly causal *social facts* such as ethnicity, social class, or race would be completely to lose sight of the creativity inherent in the practical conduct of social relations face-to-face. The nuances of social meaning available through that creativity give distinctive local significance to the "social fact." Those local meanings and local processes of production are necessarily of interest in a study of the character and outcomes of interethnic contact in gatekeeping encounters.

We have attempted to examine some of the outcomes of gatekeeping in school counseling interviews as well as some of the processes of face-to-face interaction which seem to affect those outcomes. Yet, in our analysis greater emphasis is placed on interaction processes than on their outcomes.

Looking at the interaction itself, from Sapir's perspective, one can see that distinctive shadings of social meaning are communicated in the performance of gatekeeping counseling interviews in spite of, indeed *because of,* their routine general structure. There is a similar sequential order of discourse topics across interviews—an order which manifests an underlying logic of gatekeeping decision making.

But it is not the underlying logic, the interactional *deep structure,* that is essential, for much more is manifested in performance—in communicational *surface structure*—than an underlying abstract logic of gatekeeping. Distinctive packages of social meanings and social identities are also manifested communicatively in each interview. Given the constraints set by time and by rules of conversational etiquette on what can be "said" and "not said" during the interview—explicitly and implicitly, verbally and nonverbally—the social meanings signaled in communicational surface structure are of great significance for the counselor and the student. It is because of those social meanings—the behavioral means by which they are communicated and the inferential means by which they are interpreted—that a student and counselor can come away from the interview thinking that the other person was reasonable or not—that the interview itself had made sense or not. The counselor and the student actively *make sense* in reenacting the social order of the interview. We will argue that as they do so they reenact and revivify a small piece of the social and cultural order of society at large.

2

Social Identity and the Organization of Discourse in the Interviews

BASIC CONCEPTS

The fundamental question posed by the interview is, "Who is this student?" The answer to that question does not appear all at once. It is arrived at cumulatively across real time during the course of interaction. In this chapter we will consider some aspects of what is involved in the gradual, situational revelation of social identity. Before doing this it is necessary to discuss some basic orienting concepts.

Social Identity

This notion is complex and is not considered here as unitary. Social identity can be thought of as a package with diverse contents. Technically it can be defined as a set whose components are various attributes of social status on many different dimensions.[1] A student, for example, may possess all the following attributes: He may be well dressed, be Italian–American, be of working-class family background, be an older brother, work part-time as a cook in a restaurant, have a 3.8 grade point average on a 4-point scale, be a male, look physically fit and active, play

[1] On the notion of multiple dimensions of status and role, see Goodenough, 1965.

left end on the school football team, be enrolled in a data processing program in the junior college. These attributes differ dimensionally in kind. Which subset of attributes and which dimensions will become salient in the counseling interview depends upon the exigencies of the local production of interaction in that particular encounter.

Encounter and Frame

These terms concern patterns of selective attention by participants in social occasions. The encounter has been called a *partially bounded setting*.[2] Within it there are distinct *focuses* of appropriate attention. They can differ across differing encounters. Yet, though these attentional focuses influence what is noticed and left unnoticed in one sort of encounter, as contrasted with another sort, the constraints on focus of attention are never absolute. But despite occasional "leakage" in attentional focus, there is so much more available for attention in any particular encounter than can actually be attended to, that some of what is available for attention is regarded as irrelevant and some is regarded as relevant by the participants in the encounter. In this sense there is a *boundedness* to encounters, albeit a partial boundedness. The encounter becomes to some extent a little world of its own.

Goffman provides an example from chess.[3] Within the game of chess the physical substance out of which the pieces are made is irrelevant. It does not matter for the purposes of playing chess whether a piece is made of gold or of wood. What matters—for chess—is whether the piece is a king or a pawn. Yet whether the chess piece were gold or plastic could be highly relevant in another social "game" (e.g., the "game" of being a museum curator collecting chess sets for an exhibition). Even within the game of chess as actually played, an attribute such as "goldness" that has such great salience in everyday life outside the game itself can momentarily become the object of attentional focus at the same time that one is playing the "official" game of the moment. The chess game, like other encounters, is a partially bounded setting.

The *frame* can be thought of as the boundary itself, standing between the encounter and the world of everyday life outside it.[4] Because the encounter is partially bounded, the frame can be thought of as movable. Placing the attribute of goldness inside the frame of the chess game or leaving it outside the frame as an irrelevant attribute is an option available

[2] See Goffman, 1961: 19–31; Handelman, 1973.
[3] In Goffman, 1961: 19ff.
[4] See Goffman, 1974: 21–40, 40–82; Erickson, 1976: 137–138; Mehan, 1978; Scollon and Scollon, 1980.

to chess players. Framing can also be thought of as a way of defining figure–ground relationships; putting the attribute of goldness in the foreground of distinct attentional focus is quite a different way of framing it than putting it off to the edge of the picture or in the soft focus of a background position.

The frame can also be thought of as semipermeable. Participants in an encounter can be thought of as being able to move attributes of social identity back and forth across the attentional frame boundary. Considering the hypothetical student again, one can see that at any point in an encounter only some of his many attributes of status will be attended to as relevant by the counselor. At one moment the student's grade point average may occupy the center of attentional focus. At another moment the fact that the student is wearing a particularly striking piece of clothing may be what is most salient for the counselor. A wide range of attributes of status of the student and counselor is available to be drawn within the frame of the encounter for attention, in the construction of social identity for particular purposes in the moment at hand.

Universalism–Particularism

Attributes of social identity vary along this dimension, among others.[5] Universalistic attributes are those which potentially could be achieved by any individual, given the requisite motivation, talent, opportunity, and perseverance. In the school counseling interview such attributes include current grades, scores on ability and achievement tests, the courses one has completed, and past academic performance. Ideally, the universalistic attributes of students are the only ones that are supposed to be relevant within the frame of the gatekeeping encounter.

Particularistic attributes of social identity are those which are determined by birth directly or indirectly. Those determined directly by birth include the student's sex, skin color, ethnicity, some physical handicaps, and social class rank. Those influenced more indirectly by birth include cultural attributes, such as the ways of speaking a language or dialect that were learned by the child at home, his or her religious identification,

[5] The distinction is that of Parsons, following the classic contrast in late nineteenth-century sociology between modern and traditional societies (see Toennies, 1887; Maine, 1860; Durkheim, 1893). There is a parallel in the distinction made in modern organization research between the formal and informal social structure of an organization. Parsons (1959) and Dreeben (1968), among others, have used the universalism–particularism contrast in discussing educational settings. Our argument here is that in everyday life in formal organizations such as schools the distinction between universalistic and particularistic standards of assessment is not made in practice nearly so absolutely as it is in Parsons' general theory.

his or her diet and its effects on physical appearance, his or her acquaintance networks. All these particularistic attributes of social identity,
which apply only to some or which are not ordinarily considered relevant
to school performance, ideally should be irrelevant within the frame of
the gatekeeping encounter. They should not, ideally, influence gatekeeping decisions by the counselor, or the manner in which the student
is treated by the counselor in the interview.

In practice, however, there is a tendency for particularistic aspects
of the student's and counselor's social identity to "leak" inside the frame
of the encounter, and sometimes for these attributes to occupy the center
of attention. This tendency was initially identified in earlier research on
academic counseling.[6] In a study of the junior college, Clark (1960) found
that counselors often advised students to adopt academic and occupational goals lower than those the students had when they began to attend
the junior college. This was especially true for students of working-class
background.

In a study of advising about college entrance, Cicourel and Kitsuse
(1963) interviewed high school counselors to learn how the counselors
decided to tell black and white students of various social class backgrounds whether or not they should apply to 4-year colleges at all (and
consequently anticipate a professional or nonprofessional occupation).
They found that black students who had average-to-high academic performance were consistently dissuaded from attending 4-year colleges,
while white students of high socioeconomic rank who had mediocre and
even low academic performance were consistently encouraged to attend.
The authors argued that attributes of social identity such as race and
social class—formally defined as irrelevant—become informally relevant
to counselors' gatekeeping decisions about students.

Neither Clark nor Cicourel and Kitsuse provided in these early studies
an account of the interactional processes by which "unofficial" particularistic attributes of student status became relevant within the gatekeeping counseling encounter (although that is a direction taken in later work
by Cicourel and Kitsuse). Such an account is a main emphasis here.

Performed Social Identity

Performed social identity refers to the composite social identity of
student or counselor that actually was relevant in a given interview. It
is an aggregate of officially and unofficially relevant attributes, particularistic and universalistic, which the counselor and student revealed to

---

[6] See Clark, 1960; Cicourel and Kitsuse, 1963; Trow, 1966; Karabel, 1972.

one another during the course of their encounter. The notion of performed social identity includes three main classes of constituents: (1) official and institutionalized attributes that were not previously recorded in the student's cumulative file (e.g., courses recently dropped or added, current plans to attend summer school or to change major fields, grades recently received); (2) unofficial and emergent attributes that have to do with the quality of the student's interactional performance during the interview itself (e.g., the appropriateness and effectiveness of the student's speaking and listening behavior); and (3) attributes of status that have to do with the student's unofficial and "nonacademic" life outside the frame of the gatekeeping encounter.

Comembership

Comembership is an aspect of performed social identity that involves particularistic attributes of status shared by the counselor and student— for example, race and ethnicity, sex, interest in football, graduation from the same high school, acquaintance with the same individual.[7] Because of ethnic and social class stratification in education, residence, and employment, and because of ethnic and social class culture patterns, shared ethnicity and race increases the likelihood that the counselor and student will find that they have additional particularistic attributes of status in common, but "normative" attributes of status such as ethnicity or social class do not fully predict the potential comembership resources available to any particular counselor–student pair, nor do normative attributes of status predict which aspects of potential comembership will become actual by being invoked and made relevant within the frame of the encounter by the counselor and student as they perform the interview.

Role and Participation Structure

In communicative terms, a *role* is the set of rights and obligations regarding ways of acting and ways of being acted toward which is possessed by an individual occupying a particular social identity. As performed social identity can change from moment to moment during face-to-face interaction, so can the communicative rights and obligations of the individual change from one moment to the next. *Participation struc-*

---

[7] Particularistic comembership is discussed further on pp. 35–37 of this chapter. The influences of this factor are illustrated in Chapters 6 and 7. The way in which comembership "scores" were assigned to each interviewer–student pair in the sample is discussed in Appendix A.

ture[8] can be thought of as the complete set of communicative rights and obligations in the roles of all those engaged in interaction at any moment. The roles of all participants in an encounter are reciprocal and complementary. Communicative roles are reciprocal in that one person's communicative action, such as asking a question, may summon a response by another person in a next moment in time, such as providing an answer to the question asked. Communicative roles are also complementary, in that the completion of one person's communicative action by another takes place not only across successive moments in time, in ping-pong fashion, but completing action also occurs simultaneously with the communicative action being completed (e.g., in the same moment in which a person in the role of speaker is addressing a person in the role of hearer, the hearer is showing attention and understanding through nonverbal [and possibly also through verbal] *listening behavior*).[9] Speaking and listening roles and role behavior are thus simultaneously complementary as well as sequentially reciprocal. Given this interdependence, an intimate kind of conversational cooperation is continually necessary among all the conversational partners engaged in interaction.

Just as the performed social identity and communicative roles of individual participants in an encounter can change from moment to moment as the definition of the situation changes, so participation structure—the total pattern of appropriate ways of acting by all parties engaged in interaction—can change from moment to moment. The dynamic, active quality of redefinition of social identity, communicative role, and participation structure from moment to moment is an essential aspect of the cultural and social organization of local production in interaction face-to-face. It is this which gives distinctive character to each particular occasion of face-to-face interaction (see the discussion of the inherent incompleteness of social and cultural organization in the previous chapter).

Role Conflict of the Gatekeeping Counselor

There is a basic tension inherent in the school counselor's role as a gatekeeper in the academic program-planning interview. On the one hand,

[8] For discussion, see Erickson and Shultz, 1977; Erickson and Mohatt, in press. The notion of participation structure is derived from Philips, 1972, 1975.
[9] The term *listening behavior* is that of Hall (1969). Among the researchers studying listening behavior in relation to speaking behavior, many follow the approach called "context analysis" developed by Birdwistell (1970)—notably Scheflen, 1973; Condon and Ogston, 1967; Kendon, 1977. Other approaches are illustrated in Duncan and Fiske, 1977; Mayo and La France, 1978.

the counselor is to be an objectively rational and impartial decision maker, a judge or actuary tending the gates of mobility within the institution. On the other hand the counselor is to be the sponsor and advocate of the student's interests.

This is a generic tension for the educational professional in a society like the United States. Waller[10] found the same conflict inherent in the role of teacher: tension between making impartial judgments on behalf of the general interests of the school institution and of society at large, and partiality toward the particular interests of the individual student.

One reason it is appropriate to take a dynamic, processual view of social identity and role, as strategically enacted in the counseling interview, is that the "mix" of activity of the counselor can vary considerably from one interview to the next. It may change within a single interview as well, as the counselor acts as the student's defense attorney as well as the student's judge. Variation in the counselor's role definition during the interview seems to depend on the practical circumstances of action at that time; who the counselor acts as seems to depend on who the counselor is deciding the student is as a social person.

In addition to acting as an impartial gatekeeping decision maker the counselors we studied engaged in the following kinds of advocacy activities in various interviews:

- *Teaching the social order* (Presenting the student description of the social structure of the school and of the larger society, what statuses and mobility channels there are, what rules and strategies apply to mobility processes)

- *Teaching the encounter* (Explaining the sequential discourse structure of the interview and appropriate communicative role behavior for the student)

- *Sponsoring student mobility* (Actively assisting the student by giving special help and waiving or bending formal organizational rules)

- *Fostering student self-image* (Portraying the student as competent and capable of achieving a desired goal)

- *Defending counselor self-image* (Maintaining self-presentation of the counselor as unthreatened, reasonable, well informed, attentive, and concerned primarily for the welfare of the student rather than that of the school)

We have sketched a way of thinking about some aspects of local production in the interview: definition of situation in terms of social

---

[10] See Waller, 1932.

identity and communicative role. In later chapters we will consider some aspects of the actual conduct of communication, verbal and nonverbal, by which social identity and role are performed interactionally in particular interviews. For the remainder of this chapter we will continue with orienting discussion, which though not so abstract as that of the previous section, still provides an overview of the range of ways the question "Who is the student?" gets answered in the practical performance of various interviews.

We will discuss various emergent aspects of social identity and role in the interviews. First will be considered some of the unofficial attributes of the student's and the counselor's performed social identity in the interview, attributes that have to do with communication style during the interview itself. Then will be considered attributes of the student's and counselor's social identity in the world outside the encounter, attributes that during the course of an interview are invoked and drawn within the frame of the encounter as relevant to the definition of situation there and then.

DISCOURSE ORGANIZATION AS DEFINITION OF SITUATION

A Logic of Gatekeeping Discourse

In the interview the counselor is acting as a gatekeeper. An essential aspect of his job is to grant or withhold permission for the student to enter or continue in a particular course of study. The counselor also advises the student about various available options in the college's academic program. This advice takes into account the student's future career interests.

Before the counselor can give advice or grant permission he must know specifically, in official organizational terms, *who the student is.* Determining that is what the first half of the interview is about. At the beginning of the interview the counselor can see what the student's academic major is by looking at the student's academic record card in the cumulative folder. Then the information on that card must be brought up to date. The counselor asks what courses the student completed last semester and what grades were received. After that the counselor asks what courses the student is currently taking. Then the counselor asks about the student's future plans for employment or further schooling.

Only after knowing who the student has been in the past in the world outside the interview and who the student would like to be out there in the future can the counselor proceed to the second half of the interview, making appropriate gatekeeping decisions and engaging the student in appropriate academic program planning. Choosing any course for next semester or making any judgment about how "realistic" the student's career aims are requires knowledge of the student's past performance and future plans.

Accordingly there is an invariant sequence in the topics of discourse in the interview. (See Figure 2.1.) Unless the student is a special acquaintance of the counselor, so that the counselor already knows the answer to the question "Who is this student?" conversation about the student's past performance and future plans always precedes conversation about the possibility of those plans. If the counselor already knows the student fairly well, the whole first half of the discourse sequence can be elided. Conversation can begin with the "second half"—with advice about the achievement of the student's hopes for the future. But in the interviews we studied this never happened if the counselor was meeting the student initially, or if the student was only vaguely identifiable by the counselor as one among the hundreds of students on the counselor's case load. Then the interview always began with talk about who the student was specifically, in official organizational terms. Discourse structure in the interview can be seen as manifesting an underlying logic of gatekeeping decision making.

Discourse as an Arena for Revealing Performed Social Identity

The counselor as gatekeeper is not only concerned with determining who the student has been and wants to be in the world outside the interview; the student's social identity face-to-face in the immediate present is also taken into account. Inside the encounter the student establishes a *performed social identity* through his ways of interacting with the counselor. The student's ways of speaking and ways of listening—of showing interest in, understanding of, and commitment to the interview as it is happening—are communicative means of making an impression on the counselor. That unofficial impression of the student's performed social identity becomes inextricably involved in the counselor's judgments of the student's official social identity as they inform the counselor's gatekeeping decisions.

The counselor's ways of speaking and ways of listening also make an impression on the student, and so their impressions of and reactions to one another are reflexively influenced—jointly produced. Specific details of the joint production of interactional behavior will be considered in

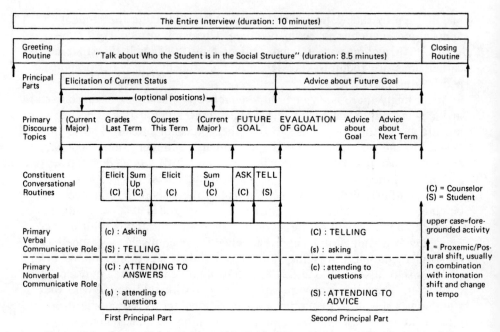

Figure 2.1. Sequential and hierarchical relations among constituent parts of the interview.

later chapters. At this point it is enough to consider *what* happens interactionally in the interview, not *how* it apparently happens.

The necessary point here is that the structure of discourse in the interview is also a structure of social participation. Changes in discourse activities, from one topic to the next, from one major section of the interview to the next, involve subtle changes in social relations between the counselor and the student. These are changes in participation structure—in the allocation of reciprocal and complementary communicative rights and obligations—communicative roles—between counselor and student.

During the first half of the interview, in which the topics of discourse concern the student's social identity in the world outside the encounter, the student's communicative role inside the encounter is mainly that of *answering,* which interactionally complements the counselor's role of *asking.* During the second half of the interview, in which the topics of discourse concern the counselor's advice, the roles of main speaker and main listener are reversed. The student now participates in conversation mainly by *listening,* which complements the counselor's role of *telling.*

The relationship between discourse structure and participation structure can be seen as mutually constitutive. This is illustrated in Figure

2.1, which shows the sequence of major topics of discourse in a typical interview, and the sequence of verbal and nonverbal role behaviors through which the counselor and student conduct their conversation together.

When interviewed by the researchers, counselors and students often referred to discourse units and conversational routines in the interview as whole, internally coherent "chunks." The following comments by one counselor are taken from "viewing sessions" in which the counselor watched videotapes of his interviews with different students:

    a. This last sequence here is enumeration of classes.
    b. At the point where we started talking about courses I think that he began to get a little bit nervous.

Both comments refer to a major discourse unit that typically occurred as the second topic of the interview, *Courses Taken This Semester*. In the first comment the counselor called this discourse unit a "sequence." He called the conversational routine by which the discourse sequence was accomplished "enumeration of classes." In the second comment, taken from a different interview, the same topic was called "talking about courses."

In viewing sessions, counselors and students also talked about the social meanings they inferred from one another's ways of speaking and listening at particular points during a discourse unit. Notice that in comment (b) the counselor mentioned the juncture between the first and second discourse topics, calling the juncture "this point." Then he reported an interpretive inference: "I think that he began to get a little bit nervous."

In the actual interview the student did not interrupt and say explicitly to the counselor, "I am getting nervous now." The student's explicit communication consisted of answering the counselor's questions about the courses he was taking. Apparently the counselor inferred the implicit social meaning, *nervousness*, from the student's *ways of answering*, verbal and nonverbal. At that point in the interview the student acquired a new attribute of performed social identity. He became *student who is nervous now*.

Participation Structure, Interactional Incidents, and Performed Social Identity

The student's display of momentary nervousness was noticeable to the counselor—an interactional "incident."[11] More serious incidents in-

---

[11] See Goffman, 1961: 45ff.

volve one or the other of the two conversational partners doing something communicatively which interferes with the other partner's ability to complete his own communicative actions. The successful accomplishment of discourse involves close, moment-by-moment cooperation. Failure by one party to do his share leads to trouble. If the counselor is engaged in asking a connected series of questions about *courses this semester* and the student fails to answer one of the questions, the counselor is unable to proceed to the next question in the series. The student's behavior at that point is not properly reciprocal with that of the counselor. If the student is explaining what his future career aims are and the counselor looks utterly bored to the student, this may interfere with the student's ability to complete his explanation smoothly. The counselor's way of listening at that point is not properly complementary with the student's speaking.

While incidents involving a momentary breakdown in conversational cooperation can occur at any point in the interview, the likelihood of certain kinds of breakdowns occurring is related to the overall structure of participation and discourse. During the first half of the interview, in which the counselor is mainly *asking* and the student is mainly *answering,* the most troublesome incidents involve a student's failure to answer the counselor's questions. During the second half of the interview, as the counselor mainly *tells advice,* the most troublesome incidents are likely to involve either (*a*) inappropriate ways of listening by the student, from which the counselor may infer that the student is not paying attention or understanding the advice; or (*b*) inappropriate ways of speaking by the counselor, from which the student may infer that the counselor is not understanding or taking seriously the student's interests and hopes.

The succession of discourse topics in the interview, each with a distinct participation structure involving slight reallocations of communicative rights and obligations between counselor and student, provides successive environments for the display of performed social identity by the counselor and the student. What the two do together in those environments of conversational cooperation influences definition of self and other in the encounter. This can be seen in Example 2.1. (Throughout, C will represent counselor and S student in dialogues.)

EXAMPLE 2.1
Discourse Topic: Grades Last Semester
(*a*) C: What did you get in your Biology 101 last semester?
(*b*) S: (speaking with marked Polish–American pronunciation) Wa'd I get?
(*c*) C: What did you get for a grade?

(d) S: "B."
(e) C: "B"?
(f) S: Yeah.

At turn *b* the student apparently failed to answer correctly because he did not understand the point of the previous question, "What did you get?" His interactional mistake came right at the beginning of the first sustained discourse topic in the interview. After the student had entered the room he and the counselor had greeted one another and gotten seated and set for official business. The counselor waited for the student to fill out the top of a registration card, then the counselor asked in turn *a* the first of a series of questions about grades in courses taken last semester.

The student failed to provide an appropriate answer (turn *b*). He responded to the counselor's question with another question instead of an answer. This was a serious breach of reciprocity. Accordingly, the counselor pressed the student (turn *c*) for an answer to the first question before going on to the next question in the routine (turn *g*). By doing this the counselor was making the absence of an answer in turn *b* a socially accountable absence. In turn *e* the counselor negatively sanctioned for a second time the student's first inappropriate answer (turn *b*). The counselor did this by questioning the veracity of the student's second answer (in turn *d*). At the beginning of the exchange the student had questioned the counselor's question. By turn *e* the counselor was questioning the student's previous answer.

Consider the social identity work being done from moment to moment. Each *ego* is telling *alter* who *ego* is. In turn *b* the student is telling the counselor that the student is a person who not only does not know the slang meaning of "get" in the question "What did you get?" but by extension does not know the conversational routine at this point. The student reveals himself as *a person who is conversationally incompetent now*.

Ego also is telling *alter* who *ego* thinks *alter* is. In turn *e* the counselor, by questioning the student's previous answer, is telling the student that from the counselor's point of view the student has now become a person who is conversationally untrustworthy—one whose answers can and should be stopped and frisked. By telling the student that he is now the kind of student whose answers are suspect, the counselor is also telling the student that the counselor is the kind of counselor who stops and frisks students who make conversational mistakes in his interviews.[12]

---

[12] Sacks (1972) illuminates the similarities between police work and other kinds of interrogatory professional activity. For the school counselor as gatekeeper, suspicion is institutionalized as part of the official role.

Thus in each successive move the counselor and the student define self and other at the same moment, in a reflexive process. The counselor's and the student's social identities are progressively being specified. As their social identities (their *statuses*) take clearer and clearer shape as the encounter proceeds, so do their mutual rights and obligations (their *roles*). The counselor and student work together in defining both who they are and how to act given who they are, continually negotiating status and role in the doing of the interview. Through the commission of interactional *incidents* each may reveal himself as "person who isn't answering now," or "person who isn't paying attention now," or "person who isn't explaining this clearly—or believably." Through the avoidance of interactional incidents he may reveal himself as "student who knows what is going on" or "counselor who is interested and who understands."

By repeated involvement in conversational incidents during an encounter, a person may establish an overall bad record as a conversational partner. Such a record is of considerable importance: If the counselor consistently develops a bad record, this reputation may spread through the student grapevine in the school and students will begin to try to avoid encounters with that counselor.

If a student develops a record during the interview, the consequences of it are immediate and potentially serious in ultimate results, because the counselor's opinion of the student carries more weight than the student's opinion of the counselor. The student's record of conversational cooperation is relevant to gatekeeping in that the counselor during an interview is extrapolating an estimate of the student's future success partly on the basis of the ways the student is acting as a conversational partner at the present moment.

In the counselor's practical gatekeeping decision process, the unofficial, interactionally emergent record of the student as a conversational partner becomes inextricably intertwined with the official, institutional record of the student's social identity as indicated by the test scores, grades, and course sequences that are documented in the student's cumulative folder.[13] This is why it is essential to take performed social identity into account in considering what is happening in the gatekeeping process.

---

[13] Official documentary records—their meanings and uses—play a crucial role in Weber's theory of bureaucratic organizations. Accuracy—or at least, believability—of the documents is essential for the technical precision of bureaucratic operation noted by Weber (1922 [1978 ed.]: 350ff). The attention paid to the cumulative folder in the school counseling interview can thus be seen as not at all trivial. For a discussion of the process by which impressions derived from face-to-face interaction are written into official institutional records, and once written down take on a hypostasized "reality," see Cicourel, 1968.

THROUGH THE LOOKING GLASS: THE SELECTIVE
REVELATION OF SOCIAL IDENTITY WITHIN
THE ENCOUNTER

We have been considering aspects of performed social identity that arise within the frame of the encounter, through the processes of face-to-face communication itself. Next to be considered are aspects of the social identity of the counselor and student in the world outside the encounter. We will examine some of the ways in which "outside" aspects of social identity become locally relevant and meaningful inside the encounter.

Just as one's ability to interact appropriately during the interview is not revealed all at once, and the sequential structure of the interview provides differing contexts across time for revealing adequate or inadequate cooperation in conversation, so some facets of social identity in the world outside the interview are more likely to be revealed in one section of the interview than in another. This is especially true for official aspects of the student's social identity. Grades the student received in courses are more likely to be revealed in the first part of the interview than in the middle. The student's plans for future education or employment are more likely to be revealed in the middle of the interview than at its beginning.

Within a given conversational routine new aspects of status in the world outside the encounter may appear suddenly, as in Example 2.2.

EXAMPLE 2.2
Juncture—Discourse Topic: Grades in Courses
Last Semester

(a) C: (The counselor changes postural position.) Now, let's have some grades...last semester, Data Processing 101. Whadja get for a grade?

(b) S: A "B."

(c) C: Data Processing 111?

(d) S: An "F."

At turn *b* the student is occupying the status "good student." By the end of turn *d* the student no longer occupies that status nearly so adequately as he had done the moment before.

Certain distinctive aspects of the counselor's or the student's ways of acting inside the encounter may point to aspects of their status outside it. In the case of the student who did not know how to answer the counselor's question "What did you get in Biology 101?" (Example 2.1), the student's ethnicity as a Polish–American, which was already apparent to the counselor in the student's last name, may have become more salient as the student said, "Wa'd I get?" The student used "nonstandard" English speech sounds and grammar—"Wa'd I" rather than "What did I." This involves phonological features characteristic of Polish–American dialect, and a syntactic feature (elision of the *did*) characteristic of "casual" rather than "careful" speech style.

Aspects of cultural style in nonverbal behavior can also point to one's ethnic identity, as in the "black power" handshake, or as in Example 2.3, in which an Italian–American student makes an expansive gesture in response to an Italian–American counselor's question about program planning for the next semester:

EXAMPLE 2.3[14]

(a)   C: ... That gives you 3, 6, 9, 12, 13 hours (for next semester). Take another class?

(b)   S: Just one I can. (In this vocal pause the student gestures iconically. In a viewing session the student said the gesture meant "A course I don't have to work hard in.")

(c)   C: What's that? (Referring to the gesture by pointing to the place in space where the student had done it.)

(d)   S: No, that's Italian. (Both laugh.)

(e)   C: O:::nly too well. (The first word is exaggerated in length, as the counselor says in effect, "As an Italian–American I know what you mean by the gesture and recognize only too well that it's an "Italian" way of using your hands in talking." This was the interpretation of what the student did and what the counselor said that was given by the counselor in his viewing session.)

Any point in the interview is potentially interruptable for a reference to aspects of status outside the encounter. This can happen in the first few moments of the encounter as in the case of the Polish–American student, or in the last few moments at the end, as in Example 2.4. There is a momentary silence as the student fills out a card to bring along on the day of registration to remind him what courses to register for.

---

[14] A set of three dots indicates a pause of approximately 1 second, while a set of two dots indicates a pause of approximately one-half second. Sets of colons indicate elongated vowels.

EXAMPLE 2.4

(a) C: All right...Now...on this stub..why don't you put your name down there. (The student is writing his name in the wrong place on the card.)

(b) S: I'm sorry. (Said overlapping the previous turn as the student writes name in correct place.)

(c) C: ...(There is a pause in speaking during which the counselor looks at student's folder as student is filling out the card. The counselor looks at the place on the record that shows the high school the student attended and then says) Roger Bacon Tech, huh?..You know Mr. O'Reilly?

(d) S: Well, not real good, but I know who he is. (There is a pause in speaking as the student continues to fill out the card.)

(e) C: You guys took the dive in your basketball game the other day, huh? (Laugh.)

(f) S: (makes hissing noise as counselor is speaking, then says) Unreal. I couldn't believe it...I'll just copy this (the information on the card) on a piece of paper, OK?

The instrumental work at hand was getting the card filled out. Interpolated within that was an expressive aside, talking about the basketball game. Instead of continuing with the normal succession of topics in the interview, the counselor departed from the usual routine and opened up a topic of small talk. The counselor may have realized, as he looked over the student's cumulative folder during the "dead air" time while the student filled out the card, that the student now in junior college had attended a high school where one of the staff, Mr. O'Reilly, was part of the counselor's acquaintance network. Opening up small talk is an option available to the counselor at any moment. The pause in speaking provided a transition slot during which that option could be taken, and official business could be suspended for a few moments. Within this conversational aside there is one discourse topic containing two related subtopics. Each of the subtopics is sustained across a pair of turns at speaking. The first subtopic (end of turn c and turn d) concerns the acquaintance of the counselor, and the next (turn e and the beginning of turn f) concerns last week's basketball game at that school. By initiating both of these subtopics the counselor shows not only that he knows the school and someone who works there, but that he "follows" the Catholic high school league sports scores in the city. This is something that Protestant upper-middle-class suburbanites in this city do not do.

Given that the counselor and the student both know that the counselor has an Italian–American last name and the student has a Polish–American last name, and that they both grew up in the city, the references by the counselor to a staff member at the school and to the sports scores could be functioning as diacritical marks of their common social identity as Roman Catholic "white ethnics" who grew up in the city. This is an invocation of shared attributes of social identity at a level we can come to call *pan-ethnicity* (see Chapters 5, 7, 8, and 9), which refers to similarity across ethnic categories that differ in terms of national origin and race but that are similar in other respects—social class level and contiguous residence patterns in the city. The students and counselors we studied fell into two pan-ethnic categories: *white ethnics* (Italian–, Polish–, and Irish–Americans) and *Third World* (black, Puerto Rican, Mexican–American).

The use of small talk in this way is literally "diacritical" in that it stands "outside the text" of the instrumental speech activity of the gatekeeping interview.[15] The very item of information that could have been of relevance for the official, instrumental work of gatekeeping—the information about what high school the student attended—is the item taken and used for an unofficial, expressive conversational purpose by the counselor—calling attention to the student's urban white ethnic, non-elite, non-Protestant "old school tie."

This use of potentially instrumental information in a relatively expressive way gives distinctive social meaning to the referential content of the topic: distinctive meaning perhaps, but not precise meaning. The social meaning pointed to by this way of speaking is not entirely clear. The counselor could have gone on to say that he knew the staff member of the Catholic technical high school because he had formerly been a teacher at another Catholic high school in the city, and that one reason he followed Catholic League sports scores was that he had been a wrestling coach at the high school. The counselor could have gone on to say that he too had gone to Catholic schools in the city, as had the student he was addressing at that moment. In these ways he could have been more explicit about the social meaning of bringing up the small talk topic.

In Example 2.4 the counselor did not try to say in so many words what the social meaning of his small talk was. He left the meaning implicit and *indexical*,[16] leaving the small talk topic only partially opened up in

[15] See Barth, 1969: 14–18 for a discussion of diacritical behavioral markers of social identity.

[16] Garfinkel claims that all speech is inherently indexical in that anything said presupposes knowledge of some larger context beyond what is said, and that consequently it is impossible to "repair" fully the indexicality of talk—to say precisely what one means "in so many words." On this issue, see Garfinkel and Sacks, 1970; Bar-Hillel, 1952.

conversation to stand for more information behind it, as does an item in an index. Because of this indexicality, interpreting the social meaning of such talk involves an inferential leap, both for the analyst of the conversation and for the participants in it. Yet whatever the counselor meant by talking about Mr. O'Reilly and the basketball game, he meant something having to do with aspects of life outside the instrumental frame of the gatekeeping encounter. He seems to have been pointing to aspects of his social identity and that of the student that stood apart from their official social identities as a gatekeeping counselor and a student in a junior college.[17]

Sometimes the pointing was quite precise and explicit, as in Example 2.5. In that interview, conducted by the Irish–American counselor, small talk was interpolated in the midst of a discussion of the junior-college student's future goal of transferring to a 4-year school offering a baccalaureate degree. The student was in a program of study leading toward a degree in engineering. He and the counselor considered the relative merits of an engineering and technical college and a Roman Catholic liberal arts college:

EXAMPLE 2.5

(a) C: What other places were you thinking of?

(b) S: Poly Tech for..I thought of that place, for one.

(c) C: Well, you wouldn't have any problem getting in there and they're good in both math and engineering.

(d) S: (pause) And..I'm in a (short laugh and pause) and then I kinda have my regrets about going there because it seems like everywhere I go is ah .. either ah..s..hi..there's, ah, all male enrollment. You know, like I went to Roger Bacon Tech and then I went into the Army (short laugh) and now I'm going to Poly Tech..There

(e) C: (interrupting) Oh. <u>Girls</u>. There are girls at Poly Tech.

(f) S: Yeah, but it's:::(drawn out "s") .. like it's few and far between (short laugh).

(g) C: Yeah..well, maybe you oughta s..(short laugh) think about something like St. Ximenes. A hundred and..it's out at a hundred and third..which is an all-girls school until y..recently they graduated five men.

[17] In a number of interviews this Italian–American counselor (and another who was also a Roman Catholic reared in the city, but was Irish–American) raised the topic of Catholic high school league sports scores as a topic of small talk for apparently similar purposes with similarly diffuse and multivocal social meaning. The counselors seemed to be pointing in implicit ways to who they and the students were outside the official frame of the encounter.

(h)   S: (overlaps end of previous turn) I know my limits (laughs, together with counselor).

(i)   C: OK. (Said as student says again, "I know my limits.") Yeah.. well, think about the..4-year school you're going to attend. I would send..the ACT's..uh, scores to Poly Tech if you think you're going there, an' maybe the State University.

Here the reference by the student to that aspect of his social identity as a young man interested in girls is quite explicit. In turn *d* the student gave special communicative emphasis to the special nature of what he was about to say. He did this through laughter, pauses, and other hesitation phenomena. The counselor's response in turn *e*, "Oh, girls," marking *girls* with volume stress and pitch stress (a high falling intonation) makes it clear that the student has succeeded in disambiguating the discourse topic that he initiated as a joke in turn *d*. In turn *e* the counselor also ratifies the student's discourse topic, making the presence or absence of girls at a school permissible to talk about. The student had already incorporated the unofficial *presence of girls* subtopic into the official topic, *choice of 4-year school,* and so this example is not one of expressive small talk that is entirely unrelated to instrumental purposes at hand. Rather, this is a mixed form, an unofficial way of talking about official business.

The shift from instrumental official business to expressive unofficial small talk involves, simultaneously, a change in participation structure, a change in performed social identity, and a change in the overall character and tone of the encounter. The change in participation structure consists of overlapping speech and laughter (see transcript). This is characteristic of turn exchange in *casual* speech style, as contrasted to more *careful* speech style. Neither party acts as if this overlapping was an inappropriate interruption by the other party. In terms of social identity, the unofficial, sexual aspects of the young man's student career appear momentarily in the foreground of attention, with the more officially legitimate academic aspects of the student career left in the background.

The shift to a more informal conversational tone involves a way of talking about the world that is not only more relaxed and funnier, but more pragmatic. This was also true in the previous example, when with a flip of the hand the student told the counselor an easy course was what was wanted. In both examples, unofficial realities of college life are pragmatically oriented toward—girls and "gut" courses. The bureaucratically organized formal organization is seen with its underlife exposed—seen in its relatively "secular" informal order rather than in its "sacral" formal order. Within the frame of the encounter the counselor momentarily joins the student as a coconspirator in the underlife, collaborating in this worldly way of talking about the world outside the encounter.

After a few moments the counselor and student stop the small talk and casual turn exchange. They return to the instrumental business at hand. As they do so, the official version of school reality—a more sacral way of regarding standard operating procedures—returns to the foreground of their talk.

Small talk is an important resource for the counselor as a means of distancing himself from his official role. In strategic terms, role-distancing as a way of acting in one's role contrasts sharply with role embracement.[18] When the counselor embraces the official role he cannot give the kinds of advice he can when he is able to be more unofficial and pragmatic. In the role-distanced mode he can avoid preaching about the goodness of the school's rules—their ultimate benefit to the student. Notice how a decision about dropping a course is talked about in Example 2.6 in which the counselor relates to the student in an unofficial way:

EXAMPLE 2.6
Discourse Topic: Courses This Semester

(a) C: Math?

(b) S: Naw, I didn't take Math (pronounced "Mat").

(c) C: Did you register for it?

(d) S: No..I registered for speech instead of Math (pronounced "Mat")
        'cause I

(e) C: (interrupting) No, we don't have to drop your Math (pronounced
        "Mat") class now. You're not registered. (Intonation level rises
        for emphasis.) See, if you're registered in it and you don't attend,
        you're gonna receive an "F" at the end of the semester!

(f) S: Naw, I didn't even get a class card for it.

(g) C: OK, all right. Data Processing 112?

When the student tells the counselor he didn't take Math, the counselor does not say in turn *c* "Why not? It's a required course! You need that background as a data processing major." (That more sermonizing way of talking was what he used at an exactly analogous point in an interview with another student.) Rather, the counselor says "Did you register for it?" and then in turn *e* he clarifies his request further. He says in turn *e* that he did not mean by the question in turn *c* to imply that the student

---

[18] See Goffman, 1961: 106.

should have registered for it (since it was a required course). He just wanted to remind the student that if he had indeed registered for the course he needed to remember to drop it. That sort of pragmatic advice shows the student how to make end runs around the formal organizational rules.

Another way in which role-distancing can be done is to speak ironically of an aspect of standard operating procedure. The communicative means used to signal irony can be lexical and syntactic (vocabulary and grammar), or prosodic (voice pitch, tempo, and volume), or a combination of the two.

One counselor, in introducing a new discourse topic in the interview, used a lexical and syntactic means primarily (Example 2.7).

EXAMPLE 2.7

(a) C: Here's another little exercise to try your patience (advising the student about a registration procedure).

That same counselor with another student used speech prosody as a means of cueing irony (Example 2.8).

EXAMPLE 2.8

(a) C: According to the rules of the (slight pause and then slower tempo, with stressed pitch shifts at the beginning of each of the next words) State Scholarship Commission (back to normal tempo and intonation) you have to....

Examples 2.7 and 2.8 have involved momentary shifts into statistically infrequent ways of speaking, termed *marked* occurrences by linguists, as distinct from statistically frequent, *unmarked* ones.[19]

Not only momentary cues of irony or informality, but topics of "small talk" themselves are statistically infrequent, *marked* occurrences within the interview. Why do they occur at all? Apparently because it is within such momentary ploys that an extremely important set of facets of un-official social identity can be revealed by the counselor and the student. This set of facets will be considered in the next section.

[19] On the distinction between marked and unmarked forms, see Lyons, 1968: 70–73, 79–80, 307–309, and the discussion in Hymes, 1974: 111–116. In linguistics the distinction entails not only frequency of occurrence but qualitative differences of function as well. For our purposes here it is sufficient to note that infrequently chosen communicative options, such as the use of prosodic cues to signal irony, have a salience that more frequently chosen alternative options do not have.

Comembership and Interpersonal Solidarity
in the Interview

Small talk is the main conversational means by which the counselor and/or the student invokes or discovers those attributes of status in the world outside the encounter that are called, in ordinary language, "what they have in common."

Within the encounter the two conversational partners constitute the status set *counselor and student*. But that does not seem to be enough for them. Sometimes they seem to be deliberately trying to discover shared attributes of status outside the encounter (as in Example 2.4 in which the counselor asks the student, "Do you know Mr. O'Reilly?"). Such a question can be glossed more formally: "Are we both people who share membership in the class of persons *those who know Mr. O'Reilly?*" Neither the counselor nor the student would talk in so technical a way about their performed social identity in the interview. But the question, "Do you know Mr. O'Reilly?" can be seen to involve an active search for those shared attributes of social identity that can be termed *comembership*.

Comembership involves attributes of shared status that are particularistic rather than universalistic (see the discussion on p. 15, note 5). In Example 2.4 that facet of the student's identity involving whether or not he knew Mr. O'Reilly should have been irrelevant to the counselor. Officially, the question never should have been asked. Yet such questions were in fact asked, occasionally, in various interviews.

Aspects of particularistic comembership were not only searched for by questioning if the counselor did not know the student; they were sometimes invoked when the counselor did know the student. The counselor who asked about Mr. O'Reilly used a question to invoke comembership more implicitly in another interview. The question came at the end of the first official discourse topic, concerning the grades the student had gotten in courses last semester. The student had dropped a number of courses during the semester. The last course mentioned was one the student had not dropped. It was in physical education, whereupon the counselor asked:

EXAMPLE 2.9

(a) C: You wrestlin'?

(b) S: (smile) Naw, I have a bad knee. I just had it operated on.

(c) C: (smiling) You sure it was the knee? (implying, "And not your head?" tying back to the student's earlier revelations of his numerous dropped courses and the "F" he had received in a course in his major field.)

(d) S: (smiling) Sure it was. I got a big cut and big scar to prove it.

(e) C: (laughs briefly, and then says, smiling) OK, now this semester...

In this case the counselor, who was formerly a high school wrestling coach, was talking to a student who had a year or so previously been a member of the junior-college wrestling team. But their comembership relationship involved more than just common participation in wrestling. The student had gone to the same Catholic high school in which the counselor had been the wrestling coach during the time the counselor had taught at that high school. While the student had not been on the counselor's wrestling team, his younger brother had been. The counselor had met the student's parents at that time. The father of the boys was Mexican–American and the mother was Italian–American. (In a viewing session the Italian–American counselor said, "He's Italian—his father is Mexican but his mother's Italian.")

During the interview, as the counselor brought up comembership in terms of wrestling, he may have been alluding indexically to all or some of the complete set of comemberships they shared. This is the same student as in Example 2.2 and 2.6, who has an "F" in a course in his major field and who didn't register for a required Math course. Not only that, but he is in his seventh semester at a four-semester junior college. He is hanging around there, partly to avoid the draft, partly because hanging around is his style. He is a Huckleberry Finn on the loose in bureaucracy. But he is not repeatedly stopped and frisked by the counselor. For although a rogue, he is an attractive one, and he is a comember.

Revelation of comembership provides a basis for special solidarity between the counselor and the student. One use of this sort of solidarity is apparent from the previous example. By calling on their comembership in terms of wrestling, and whatever else the question "You wrestlin'?" may have entailed, the counselor emphasized their solidarity and, having done so, was able to play off the student's reference to his bad knee with a rejoinder in which he jokingly reminded the student that he should not be dropping so many courses each term. The counselor was able to reprimand the student while still preserving face as friendly and benevolent. The counselor's role distancing was appropriate in the presence of a familiar comember. In the presence of a stranger whose social identity was defined only in universalistic terms (and consequently in relatively undifferentiated, "low fidelity" ways that did not permit much interactional fine tuning), such stepping out of the institutionalized definition of role would have been inappropriate on the part of the counselor.

Establishing performed social identity that is differentiated along multiple dimensions is adaptive for the counselor and student. As they draw on particularistic as well as universalistic dimensions of social status, they define the situation within the encounter in terms of emergent and expressive as well as institutionalized and instrumental aspects of status and role. This provides strategic leeway that would otherwise be lacking in so routinized an encounter as a gatekeeping counseling interview, which has so many instrumental demands placed on it by the larger institutional and societal contexts in which it is embedded.

The multidimensionality of performed social identity allows the counselor and student to call on a multiplicity of social meanings within kinds of talk whose referential meaning also serves instrumental functions. Many optional ways become available for getting business done while still saving face for both parties. The counselor and the student can preserve something of the expressive character of hospitality and mutual regard that is appropriate in relations among members of the same urban village. They can do this even though the interview must be conducted, often between persons who are strangers, in the midst of a large-scale formal organization whose purposes are primarily instrumental—an organization in which there is not much time or bureaucratic leeway available for attending to the needs of particular individuals.

THE ENCOUNTER IN RELATION TO THE WORLD OUTSIDE IT

As a partially bounded encounter, each counseling interview has, to some extent, a life of its own. The ability of the counselor and student to engage one another cooperatively in conversation seems to have an effect on how they define one another in terms specific to the encounter they are currently engaged in. This is one source of performed social identity in the encounter. Another source comes from outside the encounter. Attributes of social identity from the world outside the encounter can be invoked as relevant to social identity within the encounter. These too have meanings specific to the particular encounter in which they are employed as resources. An attribute of comembership, for example, is distinctive to the local circumstances of the encounter in that it is an attribute invoked as something shared by the particular individuals who confront one another in that particular encounter.

While each encounter has a set of distinctive internal conditions, and is thus unique, what happens in the encounter is not entirely cut off from patterns of life that exist outside it. Each counselor and student brings to the interview culturally learned ways of speaking and listening. As will be seen in later chapters, similarities and differences in their styles of interacting seem to have an effect on their ability to cooperate conversationally. Thus cultural patterns in communication style that are learned and shared within differing speech communities in the wider society play a part in the distinctive local production of performed social identity within the encounter. Each counselor and student pair also brings to the interview a different set of possibilities for the establishment of comembership. In the large city in which they live, ethnic and racial group membership and social class affect residence patterns, school attendance and tracking, recreational interests, and acquaintance networks. These affect the kinds of comembership relations a given counselor–student pair is able to invoke during the interview. Consequently the local production of talk and listening in the encounter, and of performed social identity—those emergent aspects of fine tuning in each interview that are uniquely improvised from moment to moment—are related to normative culture and social structure in the wider society.

Normative culture and social structure also seem to affect the broad patterns of issues or themes that recur across many of the interviews. Among the generally recurrent issues in gatekeeping interviews are future planning, the care with which particularism is managed during the interview, and the role conflict of the gatekeeping counselor.

Planning one's future career is an activity that is culturally distinctive. Such activity seems relatively rare when one considers a wide range of human societies past and present. Movement from one occupational category and social rank to another from one generation to the next has been possible only in some societies. The notion that one's future life is necessarily amenable to change through present effort and the notion that rational planning could be useful as a way of affecting the future course of one's life are ideas that have not had much currency in preindustrial and nonliterate societies. Moreover, in small-scale social groups, in which kinship is the essential core of one's social identity and acquaintance networks overlap a great deal, there is no need for a social occasion in which one stranger meets with another in order to answer for gatekeeping purposes the question, "Who is this person, specifically?" The answer to that question is a *given* in a small-scale traditional society.

In modern large-scale societies, one's social identity and mobility is indeed problematic. Gatekeeping interviews and other forms of social identity assessment by strangers occur throughout the life cycle as the individual engages from the moment of birth until the time of death a succession of differing formal organizations.

Also distinctive to modern societies is the tension between universalistic and particularistic criteria according to which social identity is assessed. Whether the modern society is capitalist or socialist, particularistic attributes of social identity such as skin color, kinship and ethnicity, religious affiliation (here some socialist societies are an exception), acquaintance network, and culturally stylistic ways of speaking, are all ideally irrelevant to gatekeeping decision making. Yet in practice, all these factors enter into gatekeeping decisions; there is particularistic "leakage" within the frame of the gatekeeping encounter. That this leakage occurs is not surprising, for reasons already discussed. But the fact that this leakage is to some extent surreptitious is of interest. In a traditional society it would be the particularistic factors that predominated in a gatekeeping interview, if such an interview were held at all. This indeed happens in societies in transition from traditional to modern form, such as those of the current Third World. Societies like Saudi Arabia are the exception in the Third World: technologically developing yet exceedingly particularistic and feudal in social structure. In most developing countries—Nigeria, Indonesia, and Brazil, for example—there is tension between universalistic and particularistic criteria for judging people, and there is open and often violent social conflict over the ethnic and social class status of gatekeepers in formal organizations. Analogous tensions and conflict exist in large-scale industrial societies, including the United States. The conflict may occur in less overly violent ways than it does in societies in transition between traditional and modern form, but the conflict is still present. Political dispute over the social identity of the gatekeeper is characteristic of contemporary life in the United States. Should the gatekeeper be black or white? Male or female? White ethnic or WASP? Upper-middle-class or working-class?

But in the United States this conflict is somewhat masked not only at the level of the general society but within the specific gatekeeping encounter. In the interviews we studied, the indirect ways that particularistic attributes of identity are drawn within the frame of the encounter and the brief times that these attributes are allowed to occupy the foreground of attention in the interviews, attest to the need for masking. The delicacy with which particularism is managed in the interviews points to the illicit nature of stepping in and out of particularistic content in what ideally is supposed to be a gatekeeping decision process conducted entirely on universalistic grounds.

Although planning for the future and delicate interactional management of particularistic leakage may be characteristic of modern societies generally as contrasted to more traditional ones, the counselor's dilemma concerning particularism may be especially distinctive to the United

States. In the United States not only does the normative culture maintain universalism as the ideal for just treatment of individuals, but holds that ideal in tension with the manifest presence in everyday life of particularistic treatment of individuals. Normative culture in the United States also supports another paradox, that of holding equality as an ideal in the face of manifest social inequality. This seems to have consequences for the conduct of the gatekeeping interview.

The counselor in the school gatekeeping interview is supposed to be entirely universalistic in his gatekeeping judgments, yet he cannot be, given the practical circumstances of face-to-face interaction by which the gatekeeping decisions must be made and communicated to the student. The counselor is invested with institutional authority to lead the student through the interview, make the gatekeeping decisions, and communicate them. Yet the counselor is restricted by the tension between equality and hierarchically distributed authority; he is supposed to exercise gatekeeping authority but he is not to do so in an arbitrary way. Moreover, at the same time as he is to be the student's judge he is to be the student's advocate. As one student put it in a viewing session: "A counselor's supposed to be your friend and buddy and guardian." If the American counselor were only pressed by the need to be universalistic in his judgments and not also pressed by the ideal of equality, he could operate "objectively" as a professional secure in his institutional authority. If the American counselor were pressed only by the egalitarian ideal, he could act "subjectively" as an advocate for the special interests of each particular student and not find the role of advocate contradicted by the role of judge. Simultaneously pressed by universalism and egalitarianism, the counselor is placed in a situation that is manifested interactionally in the counselor's conduct of the interview.

Telling the Bad News: A Practical Problem of Impression Management

The point in the interview at which the counselor's role conflict becomes most apparent is the point at which it becomes necessary to tell the student some sort of bad news about his current or future status.

The counselors we studied all seemed to be operating according to a conversational maxim somewhat like the following one with three corollaries:

> It is inappropriate for the counselor to emphasize or even to refer explicitly to any apparent academic deficiency the stu-

dent has, or to predict future failure because of present academic inadequacy.

1. The greater the academic difficulty of the student, the greater the inappropriateness of such talk by the counselor.
2. The general maxim and its first corollary are the "normal forms." They always apply except under special circumstances.
3. *Special circumstances* are those of high comembership. Under those conditions, talk about academic trouble is appropriate.

High comembership consists of shared membership in such particularistically defined categories of social identity as ethnicity, race, and sex. It also includes shared interest in and knowledge of unofficially relevant domains of knowledge. Among the male counselors and students we studied, these domains included sports scores, the unreasonability of traffic cops, common acquaintances, and getting girl friends to type your college papers for you. The first three classes of attributes of shared comembership—ethnicity, race, and sex—are attributes that often are implicitly or indirectly communicated face to face because they are often obviously manifest. The other aspects of comembership—common experience, acquaintance, or special knowledge—are all explicitly communicated through small talk.

The implicit and explicit revelation of comembership during the interview provided a microsocial context for empathy and rapport. Under the condition of high comembership it apparently became appropriate for the counselor to talk directly about academic trouble the student is in. In the absence of the revelation or particularistic comembership (i.e., if the counselor and student shared little manifest comembership and restricted themselves in talk to defining their social identities in universalistic terms), the counselor tended to adhere to the general operating principle which can be paraphrased, "Don't tell the bad news in so many words."

This is a profound conversational double bind. If the student was in academic trouble the counselor should have been able to point that out. Sometimes the counselor did tell the bad news. But unless the counselor and student shared comembership, the student might have resented the telling and might have discounted the truth value of the news. Usually the counselors stepped lightly around such news, avoiding its statement in explicit ways, as seen in Example 2.10, in which a student rather abruptly told the counselor his future goal and the counselor reacted with a nervously elaborated and implicitly discouraging explanation of how one could reach such a goal.

EXAMPLE 2.10
(Juncture) Discourse Topic: Courses Next Semester

(a)   C: (changing seating position)..As far as next semester...Why don't we give some thought to what you'd like to take there...? (Leans forward.) Do you plan on continuing along this P.E. major?

(b-1)   S: Yeah, I guess so. I might as well keep it up..my P.E., and

(Juncture) Discourse Topic: Future Career Goals

(b-2)   S: (shifts in chair) I wanna go into counseling too, see...you know, to have two way...like equal balance.

(c)   C: I see. Ah...what do you know about counseling?

(d)   S: Nothing. (Smiles and averts eyes, then looks up.)

(e)   C: Okay...

(f)   S: (shifts in chair, smiles and averts eyes) I know you have to take psychology courses of some sort...and counseling.

(g)   C: (leans back) Well,....(Student stops smiling, looks directly at counselor and sits almost immobile while counselor talks and shifts in chair repeatedly.) it's this is a ...It'll vary from different places to different places ...But essentially what you need...First of all you're gonna need state certification, state teacher certification..in other words you're gonna have to be certified to teach in some area..English or history, or whatever happens to be your bag..P.E. Secondly, you're gonna have to have a Master's Degree...in counseling...which as you know is an advanced degree. (Short laugh.) That's what you have to do to get a counseling..to be a counselor.

While watching a videotape of the interview the student, who was black, stopped the tape at this point and said that he inferred an implicit meaning from the relatively convoluted way of explaining used by the counselor, who was white:

> He's telling me I'm not qualified. But he doesn't just come out, "pow," like they would in the old days, you know. He uses some psychology. He puts some sugar on it.

This example of talk from an interview and the accompanying comment made in a viewing session raises a number of issues, more than can be dealt with at this point. The example will be returned to throughout the book. What is significant here is the focus by the student on the *implicit social meaning* rather than on the *explicit referential meaning* of the counselor's way of explaining.

Such a focus was found in a number of interviews, suggesting that it is a strategically adaptive response by students to the strategically adaptive tendency of counselors to avoid telling bad news explicitly in encounters in which a low comembership relation exists.

In contrast, when a high comembership relation existed the counselor often got directly to the point in warning the student about trouble that might lie ahead. The student in the next example was a data-processing major at the junior college who could be about to face a serious problem in the future. The counselor discussed that trouble explicitly:

EXAMPLE 2.11
Discourse Topic: Plans for Transfer to
Four-Year School

(a) C: How much investigation have you done of other schools that offer programs in data processing?

(b) S: Not really down to it. I've talked to students over there, that's about it.

(c) C: At (state university)?

(d) S: Uh, I've talked to one student I know, he..never really got into the courses he had started on 'em, he said that the courses they offer are pretty good as far as he could see..

(e) C: Mhm, one of the problems that I think you're gonna run into is transferability.

(f) S: Yeah, I realize that. (C: You know which) I gotta little Biology I gotta get in there.

(g) C: No, I'm not even so much worried about that as I am about these Data Processing courses.

(h) S: Why?

(i) C: As to whether they'll transfer and accept them at (state university).

(j) S: Well, if not that I'll just start all over..What can I say?

(k) C: Yeah (laughs)..ah..well, one of the things you could say is ah..(very seriously) one of the things you could do is (emphasis) check.

(*l*) S: Yeah.. I will.. I'm gonna get in on that (C: Would y...)

(*m*) C: (interrupts) would y...(with emphasis) please do that because the sooner you know, the easier it's gonna be for you to make a decision as to whether you wanna continue here and get that 2-year A.A. or whether you..you know...you're planning on transferring over to State (S: Oh, oh, oh, um, ex-cuse)

(*n*) S: (interrupts, with emphasis) Oh, oh, oh, um, excuse me, I thought you meant that after, you know, my 2 years are done here then go to State....

The student in this example may have been in more serious trouble than the previous student was. A whole sequence of courses this student had taken in his major field might not be transferable with credit to the public university he was planning to attend next. He was at the end of the third semester in the four-semester junior college. The previous student, in Example 2.10, had only taken one term of courses. While that student had not taken courses in the sequence preparatory to majoring in counseling, at least he had not already invested time and money in courses in a major field at the junior college that might not transfer at all to a 4-year school. Although this may have been by objective standards a less serious predicament than that anticipated by the counselor for the latter student, the counselor treated the former bad news (Example 2.10) as a conversational hot potato and did not do so for the latter (Example 2.11).

An additional factor affecting treatment of the student is the press of time. Given the counselor's large case load there is a need to handle each case as expeditiously as possible. This did not please many of the students we studied. For them the counseling interview was a special occasion even though it was a routine one for the counselors. Students seemed to expect that their own case would be regarded as special by the counselor, even though they may have been in no special academic trouble. In a viewing session one student commented this way:

EXAMPLE 2.12

It was too, like..systematized. You know (in an exaggerated style), "This-is-here. Pick-this. You-can-have-this-if-you-don't-want-this... Just like ah...he had a plan. That's how it felt...

At another point while watching the tape this student stopped and said:

EXAMPLE 2.13

> I think there was too fast of a pick. Like I didn't have time to really..see what I wanted or..you know.. I didn't have the book (the college catalog) to see what courses or anything so..it was like (now speaking in exaggerated prosodic style) "Well-you-have-to-pick-it-right-now,".. So I just grabbed..anything I could pick.

The expectation of students that they will somehow be treated as unique individuals rather than as instances of a general class presents a problem of impression management for the counselor. Time is short, and the situations of most students fall into quite clear general categories. Even though the student's career is usually prearranged quite tidily by course requirements, there is a need to give students some sense of being special and some sense of personal efficacy. But this must be communicated quickly. There is no time for a lengthy conversational exploration by which empathy and rapport could be gradually developed. The counselor's ability to refer to shared comembership in a highly indexical way, as in "You wrestlin'?" or "You guys took the dive in your basketball game the other day, huh?" provides a quick way to signal considerable solidarity. This makes the encounter a bit special. The solidarity established for the moment makes it socially appropriate for the counselor to talk directly about academic problems the student may have. That allows the counselor and the student to clarify what the problem is without the student's becoming defensive. Then the counselor can move rapidly on to the giving of relevant advice, which, being of a secular and pragmatic kind, makes the counselor appear concerned for the best interests of the student. Such advice is realistic and plausible. It has a quality of cordial helpfulness, a quality achieved by the counselor with a minimum of time expended (although not necessarily with a minimum of effort, for the counselor must be paying close attention to conduct the interview this way). Given the severe time constraints under which the counselor must operate, this may be the best adaptation the counselor can make.

That sort of adaptation would not be necessary in the first place if it were not culturally appropriate to behave as if the student had the right to make genuine choices about his or her future, or if it were not culturally appropriate for the counselor to act as the student's advocate as well as judge.

The interpretation that these aspects of role conflict for the counselor have a distinctively American character gains force from the only cross-national comparison we are able to make directly from our corpus of interviews. The only foreign-born student we filmed was educated in Poland through adolescence. He had come to the United States and at the time of the interview was in his mid 20s. He was living with relatives while attending junior college full-time. In his viewing session he said that what impressed him most during the interview was the opportunity to make choices among alternatives. He was ambivalent about this; while he relished the opportunity it also made him nervous during the interview.

Unfortunately, the student said this most fully as he was sitting down to begin the viewing session, before the audio tape recorder had been turned on, and so it is not possible to provide here the full text of what the student said. When the recorder was turned on the student began speaking by contrasting this school counseling interview in the United States with the ones he had had as a student in Poland. (R represents researcher; S represents student.)

EXAMPLE 2.14

R: Fine. We can talk about that (the student's nervousness about choice making) a little bit at the beginning if you want to.

S: Oh, it..no, I just.. everything.. See it different.. I mean the way—the good way of it. I never had that before. I was attending the (technical school after secondary school). It was architecture. For one se-mester..(then the student came to the United States). But, you know...I didn't have any choices..(in Poland) You take the subjects the Board of Education gives you. They got the certain subjects and then...you know, for the curriculum—and they gotta take it, you know, and that's it. And over here is beautiful. You can choose your own subject in first year or..uh..second year, and (prosodic emphasis) <u>you can take it</u>. You can't do it over there.

The student saw the interview as involving open-ended choices which were "beautiful," but frightening. The counselor, in his viewing session, said he regarded the student as frightened and confused at some of the choice points, and a bit too compliant:

EXAMPLE 2.15

C: ... This kid will go along with whatever you give 'm.

R: So that's, uh..yeah..

C: An' I think I left pauses in there where..I was tryin' to get him to say something.

R: Mhm.

C: And he wouldn't.

R: So your general run of student...tends to be more...take more initiative?

C: Uh.. it depends. I thing that, uh..certain groups, let's say the Greeks and the Italians..are very us..assertive an' they know what they want an' what they're after..an' this kid, he's from Poland an' he..uh..is different than some of the kids who've been here a little longer. He takes whatever you give him. Some of the other kids (Polish–American immigrants who have been here longer) will take whatever you give them but they uh..will do it in a little different spirit. The idea is that, "OK, give it to me, if I don't like it I'm not gonna do it anyway."

R: But here he's just taking what..

C: I'm doing all the work, uh.. I'm (not) able to pull anything much out of him.

Apparently in Poland (and, one would expect, in other European nations, whether socialist or capitalist) there was no ambivalence about the authority of the school and its officers, including gatekeeping counselors: "You take the subjects the Board of Education gives you." In the American context the European student was confused when confronted with the responsibility to choose.

But the American student in Examples 2.12 and 2.13 perceived lack of responsibility for choice during the interview. That student was Italian–American—a group characterized by the counselor in Example 2.15 as assertive. It seemed to the American student that in the lived time of the interview there was not enough time to make genuine choices. The counselor was presenting the choices in too open-and-shut a fashion. The complaint, "I didn't have the book to see what courses or anything," suggests that the student wanted to know the full range of elective courses available to choose from, not to have the information known and the choices made mainly by the counselor.

To conclude, something more than individual differences among people in temperament and cognitive style seemed to be at work in the interviews. Our interpretation is that this involves the enactment of general themes and contradictions in normative culture within the unique social microcosm of the particular encounter. This involves a large inferential leap, but we make it anyway. The tensions between equality and individual opportunity inherent in American culture and society may well be reenacted each time a counselor and a student step inside the frame of the gatekeeping encounter and begin the *realization* of the interview in interactional performance face-to-face.

3

Research Methods and Procedures:
An Overview

Before more discussion of findings it is necessary to give some view of the ways the findings were arrived at. In this chapter this is done first by stating a few of the assumptions that guided the research, and second by reviewing the main types of research procedures. Some of the types are described more specifically in appendixes.

SOME PRINCIPLES FOR THE PROCEDURES

If interactional partners are to some extent making up their social relations from moment to moment, making choices from among a range of culturally conventional communicative means that are appropriate at any given moment, and if those choices manifest distinctive social meanings, then to be able to do analytic detective work on the processes by which those meanings are made and on the ways those meanings constitute social relationships in interaction, it is necessary to have available as much information as possible about what people actually do as they communicate. Such very specific information is best derived from audiovisual "behavior records"—cinema film or videotape. This information is not directly available from narrative field notes written by a participant observer, since in the very process of writing the narrative description, one is making inferences about meaning and intent on the basis of communicative cues, not simply keeping a detailed record of the behavioral form of those cues themselves.[1] Information available from continuously recorded audiotape is not even adequate, since without a visual record many aspects of nonverbal behavior are missing, and in consequence at least half the communicative means by which interaction is socially and culturally organized is unavailable for analysis.

If, in the absence of information on nonverbal behavior, one lacks kinds of evidence that are crucially important for the study of the social organization of communication in face-to-face interaction, then the absence of information on speech behavior is equally unfortunate. While a great deal can be learned about interaction by watching a film or videotape with the sound turned off, a great deal of social as well as referential meaning is carried by speech.

Social and referential meaning seem to reside in the *complementary action of the verbal and nonverbal channels together*. They form together the total pattern and context of redundancy—the full performance on the basis of which people make sense, reading off the meanings of sentences and intonation patterns in the context of facial expression, of gesture and posture in the context of speech—what one person is doing in the context of what all the others in the event are doing. To try to study the organization of a system by ignoring any of its major component subsystems would be absurd. Yet this is the problem of linguists—even sociolinguists—who listen only to speech, and of kinesicists and other scholars who look only at body motion and other aspects of nonverbal behavior. In the Watergate hearings there would have been far fewer arguments over nuances of meaning had President Nixon's Oval Office been monitored by video camera as well as by microphone.

It is for these reasons that we believe that as complete an audiovisual behavior record as possible is necessary as a first condition for analysis—one that documents the whole social occasion continuously, without any embarrassing "gaps" in the record, for if the Nixon tapes have anything to teach the student of conversation besides the need for a moving visual image of it, it is that each conversation is a lived history. Complete knowledge of the whole history of the conversation at hand can be essential for interpreting the meaning of what is said at any given moment.[2]

[1] On the limitations of relying exclusively on participant observation and narrative field notes as a data source, see Mehan's discussion of "constitutive ethnography," an approach we are calling here "microethnography" (Mehan, 1978, 1979: 16–20).

[2] See Goffman, 1976: 291–300.

A fully continuous audiovisual document of interaction is a necessary condition for analysis but is not sufficient by itself. The behavior record is not data, only potential data, and so there are subsidiary methodological and procedural premises that follow from the primary one. The first of these premises concerning the reduction of raw information into data is that, however information from either channel of behavior is handled, this should be done in the context of information from the other channel. Keeping track of *modality redundancy* across verbal and nonverbal channels is a problem of both data conceptualization and data retrieval. The invention of analytic strategies must go hand in hand with the invention of clerical strategies by which both channels can be cross-referenced.

A second premise is that *temporal redundancy* in communicative means needs to be accounted for as well as *modality redundancy*. Since the relationship of communication events in and across time forms part of the complete context of the social occasion, it is necessary to be able to locate any communication event in real time, whether that event is a connected sequence of discourse or a single nod of one person's head. Being able to place diverse communication events on a common time line also provides a baseline for cross-referencing data from the verbal and nonverbal channels.

Key questions guiding the research have to do with relationships of covariation between (*a*) the quality and outcomes of interaction across interviews and (*b*) the social identity and cultural style of the student being interviewed. Hence it was necessary to be able to compare one interview with another.

Given the scale of the study and the number of interviews that were filmed (82, of which 25 are reported on in detail here), accounting for variation across cases could not be done only through concrete "case description," by descriptive vignettes, by exemplary texts of speech, and by exemplary charts of nonverbal behavior and speech together. A more comprehensive and consequently more abstract approach to comparison was also needed. It followed that the patterns that emerged from descriptive and other "qualitative" methods of data analysis should be quantitatively summarized. That raised issues of what to count and how to summarize the results of counting in ways that would do justice to the complexity and the locally situated meanings of what the counselors and students were doing face-to-face, and yet would comprehend the full range of variation in behavior and impression management across all interviews. We needed low-inference "etic" indicators of what the communicative forms were from which meaning was inferred, as well as more "emic" kinds of data (the etic–emic distinction is discussed in the next section of this chapter).

Finally, there was a need for evidence of the impressions of the counselors and students themselves about the social meaning of variation in communicative performance. We wanted to consider the points of view of the actors in the scene, both as they manifested their points of view to each other during the interview itself (as in holding each other accountable for a failure in conversational reciprocity such as the absence of an answer to a question) and as they manifested their points of view afterwards in comments to an outside observer. Out of this concern developed interest in microobservational ways of identifying *moments when things went wrong* in the interviews. Also from this concern came the development of the *viewing session* as a format for interviewing the counselor and the student separately after their own interviews. In the viewing session a videotape of their interview was shown either to the counselor or to the student to stimulate recall of the practical specifics of interaction. Comments about what had taken place were elicited as the counselor or student viewed the tape, and these comments were recorded and later transcribed in typescripts.

From this attempt to be both specifically detailed and generally comprehensive in studying the action that took place in the interviews came an eclectic welter of analytic frames of reference and of practical routines for data collection and data reduction. In the counselors' offices, filming the interviews involved tangles of microphone and camera cords and occasionally snarls of film and tape. In the research laboratory, reducing the data involved some people listening to tapes on headsets and making typescripts, others watching film silently forward and backward using an editor–viewer and hand rewinds, still others using slow-motion projectors, all of which equipment in the hands of fallible workers was liable to produce snarls of film and tape. Conceptually the researchers were operating in some ways as linguists, in other ways as anthropologists, sociologists, and social psychologists who were doing participant observation and interviewing. We operated in other ways as ethologists doing careful *nonparticipant* observation of fine details of verbal and nonverbal behavior. Such diversity of orientations and methods presented continual potential for conceptual confusion. Those of us working on the project were usually liable to the characterization of the unspecialized anthropologist doing ethnographic field work as "a social scientist who does nothing well."

By attempting a *microethnography of communication* we confronted in miniature the problems faced by traditional general ethnography in attempting the holistic analysis of a single sociocultural system (village, region, linguistic community) and in attempting valid comparisons between sociocultural systems. Comparison between a film record of the "microsociety" of a single gatekeeping encounter and a film record of another encounter presents the standard problem of unit definition and rules of evidence that is found in attempts at intersocietal comparison, but in our data the problems appear in nonstandard form at microscopic scale. How could one make "microethnographic" statements of general rules or behavioral consistencies obtaining in the behavior sample that had been collected? There was concern for grounding those assertions on evidence that was relatively public, and not just saying, as in effect standard ethnography often does, "I (the researcher) was there and this is what I know about it."

Most of the theoretical assumptions and methodological principles we have employed are not unique to this project.[3] What is at least unusual and perhaps unique in this work is the attempt at systematic comparisons of parts and wholes of one kind of social occasion across an extensive set of analogous cases. This comprehensive analysis of an entire *corpus* of instances of whole social occasions (rather than just looking at one or two occasions as wholes, or at only a few instances of particular communicative behaviors across a large number of cases) has been an attempt to identify multiple aspects of variation related to the social identity and cultural communication style of the counselors and students that were filmed.

The Sample: Who Was Filmed

The counseling interviews discussed here took place in two junior colleges, one public and one private, in which as part of their daily routine counselors interviewed students of the counselor's own ethnic and racial background and also interviewed students whose ethnicity or race differed from that of the counselor. Sets of naturally occurring interviews were filmed with 4 counselors and 25 students (see Table 3.1).

Table 3.1 shows the films that were eventually selected for analysis. These are all the interviews filmed with the four counselors identified, except for two films, which were incomplete because the camera jammed during filming. These 25 films with those counselors were selected for detailed analysis on the basis of three criteria: They were the best in technical quality; for them we had the most complete viewing session

---

[3] These assumptions were mentioned in the preface, in Chapter 1 (pp. 1–8), and in Chapter 2 (pp. 13–17), and the notes to these chapters provide an overview of the bibliography in the various research approaches that were mentioned.

Table 3.1
The Sample of Filmed Interviews

Site	Counselor	Student	Number of instances
Public junior college	Italian–American	Italian–American	5
		Polish–American	3
	Irish–American	Polish–American	2
		Black–American	3
	Black–American	Black–American	1
		Polish–American	4
		Puerto Rican	1
Private junior college	Black–American	Black–American	3
		White–American	3
			25

data; (with but one exception) they involved interviews between male counselors and male interviewees. The reason for this last criterion is that, whereas we filmed interviews with female counselors interacting with male and female students, intuitively these cross-sex encounters seemed to be qualitatively different from the others. Sex difference seemed to make a difference, but that issue was not part of the original research design, so we decided not to include those interviews in the sample of those we analyzed most closely.

If we look over Table 3.1, it is apparent that across the various intraethnic and interethnic pairings of counselors and students there are not equal numbers of cases in each of the "cells." This was because of chance factors. Since naturally occurring interviews were being filmed, occasionally a student would not appear for a scheduled appointment or an extra student would be scheduled at the last minute, and in consequence the distribution of instances for a particular counselor would be skewed. This did not make a great deal of difference analytically because the variation in the data is so strongly patterned.

In addition, 55 other interviews were filmed, and filming and/or participant observation was done in six sites other than the two junior colleges. Some of these sites were schools, others were companies at which job interviews were studied. Two of the research staff went through an intensive 2-week training session on hiring-interview techniques at one of the companies, studying what the job interviewers were formally taught about gatekeeping decision making in the employment interview.

Inevitably, some of the interpretations made regarding the 25 interviews are influenced by the broader perspective that came from field experience and filming at other sites. Moreover, a number of the research staff had lived for some time in the city and a *participant's sense of the city* turned out to be crucial in studying the significance of ethnicity and comembership in the interviews. Still, the main lines of interpretation given here—and all the data presented—come directly from the intensive analysis of the 25 cases shown in Table 3.1.

How the Films Were Made

Initial contact with a counselor began with a brief period of participant observation and interviewing: 3 or 4 days of sitting in the counselor's office during interviews with students, having lunch with the counselor, and asking about his work—the organizational routines involved in it and the stock of practical know-how needed in order to do the job effectively. In this period rapport began to be established, and in addition a good deal was learned about the counselor's points of view about students and about the gatekeeping process.

After this period of initial contact the cameras were set up in the interviewer's office. The filming was done as unobtrusively as possible, with cameras and microphones off to the side in one corner of the office, in the area of peripheral vision for the counselor and student. No special lighting was used. The cameras ran noiselessly, and continuously, without moving and without "zooming" the lens. They were turned on and off by remote control (the equipment and its operation is described in more detail in Appendix B).

Inevitably, the question of unobtrusiveness of filming occurs. To what extent did the participants' knowledge that they were being filmed change their ways of acting during the counseling interview?

There were two kinds of obtrusiveness present in the scene. Not only were there cameras and microphones in the counselor's office, but students were asked for permission to film their interviews just before they entered the counselor's office, and so being "on camera" was likely to be salient for them at least at the beginning of the interview.

The issue of obtrusiveness is impossible to resolve definitively, of course. The filmed interviews did not seem to be different from those observed firsthand, but even in those cases the participant observer's presence may have been affecting what was happening.

Some evidence comes from the people who were filmed. Two of the four counselors studied most intensively said they had been slightly nervous at the beginning of the first interview that was filmed and then after that were not camera conscious. One of these two said he noticed the camera in some other interviews, but only at those moments in which the student did something the counselor thought was a bit embarrassing.[4]

Evidence also comes from other school counselors and administrators who watched the films. They uniformly agreed that the films were "true to life" for the kind of interview that was being conducted.

Since there is no way to resolve through empirical evidence the issue of whether what was studied was changed in a fundamental way by the process of studying it, the argument must finally rest on logical grounds. In thinking about this issue it is important to consider the power of reflexivity in everyday life—that apparent tendency of persons engaged in ordinary ways in everyday affairs to regard those affairs uncritically as "really" happening.[5]

While immersed in doing, one does not regard one's actions from the point of view of a detached observer. The observer stance permits abstraction and epistemological skepticism of a sort there is no time for while getting practical affairs done from moment to moment. In *lived time*, the compelling power of everyday life is that people become absorbed in it and take its "reality" for granted.

In an actual counseling interview, in contrast to a role-played one, there are actual practical affairs to be accomplished. Some gatekeeping decisions must be made. Questions need to be thought of. Once asked, their answers need to be thought of. It is easy for the counselor and student to get involved in the practical work that must be done from moment to moment. It may be far more difficult to keep on paying attention to the camera and to the researchers than to focus primarily on the interactional business at hand.

The Viewing Session as a Source of Emic Data

After an interview was recorded, the videotape of it was shown in separate viewing sessions to the counselor and to the student. These

---

[4] This counselor had the most training and experience of all the counselors studied, and, more than did the other counselors, he tended in viewing sessions to talk about the interviews in terms of his subjective experience during them, only one aspect of which was his occasional sense of being "eyed" by the camera.

[5] On the role of *reflexivity* in naive realism—the usual ways of understanding employed to make sense of everyday events while participating in them—see Mehan and Wood, 1975: 8–14 for discussion and additional citations.

sessions usually took place within 2 weeks of the time the original interview had taken place. The main purpose of the viewing session (besides learning the overall impressions each party had of the interview) was to elicit each person's judgments and perceptions of the sequential structure of the interview in order to determime what points in the continuous behavior stream were regarded as especially salient by the counselor and by the student.

Such judgments of salience are *emic* rather than *etic*. This distinction is so important for the organization of evidence in this study that it deserves brief definition and discussion here.

The importance of the distinction between the etic and the emic first became apparent as linguists studied languages that were very different from Indo-European ones in the ways that relationships between sound and meaning were organized. When studying these previously unstudied languages the linguists found that, whereas variation in speech sound could be thought of as an undifferentiated range of purely physical properties of pitch, tone quality, and articulation (having to do with how the sounds are produced by the organs of speech), only some aspects of the total range of possibilities for variation in sound were regarded as meaningful by speakers of a given language. Other aspects of variation that could be measured by scientific instruments were not regarded as meaningful by speakers. Moreover, aspects of variation in sound that went unnoticed in one language system—even to the extent of going *unheard* by the culturally trained ears of speakers of that language—were very salient for meaning in other languages, that is, different aspects of language *form* had differing *functional* significance in differing language systems.[6]

In English, for example, there are two functionally significant categories and two letters of the alphabet that designate the two physically different sounds /d/ and /t/. Conversely, in English the letter /p/ is used as a single category of meaningfulness for sounds that differ in physical properties that are regarded as meaningfully significant in some other languages. Speakers of English produce more of a burst of air (aspiration) after the "p" when it is found in final position, as in /top/, than they do in saying "p" when it is found in initial position followed by a vowel, as in /pot/. When measured by a recording instrument this difference in the physical form of the two "p" sounds shows up, but it is not noticed by speakers of English. We have only one letter in our alphabet for the different sounds of /p/. It includes both "p" sounds (and others as well)

[6] See the discussions in Hymes, 1977; Erickson, 1977; Pelto, 1977: 54–65; Pike, 1967: 35–72; Sapir, 1925.

within the same unitary category. Yet speakers of another language hear
the difference between the two kinds of "p" sounds as meaningfully and
discriminably different, requiring not one symbol in their alphabet, but
two. *Phonetically,* considered in terms of physical properties of sound
alone, the two kinds of "p" sounds differ. *Phonemically,* however, the
two kinds of sounds function the same in English. They are considered
variant "tokens" (allophones) within the same functional "type" or category, the *phoneme* /p/.

This distinction between considering things in terms of their physical
form or in terms of their functional significance within a system of meaningfulness and salience is of such importance that it cannot be over-
stressed, for it has been employed by linguists and linguistic anthropologists in drawing an analogy between the organization of meaning in the
sound system of a language and the organization of meaning in the status
system of a society.

Great cultural differences have been shown between ethnic groups,
occupational groups, social classes, and groups of people with specialized
interests (such as stamp collectors or gourmets) in which aspects of *etic*
variation in the physical form of phenomena are considered *emically*
salient and meaningful. Among black young men in northern American
cities in the early 1960s, for example, differences in the physical characteristics of different kinds of shoes distinguished people recently arrived from the "country" from those who had lived longer in the "city."
These differences among shoes went unnoticed by whites. Yet for black
young people, the emic cues to social identity provided by shoes and
other items of clothing, by haircut, and by what music one liked (all
components of a person's total self-presentation of social identity or
"front")—those cues were *distinctive features* in a whole system of
social classification along the dimension country–city (acting as they do
in the "country" down South, in contrast to acting as they do in the
relatively sophisticated northern urban black ghetto).[7] In the formal social
system of the school, this informal dimension of social classification, as
well as the performance cues that were diacritical for locating persons
along that dimension, were not regarded as emically salient and meaningful in white "teacher culture." They were very meaningful in black
student culture, and in the informal student social system.

Analogously, one could expect differences among school counselors
and students in what each regarded as emically salient as each watched
the videotape of his interview. One could also expect differences between

---

[7] For an ethnographic account of these patterns of salience to teenagers, see Keiser,
1969.

informants and researchers in the ways they regarded the interviews—what communicative cues were more meaningful than others, what parts of the interviews were regarded as more important than others, where the boundaries were drawn between one part and the next.

In order to learn the points of view of the counselor and the student about significant communication cues, verbal and nonverbal, and about the sequential structure of the interview—what was most important about it and where the most significant junctures in it were—it was necessary to develop a technique of elicitation that avoided putting the researchers' words and concepts into informant's mouths and heads, to the extent that this can ever be avoided. Such questions as "When he said *that*, what did you think?" or "What did *that* posture change mean?" would have been too directive, for the research began with a search for emic definition of *functional units of interaction* as well as the *social meaning of particular forms of communicative action* by which the functions were accomplished. Our intention was, when an informant said "Look at that," to learn what a communicative *that* was, from the point of view of the informant, as well as to discover what the *that* may have meant to the informant. On the other hand, we soon found that such an eliciting question as "What was important to you in the interview?" was so general as to be unintelligible and unanswerable.[8] We searched for ways of eliciting that avoided the extremes of being too directive or too nondirective.

The search for a way to avoid extremes led to the use of the behavior record itself—the videotape—as the main stimulus and organizing device for elicitation.[9] As the videotape was played the informant was asked no direct questions. Rather, each informant was asked to stop the tape and comment wherever he wished. In an introduction to the viewing session just before the videotape was played, the researcher called attention to change points and sections, emphasizing changes in emotional tone and intelligibility. Here is a transcript of the "framing" comment at the beginning of the first viewing session with one of the counselors:

[8] In school settings, at least, that question is likely also to be implausible and therefore untrustable. Schools are settings in which people of higher rank are constantly evaluating the performance of those of lower rank, and so it is understandable for school professionals and even for students to think that what researchers (who are people of higher rank) *really* are asking is whether what they did was right or wrong, rather than wanting to know how what they did is socially organized. On this point, see Florio and Walsh, 1980.

[9] In retrospect, the approach finally chosen may still have been too nondirective, in that some informants found it confusing not to be told "how and what to answer," but the dangers of being too directive in eliciting information about semantic domains in the area of social behavior may be greater than those of being too lax.

> The routine is that I won't ask any questions, I'll just let you respond to whatever seems important to you, whatever sort of reminds you of the kinds of things you were thinking about or what you thought maybe the kid was thinking about, or how you felt, how you thought he felt....If maybe a section that wasn't so comfortable—where you thought he understood what was going on or maybe he didn't seem to understand....It's whatever seems of significance. Just tell me to stop and we'll stop the tape.

As the informants stopped the tape and commented on the segment preceding the stopping point, it became intuitively apparent that they were not stopping at random points in the interaction they were watching. They usually stopped at a point in which a discourse topic or conversational routine had just been completed (e.g., "talking about courses this semester").

This can be seen in the following example. (The slash mark in the text indicates the point in the tape at which the counselor in the viewing session called out to stop the tape.)

EXAMPLE 3.1

(a)   S: (The student has been talking about his draft status.) ...They might take me along with the first group.

(b)   C: I see. (This is said overlapping the end of the previous turn, then...) It's kind of a bad position to be in isn't it?

(c)   S: Yeah, well, it's, you know

(d)   C: (the counselor changes seating position) I see, okay

This tendency to focus on discourse topics as definable units is also illustrated by the following comment by a counselor during a viewing session: "I think we're gonna move on now to something else." Here the "something else" in the counselor's comment refers to the next "chunk" in the discourse structure—the next discourse topic—which involved the student's academic major field.

The informants would sometimes point even more directly to what they regarded as the actual point of juncture between discourse topics, as in the following example. (The slash marks indicate the stopping points and the starting point of the replay of the tape.)

EXAMPLE 3.2

(a) C: (summing up the previous discussion of what the student's academic major is) The business programmer's that 2-year degree and you're pretty well on your way to that.

(b) S: Mhm. (Student and counselor shift seating position simultaneously.)

(c) C: Okay, so you..so that's..when you say you're going into programmer that's..that's what your're/("talking about.")

| Counselor in viewing session (CVS 1): | Stop...yeah, and push it back a little bit. (The videotape is rewound a few revolutions.) |

(a) C: /You're pretty well on your way to that.

(b) S: Mhm. (Student and counselor shift seating position simultaneously.)

(c) C: Okay, so you/

| Counselor in viewing session (CVS 2): | Right there. At this particular point both (name of student) and I seem to make, you know, a very similar movement in agreement to the fact that we had, uh, accomplished something and we're going to go on from that point. |

Here the counselor directed the researcher to replay the tape ahead of the first stopping point and then called out to stop "Right there" (CVS 2) at the end of the discourse "chunk" (beginning of turn *c*). The counselor refers to the juncture as "there" (CVS 2) and as "this particular point" (CVS 2). The juncture is marked verbally by the closing formula, "Okay, so you.." and it is simultaneously marked nonverbally by simultaneous posture and interpersonal distance shifts by the counselor and student—a mutual contextualization cue whose function was identified explicitly by the counselor in the viewing session comment. Alternatively an informant might stop the tape just after a new "chunk" ("talking about courses next semester") or at the beginning of a new discourse unit that had begun. Although the informants seemed to attend primarily to verbal content, they also stopped at points at which a change in nonverbal behavior had just occurred, *even when those nonverbally defined points were parts of larger sections defined in terms of verbal content.* At the ends of sections defined by verbal content, the informant would wait past the end of the final verbal phrase in the section until the moment a shift in interpersonal distance, change in eye contact, or other nonverbal marker occurred. At that point, rather than at the last word of a phrase, the informant would stop the tape and begin an interpretative comment.

Often these stopping points were moments at which new information had just been revealed about the student or job applicant, or the gatekeeper had just changed behavior style, beginning to perform as a new "social personage" toward the interviewee.

Viewing session comments were made frequently at moments when something had just gone wrong in the encounter. Comments were made much more frequently at these "uncomfortable moments" than at moments of especially good feeling or ease. The "uncomfortable moments" seemed to be easier to find.

When viewing sessions were held with the counselor and the student, occasionally they would both (in different viewing sessions) stop the videotape at precisely the same instant (or within 1 second of each other) to make a comment about what had just happened in the interview. (Because we audiotaped the viewing sessions we were able to identify these "stopping points" precisely by noting when the audio track of the video deck was turned off.) Sometimes the comments were mutually congruent with each other. (The gatekeeper might say, "I thought he was confused there," and the interviewee might say, "I was confused then.") At other times the viewing session comments might diverge sharply in interpretive content. The counselor might fail to infer that the student was offended or confused; that the student was characterizing the counselor's advice as insulting, and was inferring that the counselor's intent was to demean the student, or to say "No" implicitly to the student's stated future goal. (See the extended discussion of this issue in Chapter 6, pp. 155–163.) Such inferences of intent are extremely interesting, given the conversational maxim that apparently prevents the counselor, in talking to a student with whom he shares little comembership, from saying "No" or from pointing out specific problems the student has that may hinder the achievement of a desired goal.

What was also interesting was that, even though the comments made by the counselor and the student might be quite divergent in their inferences regarding each other's intent, the points in time at which they stopped in separate viewing sessions to report those inferences were very similar—often within the same second, at the same syntactic juncture as it was played on the tape. If both stopped the tape to talk about the same interactional moment, they always did so within a few seconds of each other in real time.

Sometimes only one of the two parties would make a viewing session comment on such a moment. In one interview, after watching the whole interview tape the counselor harked back to an earlier moment in it: "I came to a point of total frustration there when I said, you know, 'We can take these courses,' and he said, 'Yeah, but....'" The "there" refers to a particular brief moment in time, as does the "here" in this comment by a student in an interview with a different counselor: "Here I felt like getting up and walking out."

When they stopped the tape the counselors and students talked about those moments as "times," distinct from the "time" before them and after them in what was actually a continuous stream of communicative behavior. This may be evidence that interpretive work by people engaged in interaction may be temporally discontinuous (i.e., there may be particular points in the stream of interaction that are "aha" moments at which each of the interactional partners sums up interpretively what has been happening and makes an attribution of intent that is locally relevant to that moment). In the viewing sessions, the counselors and students may have been stopping at those points most salient for them. At other moments in the continuous flow of behavior, interactional inferences may have been in the process of being made and not yet have been crystallized into a judgment of what was happening then. On this issue the viewing session data are only suggestive. The ways in which interactional inference is organized in time are an aspect of social cognition on which much additional research is needed.

CONVERTING INFORMATION FROM
THE AUDIOVISUAL RECORD INTO DATA

We have said that social relationships and social meaning are constituted in the interviews by the performance of communicative behavior, verbal and nonverbal. Of interest is the organization of the social relationships and meanings, and also the concrete details of performance of which the organization is constituted. Accordingly the films of conversation in the interviews needed to be linked up with data at other levels. Four aspects of organization were considered across two levels:

Level I. Means of Revealing Social Identity and Role
      A. Topical content and sequential organization of discourse
      B. Participation structures by which topical content is discussed
Level II. Means of Organizing Conversational Cooperation
      A. Verbal and nonverbal contextualization cues that signal turning points in discourse organization

       B. Temporal and rhythmic organization of kinesic behavior
       (posture and body motion) and speech behavior (pitch,
       tempo, and rhythm in talk)

The aspects of conversational organization in Level I, topic and sequencing in discourse and participation structures in discourse, have
been discussed at some length in Chapter 2, and will be discussed in
later chapters, especially Chapters 4 and 7. The aspects of organization
in Level II were only briefly noted in Chapters 1 and 2, and so a bit
more discussion is appropriate here.

Sources and Kinds of Evidence from Behavior Coding

A variety of ways of coding data was developed. They were separate
and distinct research operations, but they were designed so that they
could be cross-referenced and ultimately combined in data analysis.
Researchers watched film in slow motion and at regular speed, with the
sound turned off and with it left on. They read typescripts of what had
been said. They interviewed the counselors and students.

Twelve separate coding procedures were used. Each code was related
to one of the aspects of the organization of discourse and conversational
cooperation mentioned earlier: (*a*) topical content and sequencing; (*b*)
participation structure; (*c*) contextualization cueing; (*d*) timing and
rhythm of speech and body motion.

The following codes identified specific features of communicative
means and conversational organization in the interviews:

1. *Codes for Speech Behavior*
    a. Two codes for aspects of speech prosody, one for voice pitch
       and one for voice intensity and rhythm
    b. One for the number of times speakers overlapped in talk or
       interrupted each other in each interview
2. *Codes for Nonverbal Behavior*
    a. One code for gaze direction and involvement, indicating when
       speakers looked at or away from each other
    b. One code for proxemic phenomena, indicating when speakers
       moved closer to or farther away from each other
    c. A notation system for describing kinesic rhythm—the timing (not
       the quality or specific content) of body movements—at micro-
       second intervals down to 1/24 second (the interval at which
       sound cinema film is exposed frame-by-frame)
3. *Codes Identifying Natural Units of Speaking and Listening Behavior*
    a. "Etic" codes for segmentation (in which units are defined from

the "outsider" perspective of the research staff—analogous to phonetic analysis in linguistics)

1. A code for overall behavior asymmetry, identifying sections during which the smooth flow of interaction between speakers broke down

2. A procedure for identifying subsidiary segments within the whole sections of behavioral asymmetry—an "asymmetry segments" code

3. A procedure for identifying microsegments within the subsidiary asymmetry segments, employing the kinesics notation system referred to in 2c above and a machine printout of intensity levels of the film sound track over a time line segmented in twenty-fourths of a second (corresponding to each frame of film). This procedure locates voice accent patterns in synchrony with body motion patterns.

b. "Emic" codes for segmentation (in which units, demarcated as whole "events," are identified impressionistically by the encounter participants themselves from an "insider" perspective or by naive judges from a "quasi-insider" perspective)

1. The "emic" codes for the overall impressions of the encounter participants themselves, one indicating the location of a viewing session comment in relation to the flow of interaction in the original encounter, another code indicating the content of viewing session comments

2. A group of "quasi-emic" codes for overall impressions of interaction process administered as a questionnaire to naive judges who viewed videotapes of the original encounters and scored a questionnaire for each encounter

It is apparent that the data that could be gained from these codes differ both in source and in kind. "Data source" refers to the medium of recording (audiotape, film, etc.) and the sensory modality through which that medium is experienced by the coder while coding. For example, use of the audiotape by a coder (auditory medium without visual information) and use by the same coder of the cinema film with sound turned off (visual medium without auditory information) would produce differing accounts of the same interview because of the very different sensory experiences of the coder.

"Data kind" refers to the phenomenological status of the data— whether the coded information is derived "etically" by a trained research assistant attending to the formal structure of interaction as defined in technical terms, or whether the information is derived "emically" from the mind of a participant in the encounter or "quasi-emically" from the

Table 3.2
Sources and Kinds of Coded Data

Code	Data source		Data kind
(Behavioral phenomenon)	(Sensory modality)	(Information medium)	
Proxemic	Visual	Cinema (silent)	Etic
Eye contact	Visual	Cinema (silent)	Etic
Kinesic/asymmetry—segments	Visual	Cinema (silent)	Etic
Kinesic/and prosodic rhythms—microsegments	Visual (first)	Cinema (silent)	Etic
	Auditory (second)	Cinema (sound)	
Paralinguistic (pitch)	Auditory	Audiotape	Etic
Paralinguistic (intensity accents)	"Auditory" (machine printout)	Cinema sound track	Etic
Kinesic/asymmetry—sections	Auditory–visual	Cinema (sound)	Emic (encounter participants and judges)
Overlap/interruption	Auditory–visual	Cinema (sound)	"Quasi-emic" (judges)
Interaction process	Auditory–visual	Video	"Quasi-emic" (judges)
Viewing session	Auditory–visual	Video	Emic (encounter participants)
Topic (referential function of speech)	Visual	Transcript	Etic
Time reference (referential function of speech)	Visual	Transcript	Etic

mind of a naive judge, viewing a videotape to identify those "common-sense" aspects of the encounter that can be known "obviously" by members considering the encounter in a relatively unreflective way.

One of the methodological principles was to mix sources and kinds of data in the analysis to achieve a form of "triangulation" of evidence. The elements of these triangulation procedures are not new; the *etic–emic* distinction, as we have already noted, is a commonplace among linguists and anthropologists. A "triangulation" of sensory modalities in research on face-to-face communication was employed in the 1950s by Gregory Bateson and his colleagues (Ray Birdwhistell, Norman McKeown, Margaret Mead, H. W. Brasen, and G. F. Hackett) in their unpublished study of a single therapy interview from the perspectives of kinesics, linguistics, anthropology, and psychiatry, titled "The Natural History of an Interview."[10]

Much subsequent research focused on the nonverbal channel or in the verbal channel separately, and so analysts proceeded mainly by *listening* or by *watching*. In our analysis we tried to combine listening-derived data with watching-derived data. We attempted a systematic and comprehensive triangulation across diverse bodies of evidence by deliberately varying (*a*) the "insider" (emic) and "outsider" (etic) perspectives according to which the data were coded and analyzed; (*b*) the levels of inference involved in coder's judgments and in analytic interpretation of data; (*c*) the sensory modalities by which research assistants experienced the *raw data* on film and tape. Table 3.2 presents a synoptic view of the sources and kinds of coded data, suggesting the variety of triangulations of evidence made possible by such diversity of information.

[10] See Bateson *et al.*, n.d.

4

Aspects of Social Organization in Communicative Performance

An essential aim of the counselor in the interview is to determine *who the student is*. As we have already noted, this is not simply a matter of what the student has done in the world outside the encounter. Also involved is what the student does in the "local" circumstances of interaction during the encounter itself. To put it in slightly different terms, the student's social identity, the *social fact* the gatekeeping interview is supposed to identify and ratify, cannot be considered simply an inherent and stable set of characteristics of the student himself. The social identity of the student is to some extent labile, interactionally emergent within the exigencies of communicating moment by moment with the counselor. This section of the book considers the organization of the behavioral means employed in communication as the student and counselor by their actions constitute a social ecology for one another.

In the next three chapters we will consider more closely how this ecology works, and how performed social identity gets done, communicatively. This chapter will discuss some of the communicative means by which interaction is *socially organized*. These are aspects of organization that are likely to be found universally among humans as they interact face-to-face. The next chapter will discuss cultural patterning in the conduct of communication. This involves aspects of organization that are not found universally but are distinctive among particular cultural groups and speech communities. The last chapter in this section will show some of the ways of asking questions and of giving advice that are optionally available to the counselor. That chapter will discuss ways in which the counselor's optionally available choices may constrain the student's opportunities to construct an acceptable social identity in the interview.

THE SOCIAL ORGANIZATION OF COMMUNICATIVE ACTION

Face-to-face communication is social in that it is action taken by an individual in account of the actions of the other individuals present. (See the introductory discussion in Chapter 1, pp. 9–10.) If action is taken that does not adequately take account of the actions of others, we say in ordinary language that it is "out of place." Such action is inappropriate because it is *inadequately social*. The conduct of interaction from moment to moment involves such a delicate balance of cooperation among the interactional partners that inadequately social action by one of the partners throws the other partners off. Behaviorally it looks and sounds then as if the partners were stumbling over one another, as in a moment of clumsiness during the course of a ballroom dance. Conversational hesitations and false starts occur as the smooth trajectory of conversation is momentarily disrupted. Then forward motion is reestablished and the conversation continues.

How are conversational partners able to pick up the pieces of their interaction after a stumble and continue with the performance? What cooperative organization is involved in maintaining the fluent conduct of conversation so as to avoid stumbling at all? What skills would conversational partners need to be able to converse fluently? These are questions about the operation of fundamental social steering mechanisms in face-to-face interaction. They cannot be fully answered here because students of the conduct of interaction are only beginning to understand the issues and principles involved. But some partial answers can be attempted.

We can assume that whatever organizational principles and individual knowledge and skill are involved, these are at some level human universals, since we can see face-to-face interaction conducted fluently in all sorts of encounters across many different kinds of human societies and cultural groups. Some of the principles and skills we discuss here are being observed in interaction among newborn infants and their caretakers.[1] They are also being found in the studies of animal communication, from which we infer prehuman origins for these aspects of the organization of communication.[2]

People of varying ages and cultural backgrounds all seem to be actively engaged while they interact, in telling one another what is happening as it is happening. This can be called *telling the context* by means of "contextualization cues."[3] The particular ways this telling is done—what signals are used and how the signals are employed and interpreted by the interactional partners—may vary developmentally across the life cycle and may also vary from one culture to another. But some ways of telling the context seem to be present in all instances of face-to-face interaction among humans. People seem to use these ways to keep one another on the track, to maintain in the conduct of interaction what musicians call "ensemble" in the playing of music.

If this continual telling is necessary, it follows that conversational partners must be radically interdependent in their actions together. In Chapter 1 we mentioned briefly two aspects of this interdependence: reciprocity and complementarity. Both notions involve the timing and sequencing of interaction. *Reciprocity* refers to the interdependence of actions taken successively across moments in time. One party takes action in account of what another party has just done, and then in the next moment another party takes action in account of what was done the moment before. Reciprocity is a matter of the immediate past and immediate future history of the action being taken at any given moment.

Complementarity refers to the interdependence of actions taken simultaneously in the same moment. As the speaker is explaining the listener is showing attention. As the listener's attention wavers, so may, in the same instant, the speaker hesitate in speaking. In slow-motion

---

[1] See Condon, 1974; Brazelton, Koslowski, and Main, 1974; Stern, 1977; Stern and Gibbon, 1979; Beebe, Stern, and Jaffe, 1980.

[2] See Byers, 1976; Chapple, 1979.

[3] The term is that of Gumperz (see Gumperz, 1977; Gumperz and Tannen, 1979). It refers to those aspects of communicational "surface structure"—verbal and nonverbal behavior—which function as cues pointing implicitly to the "context" or "frame" of interpretation of the meaning of behavior. The notion that communication behavior contains within itself signals that point to the interpretation of its meaning was first articulated by Bateson in a discussion of animal communication (Bateson, 1972). The behavioral modes or means employed by humans to cue the context or frame of semantic interpretation include speech prosody (Gumperz, 1977), postural positioning (Scheflen, 1973), and "proxemics" or interpersonal distance (Hall, 1966; Erickson, 1975). The rhythmic organization of speech and body motion is, we will argue here, a fundamental means for contextualization cueing. On this point, see also Bennett, 1977.

analysis of film this simultaneity is dramatically evident. The synchrony among conversationalists seems not to be a matter of stimulus-response organization at microsecond intervals, but of mutual *entrainment* of all conversational partners within an overall pattern of rhythm.[4] A speaker's gesture may begin in the same split-second as a listener's nod, and then in the next moment, as the speaker's hand changes direction, the listener's head may change direction simultaneously. Speaker and listener may cross and uncross their legs simultaneously while talking. At the end of the conversation they may rise simultaneously from their chairs. During a single utterance, the listener's "mhm" or "right" may accompany in exact simultaneity a point of emphasis in the speaker's speech.

Communicative action occurs in particular moments of actual time, in particular relationships of simultaneity and sequence. These relationships in time, taken together, constitute a regular rhythmic pattern. This regularity in time and timing seems to play an essential, constitutive role in the social organization of interaction. If action is to be taken in account of the actions of others, the action must be taken not just in any old time, but in particular moments in time, moments whose time has come. Such appropriate moments and predictable next moments are defined in terms of the overall temporal context, the pattern of timing to which all conversational partners are contributing by the reciprocal and complementary pacing of their behavior in speaking and listening. Whereas there is no metronome playing while people talk, their talking itself serves as a metronome.

Two differing aspects of time are involved in the social organization of behavior in communication face-to-face. The ancient Hebrews and Greeks made a distinction between these different kinds of time. This distinction is found in the Greek terms *kairos* and *chronos*. *Kairos* means *the right time*—the *now* whose time has come. Such moments are not necessarily measurable in clock time. Right times may happen after long and indefinite stretches of not-yet-right time. The "acceptable time" for an action by God or by man in history spoken of by the Hebrew psalmists and prophets (e.g., Psalm 103(104):27 and Ecclesiastes 3:1–9) and by the Greek-speaking early Christian writers (e.g., Matthew 24:45) is called *kairos* in the Greek translation of the Hebrew Bible and in the Greek New Testament. This is cosmic time in the workings of human history and nature. The Ecclesiastes poem begins "For everything there is a season and a time for every matter under heaven, a time to be born and a time to die. . .[Ecclesiastes 3:1–2]." *Chronos,* in contrast, refers to duration of time in the ordinary space-time world apparent to the senses.

---

[4] See Condon and Ogston, 1967; Byers, n.d.

It is mechanically measurable—what we would now call clock time, or continuous *real time*.[5]

Conversation in an encounter has both a small-scale history and a measurable duration. Consequently the organization of discourse in conversation partakes both of *kairos* and of *chronos*. Sequential functional units of discourse are of indefinite duration. They can be thought of as "slots" or "chunks" which can be "filled," at various hierarchical levels of organization, by strings of successive topics, or utterances, or sentences, or words (and at all levels by accompanying nonverbal behavior). A discourse topic may be discussed briefly or at length; the answer to a question may be one word or an elaborate string of words and gestures. While the duration of communicative action in a given functional slot may vary, certain sequence relations between slots remain constant. That constancy is a feature of conversational history, part of its *kairos* organization. In English–American discourse, for example, an answer slot appropriately follows a question slot. To give an answer before the question is asked is to violate culturally conventional expectations for proper sequencing in discourse. Such an answer is not one in the *right time*; the *kairos* time for an answer is after a question rather than before it.

Similarly, *kairos* organization is involved in the regular sequence relationships among units at higher hierarchical levels of discourse. In the counseling interview, the major successive topics are part of the *kairos* organization of discourse. *Talking about courses this semester* is invariably preceded by *talking about grades and courses last semester*. Given that sequence relationship, to begin to talk about courses this semester before having begun and completed talk about grades and courses last

[5] Very little appears in the literature of communication research on the importance of studying the organization of behavior in real time, unreduced by analytic synopsis (personal communication, Albert B. Robillard, February, 1980). Analytic accounts of behavior, whether in the form of charts, transcripts of speech, or ethnographic narratives usually are not presented to scientific audiences in a form that reports the actual durations of behavior in real time. Thus the analyst works from a synopsis and loses a sense of the strategic organization of the timing of events, much as a musicologist might "read over" the score of a piece of music without playing it. Through such "reading over" one can indeed discover interesting formal patterns (e.g., sequencing, repetition of stylistic elements). But one does not identify the *strategic*, functional organization just through visual inspection. A sense of the strategic comes best from "playing over" the music—reenacting it in real time. Then the strategic organization of duration, the "now" and "not quite yet," is experienced, in lived time. This is why in the latter part of this chapter and in the next chapter we present text examples that are to be said aloud rather than "read over" silently. Another way to experience the real-time organization of interactional behavior is to mimic the verbal and nonverbal behavior of others. For additional discussion of these issues see Sudnow, 1978, 1980.

semester is inappropriate. In the unfolding history of that interview it is not yet the *right time* for that topic.

Kairos organization is also involved in the insertion of unofficial topics within the overall sequence of the official agenda. Stretches of inserted small talk in which comembership may be revealed must be followed by a return to the topic on the official agenda. Opening up the small talk topic can be done too soon, in terms of the official agenda. Closing the small talk topic down can be done too soon in terms of standards of cordiality that apply once the small talk topic has been opened up. Overall, there are right and wrong times for the alternation between official and unofficial business in the interview.

In sum, the *kairos* organization of discourse defines relationships of appropriateness in sequencing at various hierarchical levels, from pairs of adjacent utterances to pairs of adjacent discourse topics.[6] The major and minor "slots," "chunks," or "seams" of the event are qualitatively different contexts for action depending on their location in the *kairos* dimension of time: *now, not quite yet, too late.* These are strategic aspects of timing in the conduct of talk. Conversationalists need behavioral ways of telling one another what time it is in *kairos* time.

Conversationalists also need behavioral ways of pointing to time in its *chronos* dimension. This too is done within the conduct of talk itself. When conversation takes place there are rhythmic cycles and wave patterns in verbal and nonverbal behavior that are both intuitively apparent and mechanically measurable. These are durations in *chronos* time. The successful intercalation of communicative behavior between conversational partners seems to involve *staying in phase* with these wave patterns.[7] When interactional "stumbles" in verbal and nonverbal behavior occur, the behavior of the conversational partners is thrown temporarily out of phase. As the partners mutually recover from their mutually produced stumbling their reciprocal and complementary communicative behavior returns to being in phase once again.

We will discuss and illustrate the rhythmic organization of verbal and nonverbal behavior in conversation more fully later in this chapter and in the next chapter. At this point it is enough to say that the underlying rhythmic wave patterns in verbal and nonverbal behavior of speakers

---

[6] The reader is referred to Figure 2.1, which shows the overall sequence of topics for the interview. The point here is that getting through such a sequence is something done in real time, not in a synoptic representation of real time.

[7] Notions from wave theory, such as *phases* and *peaks,* are additional metaphors by which rhythmic periodicity and interpersonal synchrony and entrainment can be described. The extent to which these metaphors should be taken literally in the study of face-to-face communication is not presently clear.

and the listening behavior of listeners are the communicative means by which a relatively stable context of timing is enacted in conversation. In that context of *chronos* organization, conversational partners are apparently able intuitively to recognize and predict the onset of strategically crucial *kairos* points in conversation—the "now moments" in which certain actions are appropriate, and the "next moments" at which a redirection of action will soon become appropriate.

In question–answer pairs of utterances, for example, the sequencing relationship is a matter of *kairos* organization. But in the actual performance of these successive units of discourse there is a measurable duration of *chronos* time between the appropriate ending (or offset) of the question and the appropriate beginning (or onset) of the answer. In a given section of a conversation this same *chronos* duration may obtain between other kinds of adjacent utterances. When two successive utterances are the bridge or juncture between two major discourse units, such as one discourse topic and the next, the *chronos* duration between utterances—a regular rhythmic interval—defines the *kairos* time for the onset of the utterance that will open up the new topic. Thus in the counseling interviews, as the counselor and student move from talking about grades and courses last semester to talking about grades and courses this semester, the rhythmic interval between the last utterance in *grades and courses last semester* and the beginning syllables of the first utterance in *courses this semester* provides a temporal signal of appropriateness. Using this time interval as a cue, the person opening up the new sequential discourse slot is able to "know" intuitively the specifically right time, behaviorally, in which to do so.

Underlying *chronos* wave patterns obtain within utterances as well as between them. The patterns are outlined by points of emphasis in body motion and in the speech stream. In English, a heavily stressed language, points of emphasis in speech, called *stressed tonal nuclei,* are most distinctly marked by a combination of pitch (intonation) shifts and increased loudness (stress). These points of emphasis in speech, together with alternating or cooccurring points of emphasis in kinesic activity (e.g., points of extension and flexion in gesture, shifts in postural positioning), often occur at evenly spaced time intervals. Taken together, these verbal and nonverbal points of emphasis mark a pattern of regular rhythm. This underlying *resultant rhythm* or *cadence* is slightly freer than a metronomic "beat," but it can be reliably measured by a metronome or by other sorts of chronometric instruments. Because the points of emphasis in pitch and stress contribute to the overall pattern of rhythmic regularity, it is necessary to take them into account in analysis. This is why coding for these aspects of speech prosody was one of the elements in the research design for the study of talk in the counseling interviews—see the discussion in Chapter 3, pp. 64–67.

Conversationalists have two related practical problems in the conduct of talk together. One problem is *when*, specifically, to say what to whom. Another problem is *how*, specifically, to say what to whom. Most analysis of conversation by students of face-to-face interaction, regardless of disciplinary perspective, has been concerned with understanding the latter of these two problems of practice. But since conversation takes place in real time, the *when* of the action may be as fundamental a practical matter as the *what* of it. To "say" or to "listen" the right thing in the wrong time, verbally or nonverbally, can be as inappropriate—as inadequately social—as to say (or listen) the wrong thing in the right time.

This is why the *when* of communicative action and the communicative means by which the *when* is signalled receives such emphasis in this discussion. The telling of the context in and through communicative behavior continuously across real time seems to be crucially important for the social organization of conversational cooperation, a means by which conversationalists are able to tell one another implicitly from moment to moment what to expect from one another. It seems that it is the sequential (*kairos*) organization of communicative behavior in real time (*chronos* time) that enables conversationalists to engage in fluent discourse and to regard one another as conversationally competent. In terms of the gatekeeping counseling interview, it is in particular moments of real time that the *right times* come to introduce a topic of small talk by which the student can reveal an attractive aspect of social identity. And it is in real time that the student and counselor may reveal aspects of social identity that are inappropriate or unattractive. As the rhythmic organization of conversation falls apart at a certain moment in real time, not only may a behavioral stumble occur but the social identity of a competent conversationalist may fall apart at that moment, for the counselor or for the student. The student may come out of such a stumble being regarded by the counselor as unreasonable or disinterested.

Interactional stumbles represent a failure in the basic social steering systems of conversation. The steering signals, or *contextualization cues*, are behaviorally displayed, verbally and nonverbally. These cues signal the context in which a given utterance is to be interpreted at that moment, and they foreshadow changes of context that are about to happen.[8] In the following sections, three levels of organization will be discussed:

---

[8] The aspect of contextualization cueing that has been most fully discussed by Gumperz is signaling the context of the present moment. In a much earlier statement, Hall (1964) discussed the function of nonverbal cues in foreshadowing the interpretive contexts for subsequent moments to come.

(1) telling the context at the level of the discourse topic and of connected sequences of topics; (2) telling the context at the level of the utterance or conversational turn; (3) telling the context at the level of continuous, moment-to-moment action within turns at speaking.

SOCIAL STEERING AT THE LEVEL OF THE DISCOURSE TOPIC

Telling the context at the level of the discourse topic is a key organizing process that enables the counselor and student to coordinate their actions in moving from one principal part of the interview to the next. The problem for the counselor and the student at this level of organization is knowing when the topic and participation structure changes.

The evidence for the function of behavioral forms as "road signs" marking these major turning points in the conversation can be identified in two ways—by close examination of illustrative examples and by a more comprehensive examination of coded data in summary form. We will first examine illustrative examples and then turn to a more synoptic view.

The distribution of some kinds of contextualization cues in the counseling interview is related to the sequential structure of the encounter at each hierarchical level of organization (see Figure 2.1, p. 22). One can identify the discourse units (and the participation structures they entail) in terms of these boundary markers.

Shifts in role relationship between the counselor and the student, marked by contextualization cues, are apparent across the boundaries between major discourse topics and across the boundaries between one subtopic or conversational routine and the next within a major discourse topic. This can be seen in the following example:

EXAMPLE 4.1
(Juncture) Discourse Topic: Grades in Course
Last Semester

(a)   C: Well, let's start from scratch. What did you get in your English 100 last semester?

(b)   S: A "C."

(c)   C: Biology 101?

(d)   S: "A."

(e)   C: Reading 100?

(f)   S: "B."

(g)   C: Med Tech..."B"? (medical technology)

(h)   S: "B."

(i)   C: Gym?

(j)   S: "A."

(k)   C: Was that a full credit hour? What was it?

(l)   S: It was a wrestling..two periods.

(m-1)   C: Wrestling. (He writes this on the record card, then shifts postural position and looks up from the record at the student.)

(m-2)   C: ..OK, this semester.. (high falling intonation on "OK") English 101?

(n)   S: (Changes facial expression, but no nod or "mhm" in response to the question.)

(o)   C: That's what you've got now...

(p)   S: (Nods.)

(q)   C: Biology 102? Soc Sci 101. (The counselor is looking down.)

(r)   S: I..I.. I don't have Biology 102. I have, mm, 112.

(s)   C: (The counselor corrects the record card) Soc Sci 101?

(t)   S: (Nods.) Mhm.

(u)   C: Math 95.

(v)   S: (Nods.)

(w)   C: Med Tech 112.

(x)   S: (Nods.)

(y)   C: Gym.

(z)   S: (Nods.)

(Juncture) *Discourse Topic: Courses Next Semester*

(aa)   C: (shifts postural position and interpersonal distance to student, looks up, and says with high falling intonation on "OK" and "summer") OK, for the summer... (the interview continues).

Turns *a–z* encompass two adjacent conversational routines in which the counselor, as the leading conversational partner, determines the current formal academic status of the student. At the last turn in the example, *aa*, the overall topic shifts to the student's future plans, first in terms of registration for summer school (the interview was held during spring semester) and then later in terms of the student's future career goals.

At first glance this may seem an entirely obvious way of asking about grades and courses. But it involves two differing conversational routines whose social organization is not obvious, either to the reader of the text or, as it happens, to the student in the interview, who made an interactional mistake at the transition between the first and the second of the routines.

The counselor performs the function of *asking* in basically similar ways throughout the example (asking about a single course at a time across the series of courses the student has taken or is taking). But the student is required to enact *answering* in two different ways across the two adjacent routines. In the first routine, consisting of turns *a* through *m*-1, the student's answering role involves saying phonologically distinct words (the "letter grades") in response to the counselor's questions. In the second routine, consisting of turns *m*-2 through *z*, the student's answering role no longer involves the production of verbal utterances, but nonverbal ones: nods and the nonlexical vocalizations ("mhm," "yeah," etc.) that have been termed *backchannels*.[9]

The student apparently did not realize that at the interactional juncture between the two adjacent routines it was necessary to change to a slightly differing participation structure. This is evidenced by the student's inappropriate response in turn *n*, at which point the student expressed confusion about how (and what) he was supposed to answer. In turn *o* the counselor made accountable the absence of the appropriate answering response form by saying the clarifying remark, "That's what you've got now."

After the clarification by the counselor (which explained what the counselor was asking, but did not explicitly instruct the student in the correct behavioral form for answering), the student in turn *p* provided the correct form and content of an answer. The correctness of the student's response in turn *p* is evidenced by the counselor's next move in turn *q*, which was to go on to the next question. The counselor also continued on after the student's responses in turns *t*, *v*, *x*, and *z*. From this one can infer that, after the initial clarification by the counselor in turn *o*, the student's responses to questions were correct both in form and in content.

An analogous sequence of clarifying moves can be seen in turns *q*, *r*, and *s*, in which the student rather than the counselor was the initiator of the clarification. In turn *r* the student held the counselor accountable for going on (during turn *q*) to the next question ("Soc Sci 101?") before the student had responded to the prior question ("Biology 102?"). The

---

[9] See Yngve, 1970; Duncan, 1972.

student had not answered this prior question because it had indicated an error in the record card: The student was actually registered for Biology 112. In turn *s* the counselor indicated both nonverbally and verbally that he understood the student's clarification. The nonverbal indicator was the counselor's writing to correct the student's record card. The verbal indicator was his continuing on to ask the next question, "Soc Sci 101?"

The change in the *answering* role of the student from one discourse topic to the next was signalled communicatively in two ways: (1) by the counselor's responses to the student's incorrect behavior and correct behavior; (2) by the presence of verbal and nonverbal contextualization cues at the interactional juncture between the two different ways the student is to act (turn *m*-2). These *transition relevance markers,* the verbal "OK," the changes of intonation, posture, and of interpersonal distance, seem to be signalling not only that new informational content is about to be asked for but that the way of answering that was socially appropriate the moment before will no longer to be appropriate in the moments to come.

The functions of various behavioral forms as contextualization cues that signal boundaries between adjacent discourse topics and participation structures can also be illustrated by considering data from the various summary codes listed in the previous chapter (see Table 3.2, p. 66). Those data were arrived at by a process of analytic *decomposition.* Coders were required to attend usually to only one communication channel at a time, verbal or nonverbal, and to attend to only one aspect of semantic content or behavioral form on that channel—that is, for the verbal channel, attending only to the referential meaning of sentences on a transcript, or only to intonation shifts as heard on an audiotape, and for the nonverbal channel, attending only to shifts in interpersonal distance or only to changes in eye contact.

After such decomposition of behavioral parts of communicative performance it was necessary to bring them together again. Because all the coded data had been cross-referenced in terms of the location of the coded event in real time, it was fairly simple clerical task to retrieve the coded parts and reassemble them into an analytically reconstructed whole. This was done in a summary table (see Table 4.1) in which data from all the codes were cross-referenced according to line numbers on the typed transcripts of speech during the interview. Information displayed on the summary table is digital;[10] the table indicates only the

[10] This is true for all the codes except that for *eye contact,* which included information not only on the presence or absence of gaze but on the quality of the gaze (e.g., mutual gaze, the cause for looking at student without student looking at counselor, etc.).

Table 4.1
Illustration of a Summary Table

Line	Topic	Time reference shift	Prox-emics 1	Prox-emics 2	Para-language 1	Para-language 2	Overlap	Eye contact	Viewing session comment
28	1							1	
29									
30	1								
31	1								
32						1			
33	1			1	1	1		11	
34	11111			1	11	1		1	
35		1				1	1	1	
36					1	1		1	
37	11	1		1	1	1			
38	1	1			1	1		11	
39				1		1			
40					1	1		11	
41	1								
42	1	1							
43	11111111	111		1	11	11	1	1111	1(1)
44	111								
45	111	1			1	1	11	1	
46									
47	1	1			1			11	
48						1		11	—
49	1	1				1	1	1111	
50					1	1		1	—
51	1				1	1		1	
52									
53	1111	11			1	11	1	1111	
54					1	11			
55	111						1	1	
56					1				

81

presence or absence of change along the various coded dimensions and indicates the relationship of the changes to each other in terms of their approximate location in time.

This process of analytic abstraction provides a synoptic view of the organization of communication in the interview. The major differences in the *texture of presence or absence of change* that are apparent as visually discontinuous "chunks" when one looks at Table 4.1 represent changes from one major discourse topic to the next. Returning to the overall synopsis of the interview that was presented in Figure 2.1 (p. 22) and comparing that picture of the whole interview with the "enlargement" of one part of the picture that is provided by Table 4.1, it is apparent that the summary table is an index of the sequential order of discourse in the interview. (See also the additional summary tables and examples of discourse texts in the Appendices, pp. 227–244.)

The sequential order of discourse can be seen to be *social order* in two senses: (1) in that each discourse topic represents a particular successive step in the acconplishment of the main social purposes of the encounter—in the logic by which gatekeeping decisions are accomplished in the interview; (2) in that each shift in discourse topic involves *some change, however slight, in the relationship of communicative rights and obligations among speakers* (e.g., exchange of the roles of speaker and listener, or change to a different form of *answering role* from the one that had been appropriate during the previous discourse topic).

In the light of this evidence, social contexts can be seen not just as environments external to verbal and nonverbal communication, but as *social environments enacted in communication*—environments that may shift from one moment to the next. For conversationalists this means that new distributions of communicative rights and obligations are likely to occur each time one turns a corner in the conversation. From inspection of Table 4.1 and of the ones presented in Appendix C (pp. 227–244), we can hypothesize that shifts in communicative *form* tend to occur at points of change in communicative *function*—at the junctures between differing discourse topics and conversational routines within which differing rhetorical ends are at stake. The shifts in cue form occur simultaneously along various dimensions of communicative means, verbal and nonverbal (i.e., there is *modality redundancy* in the cluster of cues).[11] Usually such shifts occur on both the verbal and the nonverbal channels at once, and usually, as well, the greater the functional signif-

---

[11] For discussion of explicit verbal statements by which interactional partners hold each other to the social order they are collaboratively producing in their interaction, see Mehan and Wood, 1975: 101–106, 125–134; McDermott, Gospodinoff, and Aron, 1978. On the issue of modality redundancy across verbal and nonverbal channels, see Fitzgerald, 1975; Erickson and Shultz, 1977.

icance of the interactional juncture in terms of the sequential order of discourse for the interview as a whole, the greater the modality redundancy of the cluster of cues—that is, the greater the number of dimensions of performance on which shifts occur. Thus we would expect that the turning points in the interview that are most important in terms of the social purposes of the conversationalists are the points that would be most clearly emphasized behaviorally by clusters of contextualization cues, in order to maximize contrast as a kind of fail-safe device in the social steering process.

To see whether these expectations hold true across all 25 counseling interviews one can turn to the summary tables for those interviews in which shifts in verbal and nonverbal performance form for each complete interview are summarized. When all the tables are examined it appears that at the junctures between discourse topics or subtopics there is a cooccurrence of shifts across three or more out of a possible seven behavior codes. The minimal cluster of three shifts always included some shift in nonverbal behavior form as well as a shift in verbal behavior, and many junctures are marked by a cluster of shifts on more than the minimal three dimensions of difference in performance form (see Table 4.1).

The most important sequential turning point in the whole interview, in terms of its official purposes as a gatekeeping interview, was the point at which the student revealed his future academic or occupational goal (see Figure 2.1, p. 22). This was the moment of major reorganization in social relations between the counselor and the student, the moment at which the counselor's role in speaking shifted from primarily one of *asking* to one of *telling*. Moreover, the counselor's *telling* that occurred just after the student stated his future goal was the most important *telling* in the whole interview, since the counselor was speaking explicitly or implicitly then about the likelihood of the student's being allowed to take next steps toward the desired goal.

Goal statement points, in each of the 18 interviews for which data were available on all coding dimensions, were marked by an average of 5.6 simultaneous shifts in behavior from out of a total of 617 possible shifts. This average is extremely high. It suggests that in all the interviews the counselor and student were employing virtually all the communicative means at their disposal to mark the salience of the most important juncture in the interview.

The next most important kind of moment in the interviews, from the point of view of informants, as revealed in viewing session comments, and from the point of view of raters watching films and videotapes at regular speed with sound (see Chapter 3, pp. 63–67), was the conversational "incident," or uncomfortable moment. These moments crosscut

Table 4.2
Percentage of Proxemic Shifts Occurring at "Segment Boundaries"

Counselor	Interethnic encounters	Intraethnic encounters	Number of cases
Irish–American	100	91	(6)
Black–American	100	84	(6)
Black–American	97	91	(6)
Italian–American	77	71	(8)
Overall	92	80	26

the overall sequential order of the interview. Incidents could occur at any point in the interview, just as could digressions into humorous, particularistic "small talk." In interviews in which things had been going wrong and the student had already established a bad "record" as a conversationalist, the goal statement point was often an uncomfortable moment.

All the moments coded as "uncomfortable" by a pair of raters (with interrater reliability above 90%) were marked by clusters of contextualization cues. This was true for every instance of the uncomfortable moments that occurred in all 25 of the interviews coded.

Interestingly, of all the kinds of shifts that made up a cluster of modality redundant contextualization cues, the proxemic shift (a change in interpersonal distance between the speakers) was the one most likely to occur in the minimal cluster of three shifts or more. Thus a proxemic shift (or a postural shift, since a change in interpersonal distance always involves a change in posture) is the best predictor, among all the indicators coded, of a new segment in the discourse structure. The percentages of instances of minimal clusters that included a proxemic shift are shown for all 25 interviews in Table 4.2. The table shows that, despite individual differences among four counselors, and despite differences in frequency that are related to similarity or difference in ethnicity between the counselor and the student in any particular interview, all the percentages are still very high for the occurrence of proxemic shifts at major sequential turning points in the discourse structure.

In addition, proxemic shifts were also the best predictors of nonsequential "chunks" in the stream of communicative behavior (i.e., uncomfortable moments). Every uncomfortable moment in the 25 interviews without exception was marked by a rearrangement of postural and proxemic relationship between the counselor and the student.

These findings are consistent with those of a number of other researchers.[12] Despite minor differences in approach among these inves-

---

[12] Notably, Scheflen, 1973; McDermott, 1976; and McDermott, Gospodinoff, and Aron, 1978.

tigators, the consistency of this finding cross-culturally and across a wide age range suggests that shifts in postural–proxemic relationships may be the most salient indicator of principal segments of interaction and of discourse beyond the level of the sentence—even more salient than shifts in speech prosody or lexical transition makers such as "OK" or "Now." Proxemic shifts can be seen to have fundamental importance as a non-verbal behavioral means of social steering in face-to-face interaction.

In sum, modality redundant clusters of shifts in verbal and nonverbal behavioral form, especially shifts in posture and interpersonal distance, can be seen to function as contextualization cues marking the major turning points in *kairos* time in the interviews.

SOCIAL STEERING WITHIN AND ACROSS UTTERANCES—THE ROLE OF RHYTHM IN CONVERSATIONAL COOPERATION

The next set of issues to be discussed involves *chronos* time—the organization of verbal and nonverbal communication in real time within and across utterances. We have said that conversationalists must know when to do what in order to cooperate in conversation. They must know how to perform various kinds of communicative behavior. They must have a sense of the various kinds of socially constructed contexts in which sets of those behaviors are appropriate. In addition, they must be able to know, in *chronos* time, *when a context is about to happen.* The capacity to anticipate a new communicative context in the next moment to come can thus be seen as an essential aspect of communicative competence, and the *chronos* organization of communicative behavior can thus be seen as behavioral ways of telling the *kairos* organization; that is, the continual succession of *right times*—right moments for appropriate action. Behaviorally this telling of the context seems to be accomplished by the periodic placement across *chronos* time of points of emphasis in the speech and body motion behavior of all participants in the interactional event. These points, behaviorally discontinuous with what happens before and after them, and regularly spaced across time, constitute a framework of timing that can be perceived as a recurrent rhythmic pattern.

Example 4.2 illustrates this organization in *chronos* time. The example begins at the closing conversational routine at the end of one principal discourse unit (Elicitation of Courses Taken This Semester). The example continues across speaking turns within that routine and across a major interactional juncture, marked by a large postural–proxemic shift, at which the next major topic (Plans for Next Semester) is introduced.

In Example 4.2 and in all the following examples, all the stressed syllables are underlined. Most are performed at a constant temporal interval from one another, while some appear at other intervals. Elongated vowels are indicated by successive colons, as at *c*–4, "No:w."

Each dot indicates approximately one-quarter-second duration. The syllable at the left margin of each line of text occurs approximately 1 second later than the corresponding syllable just above it on the previous line. The syllable or syllables at the right margin of each line occurs just a split second before the syllable that appears at the left margin of the next line down (as in "to a total" in *a*-9, 10 of Example 4.2).

A few points of especially marked kinesic emphasis are also noted in the example, such as the point of furthest extension in a gesture or the point at which one or both conversational partners change posture and interpersonal distance. Those points of nonverbal and verbal emphasis that occur at the regular periodic interval of the resultant rhythm are displayed in the example along a vertical axis down the page (i.e., along the left margin). Each time an emphasized bit of speech, nonverbal behavior or, as in a few instances, an *absence* of behavior falls along that axis, the behavior is equidistant, temporally, from the behavior occurring on that axis on the line of text above it.

The underlying periodic interval is 1 second, with slight variation faster and slower at some points. The reader should "count out" a 1-second pulse or use a metronome and read the passage aloud to experience the rhythmic organization. (It is extremely important that the reader actually read these examples aloud rhythmically in order to be able to understand the subsequent points to be made.)

EXAMPLE 4.2
Discourse Topic:
Elicitation of Courses Taken This Semester

```
                ┌ (1)  (SHIFTS)       .              .              .
C: turn a       │      (chair)
                │ (2)  A:h            .              .      so you've got
                │ (3)  English   one-hundred    .                   .
                │ (4)  Afro-american          history
                │ (5)  Reading   .              one      -    twenty
                │ (6)  six            .              .              .
                │ (7)  Speech    .              one   -  oh  - one
                │ (8)  .                       an' then the rest are P::
                │ (9)  E::      courses         .              .     to a
                └ (10) total         of          eighteen             .
```

```
                                                              yes      a
S: turn b    ┌─(1)  total       of        eighteen   |   know   it's a
             └─(2)  total       of        eighteen
```

Discourse Topic:
Plans for Next Semester

```
                                                              A:ll
                                                              (falling
C: turn c    ┌─  (1)  right        .           .        fine     and
             │        intonation)
             │
             │       (2)  good         .           .          .
             │            (shifts    postural      position)
             │
             │       (3)  (clasps)      .           .          .
             │            (both hands together)
             │
             │       (4)  N o : w
             │            (steeply falling intonation)
             │
             │       (5)  A : : h       .           .          .
             │
             │       (6)  .             .           .       as   far   as
             │
             │       (7)  next semester       .            .
             │
             │       (8)  (reaches)    .           .          .
             │            (for book)
             │
             │       (9)  Why       don't      we      give      some
             │      (10)  thought    .       to a::: h            .
             │      (11)  .             .           .          .      to
             │      (12)  what     you'd    like    to    take    there
             │      (13)  .             .           .       . do you
             │      (14)  plan       .           .       on   con
             │      (15)  tin      uing     a     long    this    P::
             └─    (16)  E::      major?
```

Notice that the constant rhythmic interval is maintained both within a conversational turn (e.g., turn *a*) and across exchanges of turns between speakers (turns *a*, *b*, *c*). The constant interval is maintained even when no speech or accentuated body motion occurs "on the beat" (e.g., *a*-10, *c*-6, *c*-11). In these instances there is a stressed syllable at the next point in time that the rhythmic interval is repeated (*a*-11, *c*-7, *c*-12), and just preceding the stressed syllable there are a few elided syllables that are syntactically connected to the accented one and that function rhythmically as enclitic "pick-up notes" anticipating the major point of rhythmic emphasis (e.g., *a*-9, 10 "To a total," and *c*-6, 7, "as far as next semester").

Occasionally the rhythmic interval is marked by nonverbal behavior alone, as at *c*-3 and *c*-8. In those instances, accentuated gesticulation (*c*-3) or gesticulation together with a posture shift (*c*-8) provides points of kinesic emphasis that function rhythmically to maintain the constant periodic interval.

One can see that, with but a few exceptions (e.g., *a*-10, *c*-6, *c*-11, *c*-13), the recurring rhythmic interval is behaviorally marked by some form of emphasis, whether verbal or nonverbal. Such regularity functions to regulate turn exchange (see turns *a*, *b*, *c*), enabling the speakers to predict the *next moment* appropriate for such exchange of roles.

The presence of an underlying constant rhythmic interval also functions as a framework within which changes from one discourse topic to the next can receive emphasis through a change in rate of speech. Notice that at the beginning of turn *a* and at the beginning of turn *c*, each of which is a juncture between discourse topics, the counselor's rate of speech slows down drastically, but does so in the same temporal framework as that underlying the more rapid speech that follows and precedes it. At the beginning of turn *a*, the periodic rhythmic interval is still behaviorally emphasized nonverbally even though very little speech is being produced. At *a*-1 the counselor shifts in his chair, then at the next interval (*a*-2) says "Ah." Only after these pauses does the counselor begin more rapid speech.

A similar pattern of emphasis is seen at the beginning of turn *c*. There the counselor pauses at *c*-2, marks the next rhythmic interval nonverbally at *c*-3, marks the next several by saying "Now" at *c*-4 and "ah" at *c*-5, by pausing at *c*-6, at *c*-7 by saying only "next semester," at *c*-8 by reaching for the book, and at *c*-9 by beginning rapid speech. This extreme slowing of the rate of speech (together with the postural and proxemic shifts and intonation shifts) functions to mark emphatically the juncture between the two principal parts of the interview. This is the moment of transition between talk about the student's past performance and the beginning of talk about his future goal.

The change in speech rate, organized in and through the constant underlying rhythmic framework, is one element of the cluster of co-occurring contextualization cues marking this major interactional juncture. (This is the juncture that appears as the most discontinuous "chunk" boundary in the summary table on p. 81, Table 4.1, line 43. The "Now" of *c*-4, 5, 6, 7, "Now, ah, as far as next semester.." which occurs in *chronos* time after slowed speech rhythm, can be seen to be a "Now" in *kairos* time—in the *right time* for the onset of a major turning point in the discourse structure.

The previous example shows how the verbal and nonverbal speaking behavior of speakers maintains the underlying rhythmic interval within and across speaking turns. It was claimed that the rhythmic framework was maintained not only in the *speech behavior* of the speaker, but also in the verbal and nonverbal *listening behavior* of the listener. It is possible to examine the temporal complementarity between speaking and listening behavior even more closely. Figures 4.1 and 4.2 provide such a closer look. They display the conversation as it continued from the end of turn *c* in the previous example. In Figures 4.1 and 4.2 the continuous speech and kinesic behavior of the counselor and student are diagrammed. The speech appears in printed letters, with stressed syllables printed in capital letters. The motion of various body parts is indicated by slanted lines, a change in the upward or downward pitch of the line indicating a change of direction in motion. Straight horizontal lines indicate the absence of motion. The resultant periodic rhythmic interval is indicated by the straight vertical strokes appearing along a channel halfway between the top and the bottom of the figure. Real time is displayed on the horizontal axis of the figure, in units of 1/24 of a second. The data on the timing of kinesic behavior that are displayed in the figures were coded by slow-motion analysis of frame-numbered cinema film.

Figures 4.1 and 4.2 show two principal ways in which points of emphasis in the speech and kinesic (body motion) behavior may cooccur simultaneously in time:

1. Speech accents and kinesic accents may cooccur within the individual who is speaking at that moment. (See for example at 4350 the /tin/ in "continuing." This stressed tonal nucleus in the counselor's speech is accompanied on the nonverbal channel by simultaneously cooccurring changes in direction of motion of the head, right arm, and left arm, and aversion of the eyes.)
2. Speech accents by the speaker may be accompanied by simultaneously cooccurring accents in the listening behavior of the listener. (See for example 4450, at which the stressed syllable "up" in the student's speech is accompanied by simultaneously cooccurring cessation of motion—a *completion* of previous motion—in the counselor's left and right hands.)

The points of kinesic emphasis are accomplished behaviorally by means of the onset of motion and also by changes of direction in motion (e.g., the point in gesticulation at which an arm sweeps back after having moved forward, or the point in nodding at which the head changes

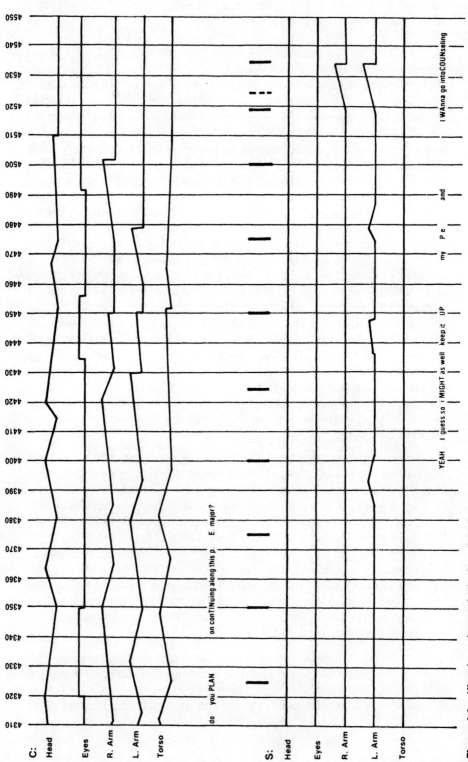

Figure 4.1. Kinesic and speech rhythm chart I.

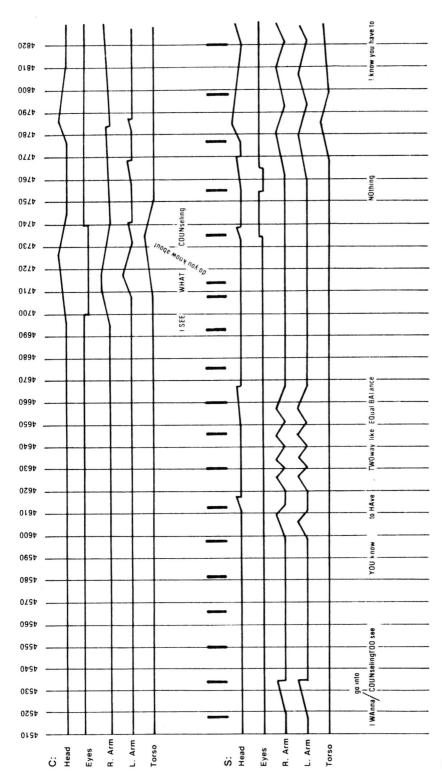

Figure 4.2. Kinesic and speech rhythm chart II.

direction of motion). These are momentary points of discontinuity in behavioral flow, discontinuity by which the emphasis of contrast is achieved.

Figures 4.1 and 4.2 show that the cooccurrence of nonverbal and verbal markers of emphasis (as at 4350) makes emphasis even more striking than it would be if marked by intonation and voice-volume shifts alone. The figures also show clearly that some of the most extreme points of emphasis—those points marked both by volume and pitch shifts on the verbal channel and also by simultaneous kinesic shifts in a number of body parts on the nonverbal channel—are points of emphasis that are evenly spaced in real time (see, for example, 4200, 4350, and 4450). When these major points are subdivided by halves (and by halves again) it becomes apparent that subsidiary points of verbal and nonverbal emphasis also appear more often than not at regularly spaced intervals in time. That interval marks the underlying *resultant rhythm*. In introducing Example 4.1 on p. 77, we claimed that the underlying resultant rhythmic interval was approximately 1 second (24 frames of cinema film, ± 1 frame). This can be seen even more clearly in Figures 4.1 and 4.2, which show the continuation of the conversation presented in Example 4.1.

The speaking and listening behavior of both the counselor and the student can be seen in Figures 4.1 and 4.2 to be organized according to an underlying resultant rhythmic interval, across turns at speaking as well as within them. The continuity of rhythmic stress across exchange of speaking turns can be seen across turns *c* and *d* (4310–4450). Within the last phrase of turn *c* ("Do you plan on continuing along this P.E. major?") the accented syllables of speech fall 24 frames apart, ± 1 frame—at frames 4325, 4350, and 4375. The prosodically emphasized tonal nucleus syllable "tin" of "continuing," which occurs at 4350, is also very saliently marked by multiple cooccurring kinesic shifts. The vocally stressed syllable immediately prior to "tin"—the syllable "plan" which occurs at 4325—is more subtly marked kinesically, with only one kinesic shift cooccurring with the vocal stress. This kinesic shift, however, is one occurring in the torso. Thus it is a shift in postural position and interpersonal distance, which as previously noted is a major interactional marker. Hence at 4325, even though only one kind of nonverbal emphasis is added to the emphasis of vocal stress, this moment of communicative performance is still set off by contrast in behavioral form from that of the verbal and nonverbal behavior immediately preceding and following it.

Sometimes vocal stress appears by itself, without a simultaneous nonvocal behavioral complement. This is the case at 4375, where the vocally stressed syllable "E" (in "P.E. major") is relatively subtly marked both because stress occurs without a cooccurring shift in pitch and also because there are no accompanying kinesic shifts. Rather, the kinesic shifts fall at 4380, at the next *minimal interval of timing*[13] in cooccurring speech and body motion behavior.

Despite its relatively subtle behavioral emphasis, the syllable "E" does mark the underlying resultant rhythm, for it occurs at frame 4375— precisely 1 second after the syllable "tin" at 4350.

Continuing on, if it were indeed the case that the underlying resultant rhythmic interval was 1 second in duration, one would expect to find some kind of behavioral emphasis occurring at the next predictable point, which would be 4400. That is what happens. At 4400, even though there is no speech occurring, the "peak" of a head nod by the counselor can be seen to be occurring. Immediately after this nod the student begins to speak: (nod) "//Yeah, I guess so," and then the next stressed syllable, "might," occurs at 4425. "Up," the stressed syllable immediately subsequent to "might," occurs at 4450, again exactly 1 second later: (nod) "//Yeah, I guess so, I might as well keep it up."

What happens next shows yet another way in which the speech and kinesic behavior of a speaker and listener are rhythmically coordinated. The accented syllable "up," which occurs in the student's speech at 4450, is followed after a pause in speaking by the accented syllable, "P" at 4475. Before the student said "P," however, the counselor performed back-channel listening behaviors: the vocalization *mhm* accompanied simultaneously by a *head nod* and *torso shift*. Notice that the initial "m" of the counselor's "mhm" occurs at frame 4462, which is precisely halfway between 4450 and 4475, ± 1 frame. Thus the counselor's back channel is rhythmically consistent with the underlying resultant rhythmic interval.

The rhythmic organization of discourse is especially obvious in the interviews in the most stylized of the conversational routines, the question–answer sequence. The successive question–answer pairs in Example 2.1 (found in Chapter 2) are performed, verbally and nonverbally, in reciprocal alternation according to a clear rhythmic cadence. This can be seen here in Examples 4.3 and 4.4, which are sequences taken from the long text that was presented first in this chapter as Example 4.1. These examples should be read aloud as were the previous ones, at a rate of approximately one "beat" per second, the "beat"

---

[13] Both Condon and Ogston, 1967 and Byers, n.d. find that the minimal time unit for body motion (kinesics) in conversation is 4–5 twenty-fourths of a second.

falling on successive syllables that are spoken more loudly than the others. Also, as in the previous examples, increased loudness, or *stress*, is indicated by underlining beneath the stressed syllable. In these examples many of the stressed syllables are also ones in which a rising or falling pitch shift occurs. Those syllables receive emphasis through both intonation and stress marking. (See the explanation of the text notation system on p. 86.)

EXAMPLE 4.3
Turn

(a) C: .   .   .   .Bi-
            ologen   one-oh-one?

(a) C: .   .   .   .Bi-
            ology   one-oh-one?

(b) S: "A".   .   .   .

(c) C: Reading   one   hundred?

(d) S: "B".   .   .   .

EXAMPLE 4.4

(a) C: Soc-sci   one-oh-one?

(b) S: mhm   .   .   .

(c) C: Math   .   .   ninety

(d)   five?   .   .   .

(e) S: (nods)   .   .   .

(f) C: Med tech . .   .   .one

(g)   twelve?   .   .   .

(h) S: (nods)   .   .   .
          mhm

(i) C: Gym   .   .   .

(j) S: (nods)   .   .   .

In some instances the question slot is accomplished within one pulse and the rhythmically appropriate answer slot occurs at the next pulse (e.g., Example 4.3, turns *a* and *b*, "Bi ology One-oh-one?" "A."). In other instances the question turn takes two pulses to accomplish (each syllable is spoken more slowly), but the rhythmically appropriate answer slot is still the next pulse immediately following the last pulse in the question slot (e.g., Example 4.4, turns *c*, *d*, and *e*, "Math Nine-ty five? (nods)").

Failure to respond in the right time can constitute a minor interactional "incident." This can be seen in the following instance at the juncture between the first two discourse topics in Example 4.1 on p. 77 of this chapter.

> (turns *m*-2 through *p*) "OK, this semester .. English One-oh-two?" (no answer) "That's what you've got now." (nods)

In Example 4.1, the student, by failing to respond with an appropriately timed answer at turn *n* (/no answer/) revealed himself as *a person who does not know that he is in a new conversational routine now—one that involves a role shift in the form and meaning of answering behavior.* At that point a minor interactional "incident" occurred. During that incident the counselor responded by clarifying the discourse topic. (Since "what you've got now" is not courses for which final grades have been received, the student can respond with indications of "yes" rather than with "letter names of grades," as was required in answer slots during the previous discourse topic.)

In this instance, apparently, the student's hesitation was interpreted by the counselor merely as an indication of unfamiliarity with the sequencing and contextual cueing of conversational routines in the interview. But sometimes a hesitation had a social meaning with serious consequences for the interview as a whole. This is illustrated in the next example.

In viewing another interview the counselor commented that he had given a particular student (not any of those in the previous examples) an interactional "mini-test" to see how the student would react. The counselor did this by asking the student to say what grade he expected to get in a remedial math course (remedial courses are prerequisites to entering the regular level of academic math courses that count for credit in transfer to 4-year colleges). In the viewing session the counselor stopped the tape at that point and said:

> "I got the impression he was doing well (so) I'm gonna chance him" (i.e., let him skip the next math course in the sequence, which was an "academic level" course [101], and register him for the next academic math course in the sequence [math 102], thus helping him to graduate on schedule).

> (If he had) "hesitated to give me just the slightest impression, "Well maybe not—I'm not doing *that* well.." (then the counselor would require the student to take the next course in the regular sequence, which would mean it would take him an extra semester to get his Associate of Arts degree).

The student in the previous example did not hesitate, and so he "passed" the interactional mini-test, but other students "failed" such tests. The counselor interviewed pointed out additional social meanings for hesitancy when he said in another viewing session,

> judging them on the basis of nothing but outward signs I figured, "O Lord, what did I get here?" And I really think that some of this hesitancy comes across in the beginning of the interview..on my part as well as these kids. Both of them seemed to be rather nervous when they came in...but I think the hesitancy was mutual (i.e., the interviewer was nervous as well).

Considered at a surface level—one that people talk about spontaneously in viewing sessions—the organization of interactional timing is related to social organizing work in that it provides opportunity for the administration of interactional mini-tests by the counselor, and for the revelation of nervousness through hesitancy. But as we have seen, the temporal organization of behavior also has fundamental, constitutive importance for the social organization of interaction.

DISCUSSION

Reciprocal and complementary action in face-to-face communication appears to proceed by a remarkably fine-tuned system of temporal regulation. Conversational partners are literally completing one another's actions in and across time; they are forming behavioral environments for one another in real time.

In our own research and in that of others, the ubiquity of the finding that communicative action is organized synchronously and rhythmically across real time suggests that this phenomenon is likely to be found universally in human interaction.

We contend that this rhythmic complementarity in behavior has social meaning—indeed, that it is constitutive of social meaning. It seems to permit a complementarity of interactional inference that would otherwise be impossible to accomplish during the course of conversation.

The function of temporal redundancy in communication seems to be the interpersonal coordination of social action face-to-face. Among individuals engaged in interaction, coordination of communicative *action* can in turn be presumed to involve coordination of communicative *inference* and communicative *choice*, all within a framework of real time.

At each level of organization of kinds of communicative choice, from the sequencing of the principal part of the social occasion, through constituent discourse topics, turns at speaking, syntactic clauses within utterances; through the level of speech prosody and accompanying *kinesic prosody*, all the way "down" the levels of hierarchical embedding to the microsecond level of phonological choice of speech sounds and of "kinological" choice of body motions, decisions are apparently made at some moments and not at others. These are apparently not conscious decisions, but they can be thought of as decisions nonetheless. Because of the need to decide *in time*, some continual sense of *what time it is* would seem to be crucial for moment-to-moment decision making in face-to-face interaction. It seems that temporal redundancy permits an interpretive sense of where one *is* in interaction, of what was a *moment before* and what will be a *moment to come.*

We are assuming that such a "retrospective–prospective" awareness is a process of interpretive inference that is "read off" communicational surface structure. Our ability to know when something should happen next in *kairos* time (and when to decide about what to do next) would seem to depend on the presence of cueing devices in the communicative behavior performed in *chronos* time. In this chapter two aspects of that cueing process have been shown—the "major" cues of postural/proxemic shifts at the boundaries between principal conversational units, and the "minor" cues by which an underlying resultant rhythm of interaction is maintained.

Our analysis underscores the importance of not abstracting prematurely from the actual behavioral organization of communication in actual time. The performance of an actual interview is much more complex than an abstracted, synoptic view of it can show. Tremendous complexity of behavioral integration between speakers is involved from moment to moment.

Moreover, between *synopsis* and *performance* there are not only differences in degree of complexity but in kind of complexity as well. A dimensional shift is involved. One moves from a universe of analytically frozen time in which relationships of sequence can be comprehended all at once, into a universe of actively lived time in which choices from among optional ways of acting must be made from moment to moment across real time. The interactional consequences of many of these choices are never fully clear, to participants or to analysts. The choices and their consequences cannot be clear, for there is so much happening interactionally that it cannot all be consciously apprehended at any given moment, much less across those moments in time.

Seen from the theoretical point of view enabled by the close analysis of behavior as it is organized in real time, sequences of social action can be seen to have a special character. They are not simply chains of sequentially linked units whose relationships of sequential connection (literally, *syntaxis*) can be simply accounted for abstractly by expression in symbols of formal logic, allowing a whole sequence of actions to be read off at a glance. To be sure, one can do this appropriately for some purposes of abstract sequential analysis (such as those conducted by linguists of a Chomskyan persuasion). One can do this for language just as one can read off a whole phrase of music in an instant while looking at a musical score without actually "playing the music through" in real time. But performing the music actually is a fundamentally different sort of activity from reading it over at a glance. That analytic abstraction, literally a "pulling out" of relationships of sequence from their temporally local contexts, is not appropriate for the construction of theories of social organization of *performance* in interaction, nor for theories of the underlying *social competence* persons must have in order to enact such performance. Since sequences of actual events in the performance of social interaction *occur in and through* chronos *time* (not outside it in some universe of merely logical possibilities of sequential connection among adjacent units of communicative action), theories that attempt to explain the practical conduct of interactional performance (and empirical methods of testing those theories) must take account of the organization of communicative behavior and communicative inference in *chronos* time as well as in *kairos* time.

5

Cultural Organization and Its Effects on the Social Organization of Performance

CULTURAL ORGANIZATION IN COMMUNICATION

The Distinction between Cultural and Social Organization in Communication

In the previous chapters we have used the term *social organization* to refer to the structure and process of cooperation in communication face to face. This cooperation has been viewed as literally *interactional,* involving relationships of interdependence between speaker's speaking and listener's listening, and relationships of meaning and connection between what one conversational partner said the moment before and what the other partner is saying now.

We have assumed that cooperation in conversation is a human universal. How the cooperation is done, however, may vary from one human group to the next, depending upon the cultural standards of appropriateness and effectiveness in the conduct of interaction that are shared within a given human group. *Cultural organization* refers to the shared standards or communicative traditions governing the use of communicative means, verbal and nonverbal, in accomplishing communicative ends in social interaction. (See the initial discussion in Chapter 1, p. 5.)

Both the means and the ends of communication are culturally defined as appropriate, effective, and intelligible. When persons meet who have learned different communicative traditions regarding intelligibility, effectiveness, and appropriateness, troubles can result in the social organization of their interaction. The conversational partners may "miss" one another repeatedly in their attempts at social steering in conversation. This can happen if they are using different standards for action and interpretation—different communicative means of accomplishing the interactional function of *telling the context*. (See the discussion in the previous chapter.) The partners also may misunderstand one another at the level of explicit and implicit *message content* of their talk. This can happen if they are using different standards for action and interpretation in the telling of explicit and literal meaning (referential meaning) or implicit and metaphoric meaning (social meaning) to one another.

The Distinction between Speech Community and Linguistic Community

A *linguistic community* is a set of persons who share common standards for interpreting the literal (referential) meaning of utterances. These standards of interpretation may not necessarily be identical among all the members of a linguistic community, but speakers must share at least sets of standards which are at least functionally equivalent[1] if they are to be able to hear one another's speech as intelligible in terms of the explicit referential meaning of their utterances. Between people who are members of differing linguistic communities—speakers of Hindi and of English, for example—there is not enough sharing in standards of interpretation (knowledge of grammar and sound system) for their speech to be mutually intelligible in terms of literal meaning.

A *speech community*,[2] in contrast to a linguistic community, is a set of persons who share functionally equivalent standards not only for the interpretation of referential meaning, but also for the appropriate and effective uses of speech and of styles of performance in speaking. The notion of speech community is both more inclusive and more restricted than that of linguistic community. It is more inclusive in that it encompasses more aspects of communicative knowledge and performance skill

---

[1] On this point see Wallace, 1970:9–34. He argues that culture-sharing and socialization provide for the *organization* (here, read "articulation") *of diversity* among individuals rather than the *replication of uniformity* among them. See also Goodenough (1971, 1976), who maintains that knowledge of multiple interactional subcultures is not only characteristic of individuals in large-scale modern societies but in small-scale traditional ones as well.

[2] See Gumperz, 1962, 1968.

than does the notion of linguistic community. Members of the same speech community knows *ways of speaking* and *ways of listening* that communicate social as well as referential meaning, in implicit as well as explicit ways. The speech community is also more restricted than the linguistic community in that the set of persons who share communicative traditions regarding ways of speaking and ways of listening that have distinctive *social* meaning may be a subset of the people who share common knowledge of the standards for interpreting the literal, referential meaning of utterances. In other words, people who "speak the same language" may not necessarily mean the same things by what they say, verbally and nonverbally. They may belong to the same linguistic community but to differing speech communities within the linguistic community.

The distinction between linguistic community and speech community is especially relevant in considering large-scale, multiethnic societies, such as the United States. People who meet as strangers in institutional settings, such as hospitals, social service agencies, work places, and schools may understand the literal meaning of the English spoken by one another. Yet if they are members of differing speech communities they may misinterpret subtleties of social meaning in what they are saying. They may also misinterpret the things they have left unsaid "in so many words." Moreover, people from differing speech communities within the same linguistic community may be employing differing kinds of social steering devices in conversation. The ways they use to tell the context from moment to moment may be mutually unintelligible, even though they understand the referential meaning of each other's talk.

Cultural differences in communicative traditions between differing speech communities may be quite distinct and obvious, as in the difference between the "East Indian English" spoken by native speakers of Hindi and other languages of India and the "British English" spoken by native speakers of the cosmopolitan, middle-class dialect of southern England.[3] Ways of speaking and listening—in terms of speech prosody, rhetorical strategy, and attention behavior—are so different between "British English" and "East Indian English" that communicative difficulties often arise between members of these groups. When one considers that, in addition to these difficulties of interpretation, political tensions between members of the two speech communities in large industrial cities of England exacerbate the unwillingness of members of the two groups to tolerate the difficulties in understanding one another

---

[3] See Gumperz, Jupp, and Roberts, 1979. Their discussion provides background material and notes for a British television film titled "Crosstalk: A Study of Cross-Cultural Communication." The film was produced by John Twitchin and broadcast on the BBC, May 1, 1979.

that continually arise in face-to-face relations, the likelihood of mutual misunderstanding is great indeed.

Cultural differences in communicative traditions between differing speech communities may be quite subtle and still be a source of misunderstanding in face-to-face relations. Under conditions of intergroup conflict, even slight differences in ways of speaking and listening that are small (by scientific standards) may be regarded as large differences that make it difficult to communicate. The very existence of the subtle differences may not be recognized by members of differing speech communities. If things repeatedly go wrong in face-to-face interaction across speech communities, members of those communities may come to stereotype one another as unreasonable or difficult, rather than identify one source of their recurring troubles in the differing ways they have of speaking and listening.

Our expectation is that in formal organizations such as schools, when one category of persons there (such as counselors) repeatedly finds that members of another category of persons (such as "black students," "Polish–American students," "Latino students," "custodians," "members of the board of trustees") repeatedly come across face-to-face as acting unreasonably, or inattentively, or too aggressively, some aspects of these interactional troubles are due to cultural differences in ways of speaking and ways of listening. The "cultural difference" explanation may not account for all the sources of trouble—differences in political and economic interest may also be involved—but our supposition is that the cultural explanation usually accounts for some of what goes wrong recurrently, whether one views cultural differences in ways of acting as mainly a *cause* of conflict, or as mainly an *effect* of other sources of conflict.[4]

A fundamental problem in the gatekeeping counseling interview is that the counselor's authority to make official judgments of the student's identity enables the counselor to designate officially those students whose ways of acting are inappropriate during the interview *as less "competent," socially and academically,* than those students whose ways of acting are appropriate. To the extent that the student's ability to act appropriately during the interview depends on the similarity or difference between the counselor and student in their cultural knowledge of ways of speaking and ways of listening, the process of official gatekeeping decision-making by the counselor is influenced by speech community

---

[4] Barth (1969:13–16) can be interpreted as arguing, as do McDermott and Gospodinoff (1979), that cultural differences are best seen as epiphenomenal of more fundamental political conflict among social groups rather than as causes of the conflict. This issue goes beyond the scope of our inquiry here. The point will be returned to in the final chapter.

membership. In the interview how the student acts is what the student gets, in help from the counselor and in official labeling as competent or incompetent.

This introductory discussion, which presents a case for the possible importance of cultural difference and speech community membership for the conduct of interaction, still stops short of showing *how* culture comes to make a difference in the conduct of interaction. To that issue we now turn.

Because the social steering processes discussed in the previous chapter seem so fundamental to the successful conduct of interaction face-to-face, we will consider here the ways in which cultural differences seem to affect two aspects of these steering processes. The first aspect involves the rhythmic organization of verbal and nonverbal behavior during *uncomfortable moments* in the interviews. The second aspect involves relationships of interdependence and mutual regulation between the speaker's ways of speaking and the listener's ways of listening during *explanations* in the interviews.

CULTURAL DIFFERENCE AND
INTERACTIONAL RHYTHM

A radical interdependence between conversational partners seems necessary to accomplish interaction face to face. One important aspect of that interdependence involves the coordination of action in and through continuous, "real" time. As we saw in Chapter 4, that coordination seems to take place through rhythmic patterning of speech and body motion by the parties engaged in interaction.

Disturbance of this underlying redundancy in the timing of interaction may indicate that conversational partners are in serious interactional trouble. This discussion considers some of the troubles that result when the regular timing of interaction is distorted.

If the structure of mutual timing between speakers is a kind of mutual calibration between them by which they are able to make accurate predictions of what will be happening next, then instability in timing presents a fundamental social problem for conversationalists. It would interfere with conversational inference. It would make the continuation of social action in conversation as difficult as it is for a group of performing musicians when one or two of them play in a temporally irregular way and upsets the underlying rhythmic structure of the music. For musicians the loss of rhythmic *ensemble* is so serious a problem that during rehearsal the playing must be stopped and begun again, not necessarily

"from the top," but at the first major sequential juncture prior to the
moment at which the playing of the music became rhythmically disorganized. For musicians this involves going back to the previous phrase
or chorus and starting again. But that is possible only in rehearsal. In
performance before an audience they must keep playing, wobbling along
for a few seconds until the "beat" is reestablished by all the players
together.

In the counseling interview, which is also a performance in that the
counselor and student are audience for one another, when the rhythm
of conversation falls apart the counselor and student do not stop everything and begin again at the previous speaking turn or discourse topic.
They keep talking, but do so hesitantly, by fits and starts. While they
are doing this interactional stumbling they look and sound clumsy and
uncomfortable.

Analysis of Uncomfortable Moments

Often as the counselor or student watched their videotape in a viewing
session, it was at moments of conversational stumbling that the counselor
or student would stop the videotape and say that something had gone
wrong in the interview. Since these moments of interactional stumbling
seemed important to the counselor and student, we investigated them
more closely. The transcripts of all the viewing sessions were searched
for every instance in which the counselor or the student (or both) had
reported some kind of discomfort or misunderstanding. Then independent
raters were asked to view each whole film of an interview at regular
speed and to identify each uncomfortable moment they saw and heard.
With that simple instruction and very little training, the raters were able
to identify uncomfortable moments at a very high level of interrater
agreement. (See Appendix D for additional discussion.)

Not only did the raters agree with one another, their judgments con-
curred with those of the counselors and students. The raters identified
every instance of an uncomfortable moment that had been noted by the
counselors and students in their viewing sessions. It seemed that the
uncomfortable moment was a unit of interaction that could be identified
in valid and reliable ways. Relatively comfortable moments (sometimes
but not necessarily including small talk that revealed particularistic comembership between counselor and student—cf. Chapter 2, pp. 35ff.)
were not nearly so easily identified by pairs of judges and by the counselor
and student themselves as had been the uncomfortable moments.

This was intriguing. The *uncomfortable moment* and the *comfortable
moment* are units unlike those we had identified as primary constituent

units in the discourse structure of the interview. Such units as *discourse topics* and *elicitation routines* are partly defined by their sequence positions in relation to one another, and to the interview as a whole. If one knows the overall sequential structure of the interview (cf. Chapter 1, pp. 11–12), a given topic or conversational routine can be expected in the moment to come as the next stage in the interview's "future," or remembered as part of an intelligible "past."

Uncomfortable moments and especially comfortable ones are distinctive in that they are not part of the overall sequential order. They can occur at any sequential place in the interview.

To be sure, these kinds of units are not completely unrelated to the sequential order of the interview. Small talk, which characterized some of the comfortable moments, happens more often than not near the beginning of the interview. The *most* uncomfortable uncomfortable moments often happened during the counselor's advice about the student's future goal, if the counselor was denying the student access to a desired future goal or was pointing out some of the student's inadequacies that made the achievement of the desired goal unlikely. Those moments of explaining by the counselor were most likely to occur after the major sequential turning point of the interview, after the student had identified a future goal.

Still, moments of special uncomfortableness or comfortableness in the interview are not subject to the constraints of obligatory series position. Potentially they can precede or follow any other unit, and so their occurrence is not easily predicted by knowledge of the overall sequential order.

How, then, were the uncomfortable moments identified so readily by independent raters, and by the participants in the interviews themselves? Why were comfortable moments apparently more difficult to distinguish than uncomfortable ones? One reason may be that comfortableness— easy fluency and regular flow—is the normal condition for interaction face-to-face. As the normal state of affairs it may not be marked by special communicative cues; it may simply be indicated by the absence of cues of discomfort. If interactional discomfort—difficulty and irregular stumbling—is the exceptional condition, occurring much less frequently than does interactional comfort, it would be adaptive for conversational partners to be able to identify readily the special circumstance of interactional discomfort as it occurs. One would expect, then, that moments of special discomfort would be marked somehow in the communicational surface structure by cues that functioned as warning signals that something was going wrong. Consequently it seemed to us that raters' and participants' intuitions about uncomfortableness must have come from something in the communicational performance—the surface structure. It was not clear, however, what aspects of communicative behavior were functioning as cues of discomfort.

The content of speech was one obvious candidate as an indicator of discomfort between the counselor and the student. In Examples 5.1 and 5.2, the text of the original interview is on the left, and the text of viewing session comments at that same point is on the right. In Example 5.1 the literal, referential content of talk seems to be a source of interactional discomfort. In Example 5.2 that does not seem to be the case.

EXAMPLE 5.1
Juncture Between Talk about Courses Last
Semester and Courses This Semester

(a)   C: OK, Joe. Tell me what courses you're taking this semester.

(b)   S: Uh, strings...

(c)   C: Now when you say strings, what's that? Music 113? Or 114?...you have?

(d)   S: One...I believe it's 113.

(e)   C: 113 or 114 now?...I think it's 114.

(f)   S: Uh, 114?

(g)   C: You see I spoke with Mr. Jones...prior to you coming in...and asked him to help me out with the, uh, music...courses for next semester. And he...claims you're taking Music 114, string instruments?

(h)   S: I must have said 114, I thought it was 113 but it was 114.

(i)   C: But he wants you to take 113 next semester.

(j)   S: All right. He wants me to take 113?

(k)   C: Yeah, so you're taking 114, now that's 1 hour of credit. What else?

This exchange, in which the counselor is attempting to have the student list the courses he is taking this semester, turns into a comedy of errors as the two participants try to decide on the correct number of a course. The student appears not to remember the number of the course (turn *h*) and the counselor reveals that he knew the number of the course all along (turn *g*) through having spoken to someone in the Music Department. The student had been mousetrapped in this exchange, and the raters seem to have relied on the verbal content of the interaction in identifying this segment as an uncomfortable moment.

In contrast, consider Example 5.2.

Juncture Between Talk about Courses This
Semester and Courses Next Semester

(a)   C: OK, let's see what we've got going for next semester. How
          about summer school?

(b)   S: I don't know. What do I have to take?

(c)   C: Well, let's start from scratch. What did you get in your English
          100 last semester?

In this example the uncomfortable moment cannot be tied to anything specific in the explicit content of talk—in the grammar and vocabulary of it. Though it is true that the student answers the counselor's first question with a vague answer (turn *b*), it also seems that the student wants to base his decision on whether or not to attend summer school on how many more courses he needs to take in order to graduate. In order to answer the counselor's first question, the student needs more information from the counselor. In (turn *c*) in order to answer the student's previous question, the counselor must ask the student a series of questions that will help bring the student's official record up to date and will then make the counselor's advising job easier. Consequently, there is a redirection of the discourse topic from *this semester* to *last semester.* But this is a fairly routine redirection. The rater's sense of an interactional stumble, therefore, does not appear to be a function of the verbal content of the interaction. It was more likely related to something in the nonverbal behavior of the participants.

Pitch and stress (loudness) patterns and voice quality might have been another way in which discomfort was cued, yet as the uncomfortable moments segments were watched and listened to, some seemed to be marked by distinctive "paralinguistic" vocal patterns but others did not seem to be. It seemed that aspects of nonverbal behavior other than vocal aspects might also be functioning as cues of discomfort.

Accordingly a viewer was assigned the task of looking more closely at uncomfortable moments using a cinema projector with the sound turned off. The most uncomfortable moment in each interview, as identified by the other raters, was viewed by projecting a strip of film that began at a point 45 seconds before the uncomfortable moment occurred and ended at a point 45 seconds after the time the uncomfortable moment was judged by the pair of raters to have ended. This provided contrast between the initial *steady state* of comfortable interaction, the moment of discomfort, and the return to a relatively steady state of more comfortable interaction again.

The research assistant viewing the film did not know all this, however.

The assistant's instructions were simply to make intuitive judgments of the relative level of interactional discomfort, identifying as precisely as possible the points on the film at which the level of discomfort changed. This was called the asymmetry segments code (ASC). The viewer looked at each strip of film repeatedly, playing forward and backward, at regular speed and also in slow motion, but without sound. Since the film was continuously printed with a time code (each frame of film was numbered), it was potentially possible to identify very precisely in real time the location of shifts in the level of interactional discomfort.

Such points of change in the level of discomfort were indeed apparent. The research assistant's judgments showed high consistency across separate codings of the same strip of film. Something in the kinesic behavior of the counselor and the student—in the quality of body motion as they talked (and possibly also in posture and facial expression)—seemed to be indicating shifts in the emotional tone of interaction. Figure 5.1 indicates such shifts before and during the major uncomfortable moment in Example 4.1 (pp. 77–78).

We decided to look in even greater detail at each strip of interaction before, during, and after the most uncomfortable moment in each of the 25 interviews. Two other raters, different from the previous research assistant, charted for each frame of film the body motion and speech of both the counselor and the student (sound cinema film is exposed at 24 frames per second). This coding produced a kinesic and speech rhythm chart (KSR chart), two of which were shown in Figures 4.1 and 4.2 (pp. 90–91).

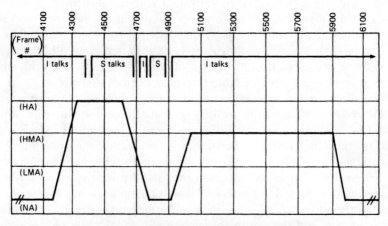

Figure 5.1. Asymmetry segments code (ASC) chart (200 frames = 8.3 seconds [24 f.p.s.]. Abbreviations: NA = no asymmetry; LMA = low-moderate asymmetry; HMA = high-moderate asymmetry; HA = high asymmetry).

When the KSR charts were examined a pattern of underlying, "resultant" rhythm was identified. (See the discussion in Chapter 4.) As the underlying rhythmic pulse was identified in each chart, it appeared that in some instances the pattern was entirely continuous across the whole chart and that in other instances the pattern would become momentarily unclear, only to be reestablished a few moments later. It began to seem as if there were moments of instability and disruption of interactional timing in the midst of some of the uncomfortable moments in the interviews. When the temporal location of these points of rhythmic instability was compared with the temporal location of moments at which the level of discomfort in the uncomfortable moment had increased, as judged intuitively by the research assistant doing the "level of discomfort coding," that assistant's judgments turned out to have coincided exactly with the temporal location of moments of rhythmic instability indicated on the KSR charts.

This did not mean that rhythmic instability was necessarily the only cue of discomfort, or even the main cue. There was often *modality redundancy* in the signaling of discomfort through a combination of verbal content, intonation cues, sudden postural and proxemic shifts, facial expressions, eye contact, and other aspects of communicative performance. But rhythmic instability did occur often at uncomfortable moments when the student and counselor came from culturally differing social groups.

An example that illustrates this is the most uncomfortable moment in interview 9-2-5. KSR charts of that moment were found in Figures 4.1 and 4.2, pp. 90–91. Compare these charts with the more synoptic view provided by the chart in Figure 5.1 on p. 108. Notice that the strip of time marked by highest uncomfortableness is coded for frame numbers 4320–4729. This is also a strip of time in which rhythmic asymmetry appears on the KSR charts. The regular periodicity of speech and body motion rhythm is disrupted.

Turning to the KSR chart in Figure 4.2, p. 91, notice that at frame number 4519 the "beat" shifts 5 frames "ahead." Before 4519 the periodic interval (indicated by the vertical strokes across the middle of the chart) is 24 frames ± 1 frame. If that periodic interval had been maintained, the next "beat" would have occurred at 4524. Instead, at 4519— 5 frames *too soon*—there is vocal stress and kinesic stress provided by the onset of motion in the student's right and left hands. Not only does the stress appear rhythmically too soon, but in addition the *tempo* of speech changes from that point on. The next point of stress in the student's speech—the syllable coun—appears at frame 4530. Here again verbal stress cooccurs with kinesic stress in the motion of the student's right and left arms.

This is an interval of 15 frames ± 1, where before frame 4519 the interval was 24 frames ± 1. Looking ahead to frame 4598 we can see that the student's speech resumes here after a pause, yet the point at which speech resumes still can be described in terms of an underlying resultant rhythmic interval of 15 frames ± 1. This interval is shown in Example 5.3, in which dots stand for pauses and an underline indicates increased loudness (see the explanation of transcription notation on p. 86).

EXAMPLE 5.3

S: (a) .   .   you k<u>now</u>

   (b) .   .   .   .   to

   (c) <u>have</u>   .   .

   (d) <u>two</u> way .   .   like

   (e) <u>equa</u>l   balance

Returning to Figure 4.2, notice on the verbal channel that the "<u>two</u>" of "two-way" (frame 4630) and the "<u>e</u>" of "equal balance" (frame 4645) are 15 frames apart in time. The student has "tugged" the rhythm 5 frames ahead, beginning at frame 4519, and then shifted the periodic interval from 24 frames to 15 frames, speeding up the tempo of interaction by approximately 39%.

Notice that the student's tugging is matched by the counselor in the next speaking turn. At 4690 the counselor responded to the student's previous turn by saying "I see," with stress falling on "<u>I</u>." The counselor's response was made in the same time frame as that which had been established by the student—a periodic interval of 15 frames ± 1. Then at 4714 the counselor said "<u>what</u>"—the first word of the question, "What do you know about counseling?" The "<u>what</u>" occurred 10 frames too soon. If the counselor had continued to speak in the rhythmic cadence established by the student in the previous turn—the cadence of 15 frames ± 1—the counselor's "<u>what</u>" would have occurred 15 frames after the "one-beat" pause which occurred at 4708 (see Figure 4.2). That would have placed the "<u>what</u>" at approximately frame 4724. Instead the "<u>what</u>" occurred at 4714—10 frames too soon.

The counselor at that point not only answered abruptly, but the counselor had shifted the rhythmic interval from 15 frames ± 1 to 20 frames ± 1 (see 4724–4820), slowing the cadence by 25%. This time the student adjusted to the rate of interaction established by the counselor. In the student's turn beginning at 4750, he continued with the cadence the counselor had established at 20 frames ± 1. (The student's response, "Nothing," his eye aversion and kinesic activity beginning at 4760, and his next utterance and kinesic activity beginning at 4810, all occur precisely on the new "beat" that had been established at 4705–4710 by the counselor.) In the next turn (this turn is not shown on the KSR chart) the counselor began an explanation of how the student might become a counselor. At that point the resultant rhythmic interval shifted again, back to the interval of 24 frames ± 1, which had been the rate of the counselor's speech and body motion in the turn before the uncomfortable moment began. (See frames 4310–4424 in Figure 4.1, p. 90.) By 5900 (on Figure 4.2) the interpolated uncomfortable moment was over, the tempo of interaction prior to the uncomfortable moment had been reestablished, and regular rhythm was restored. Interaction proceeded more smoothly from then on.

Further Illustration and Discussion

The rhythmic relationships we have been discussing are illustrated further in Example 5.4, which shows the text previously displayed in the KSR charts. In Example 5.4 each successive resultant rhythmic interval is indicated by a number in parentheses. Notice that this interval is often marked by vocal stress (increased loudness), shown in the example by an underline, as at (2), (3), and (4). Sometimes the rhythmic interval consists of a regularly timed pause, as at (5). In the example a "full-beat" (sentence terminal) pause is indicated by four successive dots. A "half-beat" (phrase- or breath group-terminal) pause is indicated by two dots (see the explanation of transcription notation on p. 86).

The beginning of the new resultant rhythmic interval always occurs at the left-hand margin of text. The shifts in horizontal placement of that margin (which produce "chunks" of text on the page) indicate the points at which abrupt "tugs" occurred that changed the rhythmic periodicity and tempo. (Again, as in the previous examples, the reader is urged to read the passage aloud, exaggerating the rhythm slightly.)

EXAMPLE 5.4

C: (1)   Do   you

(2) plan   on   con-

(3) tinuing along this P.

(4) E. major?

(5) .   .   .   .

S: (1) Y<u>eah</u> I guess so I
   (2) <u>might</u> as well keep it
   (3) <u>up</u> (C:mhm)   my
   (4) <u>P</u>. E. and   .

(Cinema Frame 4519) (5) I <u>wanna</u>   go   into
                     (6) <u>counseling</u> too see
                     (7) .   .   .   .
                     (8) .   .   .   .
                     (9) .   .   .   .
                     (10) .   .   you know
                     (11) .   .   .   to
                     (12) ha<u>ve</u>   .   .
                     (13) <u>two</u>- way .   .like
                     (14) <u>equal</u>   <u>balance</u>
                     (15) .   .   .

(Cinema Frame 4714)
       C: (1) <u>I</u> see   .   ah   .
           (2) What do you   know about
           (3) <u>counseling</u>?   .   .
       S: (1) <u>Nothing</u>   (C: <u>O</u> K)
           (2) .   . I know you have to take psy
                            (rapidly)
           (3) <u>chology</u> courses of some sorts
           (4) .   .   .   and
           (5) <u>counseling</u>   .   .
       C: (1) <u>Well</u>   it's   .   .
           (2) this   is   ah   .
           (3) .   .   .   it'll   de-
           (4) <u>pend</u>   on   different
           (5) .   .   .   it'll
           (6) <u>vary</u>   from   different
           (7) <u>places</u>   to   different

(8) places .   .   but   e-

(9) ssentially what you'll need

(10) .   .   .   .

(11) First of all you're gonna need

state   certification   state

(12) teacher   certification

Just as the KSR chart shows that during the uncomfortable moment the counselor and student, by beginning their turns at a pace faster than the pace they had previously established as normal, had in effect each "tugged" the beat ahead one-fifth of a second—the student at cinema frame 4519 (point [5] in the student's turn) and the counselor at cinema frame 4714 (point [1] in the counselor's next turn).

That this tugging was competitive is suggested by the fact that the rhythmic fabric was "torn" by both speakers in succession. After the student had tugged at the beat and shifted it forward, the counselor did not adapt to the new rhythmic base, but tugged it ahead himself. After this second distortion of the beat the student (who was the subordinate) adapted instantly to the new rhythmic cadence established by the superordinate counselor.

To return to an issue of overall organization in the interview, the issue of *who the student is,* notice that the point at which the previous pattern of rhythmic flow was disrupted—frame 4519—was the exact point at which the student suddenly revealed a new aspect of his social identity. Before that moment he had been a *black physical education major.* Suddenly he was telling the white counselor that he was a *black physical education major who also wanted to become a counselor!* The new revelation was literally abrupt and sudden; the black student began his speaking turn one-fifth of a second too soon. The white counselor's response was also abrupt and interactionally disrhythmic, both in the patterning of kinesic activity and in the hesitations and false starts in speech.

Types of Interactional Arhythmia

We can call the disturbance of regular rhythm interactional *arhythmia.* Aspects of communicative behavior besides arhythmia have been previously identified by researchers as indicators of interactional discomfort and negative affect. These are phenomena that have a place in the folk lexicon of behavioral cues—the *false start,* the *double take,* and *startling*

expression, the *nervous gesture,* the *stammer.* But arhythmia as such is not mentioned in the folk lexicon, except indirectly, as *hesitating* or as *uncomfortable pause.* Nor has arhythmia received much attention in the research literature, except in work on so-called *hesitation phenomena.* The identification of arhythmia as an interactional phenomenon suggests that what is disturbing about hesitation may be not so much that communicative signals stop and start intermittently, but that they do so in a temporally unpredictable way, making it difficult for others to coordinate joint action with the person who is hesitating. Moreover, the continuation of interaction across time under conditions of relatively less temporal integration than usual may in itself be a signal to those engaged in interaction that something is going wrong.

In examining the KSR charts, four types or levels of arhythmia became apparent in the interaction between the counselor and the student.

Type I—Individual Rhythmic Instability. Momentary rhythmic disorganization in the behavior of one individual while the other individual maintains the previous resultant rhythmic interval.

Type II—Mutual Rhythmic Instability. Rhythmic disorganization in the behavior of both individuals, lasting a few moments, involving a distortion of the regular periodicity of the rhythmic interval ± 5–7 twenty-fourths of a second. This apparently irregular acceleration or retardation in the timing of communicative behavior has the effect of "wobbling" the underlying rhythmic interval.

Type III—Mutual Rhythmic Interference. A kind of rhythmic mismatch between the behavior of one individual and the other, lasting a few moments, involving the persistence by each party in rhythmic patterns that are regular for each individual but different across individuals, for example, individual A's behavior patterned in a rhythmic interval of 1 second duration, while individual B's behavior over the same period of time is patterned in a rhythmic interval of .75 second duration. The incongruence of the two patterns together produces a "rough" resultant rhythmic flow.

Type IV—Mutual Rhythmic Opposition. (An example is found in frames 4530–4720 on Figure 4.2, p. 91). Momentary rhythmic disintegration between the behavior of one individual and the other, involving deviation of 4–5 twenty-fourths of a second from the previously established periodic interval. Coming in this much too soon or too late at turn exchange has the effect of "tugging" at the underlying rhythm. The tugging is seemingly competitive; at the very least it indicates a lack of cooperation or integration in the mutual behavior of speakers, since one speaker does not participate in the rhythm used by the previous speaker.

After the momentary tug occurs, however, the previous speaker adapts to the new rhythmic interval, and so the lack of temporal integration between them involves momentary opposition rather than continuous interference, as in Type III above.

Some Research Evidence

When the type of arhythmia was identified for the most uncomfortable moment in each of 25 interviews, it was clear that the most levels of greatest rhythmic instability (Types III and IV) were found in those encounters in which the counselor and the student were from differing ethnic and racial backgrounds. The least severe type of arhythmia (Type I) was found in those encounters in which the counselor and the student were similar in ethnic background. (See Table 5.1, in which High = Type III and Type IV arhythmia, Medium = Type II arhythmia, and Low = Type I arhythmia or none at all.)

Notice first of all that in the intraethnic–interethnic comparison there are no instances of high arhythmia (Type III or IV) in the top horizontal row labeled "intraethnic." There are, however, eight instances of low arhythmia (Type I) in that row. The pattern is very different in the "interethnic" row, with seven instances of high arhythmia. The table shows that even though low arhythmia is the usual "unmarked" occurrence—it occurs in twice as many of the interviews (14) as does high arhythmia (7)—all of the less usual, "marked" instances of high arhythmia occur in the interethnic interviews. This distribution is not only striking on inspection, but it is statistically significant as well ($p > .05$).

Cultural Difference and Arhythmia

The classification by social identity in terms of ethnicity is the only way in the aggregated data to get at the dimension of culture-sharing and culture difference between counselors and students. All persons in an ethnic or racial category are not necessarily similar culturally. (This point will be discussed further at the beginning of the last chapter.) Still, the "intraethnic" category includes the pairs of students and counselors who are most likely to share similar communicative traditions as members of the same speech community, whereas the "interethnic" category includes those pairs of students and counselors least likely to share those traditions.

Looking in the table at the alternative ways of classifying the interviews by social identity—by panethnicity and by comembership—one can see

Table 5.1
Arhythmia Levels by Social Identity[a] Classifications

Social identity	Low	Med	High	
Intraethnic	8	1	0	9
Interethnic	6	3	7	16
	14	4	7	25

$(\chi^2 = 6.86; p < .05)$

	Low	Med	High	
Intra-panethnic	10	3	2	15
Inter-panethnic	4	1	5	10
	14	4	7	25

$(\chi^2 = 4.02; NS)$

	Low	Med	High	
High Comembership	5	1	1	7
Med Comembership	6	1	2	9
Low Comembership	3	2	4	9
	14	4	7	25

$(\chi^2 = 3.12; NS)$

[a] Brief definitions of the social identity categories presented in this table are necessary here. *Ethnic* refers to commonly labeled categories of national origin and race (e.g., Irish–American, Italian–American, Polish–American, Mexican–American, Puerto Rican, black). *Panethnic* refers to two more inclusive categories within which the national origin groups are classed, on the one hand, and the remaining ethnic and racial groups are classed, on the other. The two categories of panethnicity are *white ethnic* (all the groups of European origin) and *Third World* (the groups of New World and African origin). These panethnic categories overlap with social class—with the *white ethnic* category including mostly persons of lower-middle-class and upper-working-class rank, and the *Third World* category including mainly persons of lower-working-class rank. But ethnicity is highly salient in the city in which the films were made; a distinction between "white ethnic" and "nonwhite" was current at the time the films were made, and continues to be made at this writing. In addition, when the interviews were classified by panethnicity, some patterns in the data showed more clearly than when the interviews were classified by social class, or by ethnicity. Further discussion of those findings is in Chapter 7. An interview labeled *intra-panethnic* was one in which both the counselor and the interviewee were either members of the same racial or ethnic group, or members of groups classed within the same panethnic category (e.g., an Italian–American counselor and a Polish–American student, or a black counselor and a Puerto Rican student). An interview labeled *inter-panethnic* was one in which the counselor was of one panethnic identity and the student was of another (e.g.,

that in none of the other rows and columns are the patterns of difference in arhythmia discriminated so clearly as they are when compared according to ethnicity. This is especially so when the instances are compared according to comembership—which is the most differentiated social classification used in the study, involving aspects of social identity made situationally relevant in each interview. As will be seen in Chapters 6 and 7, classification of the data according to comembership discriminates all other aspects of overall difference in interactional character and outcome in the interviews more clearly than does classification by ethnicity. But this is not so for types of interactional arhythmia. That is best discriminated by comparison according to *ethnicity*, which was our best index for cultural difference and cultural similarity in the aggregated data.

Whether arhythmia is best seen as a cause or as an effect of other troubles in face-to-face communication, it does seem to be related to cultural differences in communicative competence among speakers. Since *arhythmia* is an indicator of level of *uncomfortableness*, the relative uncomfortableness of uncomfortable moments varies systematically according to the ethnic and racial difference or similarity between the counselor and the student. In this respect, ethnic and racial differences clearly make a difference in the character of interaction in the counseling interviews.

CULTURAL DIFFERENCE AND CONVERSATIONAL COOPERATION DURING EXPLANATIONS

We turn now to consider the influence of cultural difference on the conduct of *explanations* by the counselors. We will examine cultural differences in the *ways of speaking* by which an explainer signals to the listener that a listening response is appropriate. We will also examine cultural differences in the reciprocally linked *ways of listening* by which the listener provides a listening response. In so doing we will be examining the forms of verbal and nonverbal contextualization cues and the *kairos* (sequential) organization and *chronos* (rhythmic) organization of *explaining* and *being explained to*. Cultural differences in the form

---

a black counselor and an Irish–American student). *Comembership* is a classification of the degree of similarity between counselor and student in ethnic and panethnic status, but also in other aspects of commonality that were situation-specific and revealed during the interview (e.g., both counselor and student having been wrestlers once, or history majors). Classification of the dyads by comembership level is discussed in Appendix A, pp. 219–224. The notion of particularistic comembership itself is discussed in Chapter 2, pp. 35–37.

of cues will be shown to produce interaction during explanations that is not adequately social.

In the reciprocal and complementary social organization of communication there are at least two ways in which an interactional partner can perform in inadequately social ways toward the other partner: One of these ways can be thought of as doing the "wrong thing," even though doing it at the right time; another can be thought of as doing the "right thing," but at the wrong time. Both kinds of interactional missing seem to be involved in producing the kinds of occurrences to be discussed here—times during a conversation in which the listening behavior of the listener and the speaking behavior of the speaker fail to be reciprocal and complementary.

Given the analysis presented in the previous chapter, a failure to articulate one's actions properly with the interaction rhythms of others can be thought of as a fundamental kind of alienation from interaction. If, as we have claimed, patterns in the timing of behavior function not only to organize the behavior itself but also to organize the inferences that interactional partners are making about each other's actions, then we would expect to see one person being held accountable for failing to act at the right time—or for doing the wrong thing at the right time— by other partners in the interaction; that is, we would expect to see partners displaying their expectations for socially appropriate action in their reactions to the immediately previous actions of others.

Speaking in Relation to Listening: An Aspect of "Recipient Design" in Interactional Behavior

If the speaking of speakers were genuinely interdependent with the listening of listeners, then the listeners' failure to act at the right time would have some consequences for the speaking of the speaker, and that speaking would have consequences for the subsequent listening behavior of the listener. Ways of speaking and ways of listening would thus be mutually constitutive.

We found in a detailed analysis of some of the films in the research corpus that ways of listening and ways of speaking do indeed seem to regulate one another. Analysis shows that the listener's failure to act at the right time in the right way literally prevents the speaker from finishing what he was trying to say—at least from finishing it in the way he was previously saying it. The speaker, in continuing to speak socially (i.e., in taking account in speaking of what the other is doing in listening), makes *accountable* the listener's violation of expectations for appropriate listening behavior. The speaker does this by hesitating or by repeating what was just said, or by some other deviation from the normal forward-moving trajectory of discourse.

In deciding what to do next, the speaker depends on the listener's performance of contextualization cues, and thus the speaker allows his speaking to be regulated by the listener's listening. Through close behavioral analysis it is possible to infer apparent patterns of inference by which this regulation takes place, and the analyst can discover the system of contextualization cues functioning as signals, by paying close attention to the reactions of the speaker and the listener to each other's behavior from one moment to the next.

Here is another version of the example from the interview that was discussed in the previous chapter as Example 4.1 and in this chapter as Example 5.4. (see the explanation of transcription notation on p. 86). The counselor had just introduced the topic of the student's goal for the near future (next semester). Then the student brought up his goal for the longer term, which was that he himself wanted to be a counselor. The student introduced this new topic abruptly, and the counselor responded with a long explanation.

EXAMPLE 5.5

C: (1) First   of   all   you're   gonna need

(2) state certification   state

(3) teacher   certification

(4) .   .   .   in

(5) other words you're gonna have to   be

(6) cer   ti   fied   to
    (slower)

(7) teach   in   some

(8) a r e a   .   .

(9) English   .   .   or

(10) History   .   .   or
                                (rapidly)

(11) whatever   else   happens to be   your

(12) bag   .   .   .

(13) .   .   .   .

(14) P.E.   .   .   .

(15) .   .   .   .

(16) Secondly your're gonna have to get a
(rapidly)

(17) Master's degree   .   .

There were considerable differences across interviews in the amount
of repetition of the same point by the counselors during explanations to
the students. With some students some counselors would persist at the
same point over and over, as in the previous example at (5) through (14).
It was as if a phonograph needle kept jumping back a few grooves on
the record. With other students this sort of recycling never occurred.

It was usually the counselor who was doing the explaining. Explanation
was an important speech function for the counselor. In the first principal
part of the interview the counselor's explanations had to do mostly with
future courses of action within the interview itself, clarifying the sequential order of topics at major junctures in the discourse structure by
explaining to the student what the counselor would be asking about next.
In the second principal part of the interview in which the counselor's
role shifted from that of primarily asking to primarily telling, the counselor's explanations had to do with giving the student advice about future
courses of action outside the interview—in planning the course schedule
for the next term or considering options for transfer to a 4-year college.
In both parts of the interview the counselor's explanations were central
to the successful accomplishment of the gatekeeping purposes of the
encounter.

Often when the counselor kept repeating an explanation, especially
if it happened during the second part of the interview, that segment was
judged an "uncomfortable moment" by raters. During the moment there
would often be hesitation in the counselor's speech. The salience of the
moment was often marked by an abrupt change in postural and proxemic
positioning. Occasionally the counselor or the student would stop the
videotape during a viewing session at one of these moments of repeated
explanation and make comments on it. That was the case in the previous
example.

What was happening interactionally that might have produced the
counselor's convoluted way of explaining? First let us consider some
key terms: explanation, making a point, persisting at the point.

An *explanation* can be defined as a speaking turn (or a part of a turn,
or a series of turns) whose function is to clarify something that has
already been stated, explicitly or implicitly. The subject of an explanation
has been called a *discourse topic* by other researchers.[5] Maintenance of
the discourse topic is sustained within and across sentences by various

---

[5] See Keenan and Schieffelin, 1976.

grammatical and prosodic devices. An explanation can be defined as an attempt to disambiguate the discourse topic.

The simplest type of explanation can occur within a single sentence in the logical and grammatical form of predication—a statement made about the subject of a proposition. For example:

The explanation is an attempt to disambiguate the discourse topic.

Making an *explanation point* is done by stating in a verb phrase the logical and grammatical predicate of the subject. Predications can be linked together in series, each new predication "tying" back to the preceding noun that functions as the "subject" or "topic" of the previous phrase. Such linked predications are progressive attempts to disambiguate the subject of the initial proposition in the series. As these predications are strung together, the explainer is *persisting at the point*.

This can be seen by rearranging the text of the previous example:

First of all you're gonna need *state certification*
    state teacher certification
        In other words you're gonna have to be
        certified to teach in *some area*
                                History or
                                English or
                Whatever else happens to be your bag
                            P.E.

Hyperexplanation can be defined as persisting twice or more within the same speaking turn at the same explanation point. In our data there seem to be two interchangeable forms of hyperexplanation: (1) *talking down* (lowering the level of abstraction from one repetition of the explanation point to the next); (2) *giving reasons* (each successive reason justifying the proposition asserted by implication in the discourse topic).

The Mutual Regulation of Speaking and Listening

In Chapter 4 we argued that the underlying pattern of interaction rhythm seems to function together with other contextualization cues as a way of signaling the location in real time of moments of transition relevance. At this point we are primarily concerned with moments of transition relevance that occur within a single speaking turn.

During an explanation in a single speaking turn there seem to be three key moments of transition relevance. At these successive moments it becomes appropriate for the speaker and hearer to signal reactions to one another. The first is the *moment of making a point* (MMP). The second is the moment of *listening-response relevance* (LRRM). The third is the moment of the *speaker's next move,* either persisting at the point (PP) or raising the next point (RNP). Each of these moments of transition relevance appears in invariant sequential order (in *kairos* time) as well as in a consistent rhythmic pattern (in *chronos* time). The overall sequential order is illustrated in Figure 5.2 as a series of decision points and alternative courses of action, or "paths." The most frequently occurring "unmarked" paths are represented in the model by solid lines, while the less frequently occurring "marked" paths are represented by broken lines.

The model in Figure 5.2 predicts that one frequent, "unmarked" path will be the sequence MMP → LRRM/+LR → RNP, in which the listener provides listening response (LR) at the next appropriate moment (LRRM) after the moment in which the speaker made an explanation point (MMP). Failure to provide listening response would normally be followed by the speaker's persisting at the same point, as indicated in the following "unmarked" path: MMP → LRRM/−LR → RNP. This is what we have called *hyperexplanation.*

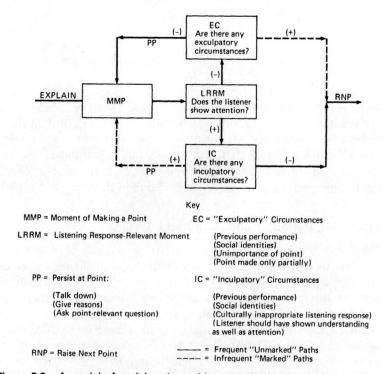

Figure 5.2. A model of social and cognitive organization in making a point.

One of the things that is distinctive about hyperexplanation in our corpus of films of school counseling interviews is that *this way of explaining only occurred in interviews between white counselors and black students.* Intuitively it seemed that there were cultural differences in the ways the white counselors and black students were providing contextualization cues to each other in their listening and speaking during explaining. It seemed that these cultural differences in cue form might account for the frequency of hyperexplanation in the interracial interviews.

To test that supposition a sample of instances of explaining was taken from nine of the films of interviews. Five of the films were of interracial encounters and four were of intraracial encounters—two between two whites and two between two blacks. (In the interracial encounters, as it happened, the speaker doing the explaining was always the white counselor and the listener was always the black student.)

All major explanations in the nine films were examined. As the films were viewed repeatedly, transcripts of each instance of explaining were prepared. On these transcripts were noted salient aspects of the verbal and nonverbal behavior of the speaker during the tripartite sequence consisting of the moment immediately prior to the LRRM, the LRRM, and the next moment after it. A total of 133 instances of these three-part sequences were found and analyzed.

In every one of the instances the three constituent "moments" were regularly spaced in real time—*chronos* time. Their spacing was related to the resultant rhythmic interval that was discussed in Chapter 4. This can be seen in Example 5.6 in which elongated syllables are indicated by successive colons, as in "July:::"(see the explanation of transcription notation on p. 86):

EXAMPLE 5.6

```
C:    (1)  .        .          what    we're
      (2)  gonna  have      to   do
      (3)  first  of    all    .      is to
      (4)  get    you   set    up
      (5)  .        .          .      for an
      (6)  A::            C::
           (twice  as  slow  as  before)
      (7)  T::        test    .        .
      (8)  .        .          .        .
           (student   nods)
      (9)  .        .          .        .
```

(10) .   .   in   .
(11) .   .   ah   .
(12) .   .   .   .
(13) .   I   believe   the
(14) next   one   will be in Ju-
(15) ly::

In this example, the next *moment* after the phrase "get you set up" was a moment of transition relevance, a moment of listening-response relevance (LRRM). But the student gave no listening response. The counselor then made accountable that absence of response (1) by repeating the same point at a lower level of abstraction (what the student is to be set up for is "an A. C. T. test") and (2) by slowing his speech to exactly half its previous rate. (This slowing of speech rate by half is a means of emphasis that was also used by speakers to mark the transition from one major discourse topic to the next.)

In the *next moment* after the phrase "A. C. T. test," another moment of listening-response relevance occurred. This time the student provided listening response by nodding precisely at the beginning of that *next moment*—"on the beat," as it were. After the listener's nod the speaker continued on at (9) through (13) to raise the next point, which was the date the test would be given.

This rhythmic relationship between the moment of making a point in speaking and the moment of providing listening response to the point made is the same sort of timing relationship as that discussed briefly in Chapter 4, in which the student made a point and the counselor responded with a vocal back channel and a slight nod (Example 5.7).

EXAMPLE 5.7

S: (1) Yeah I guess so.   .   I
   (2) might   as well keep   it
   (3) up   .   .   . my
              (C:nods and says "mhm")
   (4) P::   E::   and .   .

In that instance the back-channel listening response occurred in the middle of interval (3), halfway between the beginning of one resultant rhythmic interval and the next. The full interval was 1 second in duration and the counselor's "mhm" occurred exactly at the half-second point— on an "afterbeat," in musical terms. This is the same duration unit as that in the previous example after the phrase "get you set up." In all the instances examined, the listening-response relevance moment occurred at one of two duration units later in time than the moment of making the point: It occurred either at the onset of the full resultant rhythmic interval (indicated by four dots) or at a point halfway between two of those onsets (indicated by two dots).

It seems that the placement of stressed tonal nuclei and of kinesic accents in the speech and body motion of the speaker provides an environment of timing for the placement of moments of heightened listening activity by the listener. It seems to be more than just a generalized rhythmic environment that is being provided for the listener. The speaker seems to be providing moment-specific contextualization cues signaling that a particular next moment will be one of "listening-response relevance," in which for a moment there is a subtle shift in the allocation of communicative rights and obligations between the speaker and the listener. By signaling that the next moment is a *listening-response relevant moment (LRRM)* the speaker indicates that the appropriate listener role behavior is being momentarily redefined from that of less active to more active listening.

The communicative means by which the speaker signals this to the listener often includes (a) coming to a clause-terminal juncture in syntax; (b) a temporally periodic resultant rhythmic interval of one *full* or one-*half* a sentence-terminal pause in speaking; (c) other prosodic cues, including coming to the end of a falling or rising "tune" in speaking as marked by intonation shifts. These elements of behavioral form appear in differing clusters as contextualization cues, usually at a clause-terminal juncture in syntax, but sometimes at a point of syntactic ellipsis or of hesitation in speech. The presence of these markers, in the context of the overall interaction rhythm pattern that has been established between the speaker and the listener, seems to signal to the listener that *the next periodic time interval after the speaker's pause will be a moment in which active listening is appropriate.*

To summarize, active listening activity by the listener seems to be appropriate at the LRRM. The LRRM occurs at a regular rhythmic interval in relation to the end of the speaker's speech. This is evident not only from the extreme consistency found in the temporal placement of listening response. The obligation to respond at the right time is also evident in what the speaker does next if a listening response was absent. Speakers consistently make accountable the absence of listening response during a LRRM, as the counselor did in Example 5.2.

Because of the speaker's making the absence of timed listening responses accountable, the listening activity of listeners (and the absence of such activity) is thus able to function as a mechanism regulating the speaker's speech. Apparently, speakers infer that the presence of appropriately timed listening response indicates attention (and perhaps understanding) on the part of the listener. In the absence of this attention the speaker will usually not proceed to the next unit of speaking activity—whether it be the clause, sentence, or discourse topic—but will persist in reiterating the same "point" being made. Alternatively the speaker may call attention to the absence of listening response more explicitly, by saying "You're not listening!" or "Maybe you don't understand what I've just said."

But people do not usually say such things so explicitly, especially in a formal interview. What one usually finds in the formal interview is the use of an indirect and implicit means of making accountable the absence of a listening response. The most typical of those means is to persist at the point, or to state reasons justifying the proposition previously stated.

EVIDENCE RELATED TO THE MODEL

Hyperexplanation occurred often in the interviews in which the counselor was white and the student was black. In those interviews the listeners (who were always black) failed much more often to give listening response than did listeners who were of the same race as the speaker. This is shown in Table 5.2. (Of the four "intraracial" dyads shown, two were from interviews between pairs of whites and two were from interviews between pairs of blacks.)

The most frequently occurring condition is that listening response (LR) is provided at a LRRM. This happens in 74 out of 133 instances. But

Table 5.2
Listening Response at LRRMs by Racial Composition of Interview Dyads[a]

	LLRM + LR	LLRM − LR	
Interracial dyads ($N = 5$)	44 (33%) (45%)	53 (40%) (55%)	97
Intraracial dyads ($N = 4$)	30 (23%) (83%)	6 (4%) (17%)	36
Total	74 (56%)	59 (44%)	133

[a] Number of instances = 133

there was also a high proportion of absence of response ($-$LR) after a LRRM (59 out of 133 instances).

The frequency of $-$LR occurrence was much greater in the interracial dyads than in the intraracial ones (53 times in the former case, 6 times in the latter). Analysis shows that some features of cultural style in the behavioral form of contextualization cues seem to be producing this result.

In the interracial dyads (in which the speaker was always white and the listener was always black) the white speakers used the same forms of LRRM cues during the moment of making a point that they used when talking to white listeners. These were different LRRM cue forms from the ones black speakers used when talking to black listeners. The differences in LRRM cue form seem to be culturally conventional.

In the white cultural style of making a point, the point itself is generally made in one syntactic "chunk" that is immediately followed by a pause during which the LRRM occurs. This can be seen in Example 5.8, which displays the text shown previously as Example 5.6. Example 5.8 shows rising and falling pitch patterns as well as the rhythmic intervals and pause structure.

EXAMPLE 5.8

From this example it is apparent that LRRM cues involve an economic use of communicative means—the presence at (3) and (4) of just the end of a syntactic clause and a pause (''get you set up [pause]'') *without a large shift in intonation* is sufficient to signal a LRRM. The first LRRM at (4) was signaled by a relatively sustained intonational contour at (3) (''get you set up''). There is only a slight *fall–rise* at the end of that phrase. The absence of listening response during the LRRM cued in that way was made socially accountable by the speaker, who persisted at the point in (5) and (6) and slowed down the rate of speech, ''for an A. C. T. test (pause, +LR),'' again without a steep rise or fall in intonation. The listener at that point provided a nod.

This intonation pattern was typical for the instances examined; white speakers used both a steeply falling intonation contour and a relatively sustained contour at clause-terminal junctures. They used the sustained contour much more frequently—11 times as opposed to 3 times for the high falling contour at the moment of making a point.

In the black cultural style the speech behavior used to cue a LRRM was quite different from that used in the white style. In the films of black speakers talking to black listeners, the speakers never used sustained intonation contour in cueing a LRRM. The LRRM was always preceded by a high steeply falling contour. This falling contour always appeared somewhere in the syntactic clause preceding the pause during which listening response was mandatory, but the falling contour did not always occupy final position in the clause, as it always did in the white style. In the black style there may have been an interpolated ''filler'' such as ''you know'' between the high fall and the LRRM, but somewhere before that filler there was always a high falling intonation contour. This can be seen in Example 5.9.

EXAMPLE 5.9

S: (1) An'   then   when   I   get

    (2) he ::: re

    (3) .   .   .   .
        (pause, but no LRRM)

    (4) they   tell   me   they

    (5) ⎣o:ˢt   .   . you   kno:w

    (6) .   .   .   my
        (pause, but no LRRM)   all

    (7) ⎣Pa::ˊpers   .   .

(8) $\left[\begin{array}{l}\text{y\underline{ea}h} \quad \text{LRRM} \qquad \underline{\text{nod}} \\ \end{array}\right.$ $\left.\begin{array}{l}\\ \end{array}\right]$ 'n

(9) <u>then</u>   I   had   to   re   .

(10) .   you   know   re   a-

(11) P\y.

(12) $\left[\begin{array}{l}\underline{\text{nod}} \\ \end{array}\right.$ LRRM $\left.\begin{array}{l}\\ \end{array}\right]$ so

(13) then   they   told   me   to   resub-

(14) <u>mit</u>

In this example, after the first pause at (3), which is not a LRRM because the point has not yet been fully made, the speaker continues on at (4) and does not make accountable the absence of listening response at (3).

Despite the preceding steeply falling pitch shift before the second pause at (6), "they lost, you know (pause)," this pause did not count as a LRRM because it was preceded by the filler "you know," and also because the point had still not fully been made syntactically (what was lost was the "<u>papers</u>"). Again, the absence of response in the pause at (6) was not made accountable. The speaker continued on to complete the point at (7), doing so with a steeply falling intonation shift on the words "all my papers." The pause at (7) functioned as a LRRM, and listening response was provided by the listener at (8). Then at (9) the speaker proceeded on to raise the next point. Again the next LRRM was preceded by a brief rhetorical pause and an interpolated "you know" at (10). This was followed by a steeply falling pitch shift at (11), which was followed by a nod from the listener at (12).

This is the pattern of cueing a LRRM that was typical in the films of black speakers with black listeners. In those films the black speakers used the steeply falling intonation contour 16 times as a LRRM cue. In 13 of those instances the black listeners provided listening response, and in three instances they failed to do so. In those three instances the speakers made the absence of listening response accountable by persisting at the point until listening response was provided. *Black speakers never made the absence of listening response accountable in a pause after a sustained intonation contour,* however, and from this one can infer that in the black cultural system for organizing listening response, such nonintonationally marked pauses did not function as LRRMs. They did have that function in the white system; white speakers almost always made accountable the absence of listening response after a pause preceded by sustained intonation contour.

It seems apparent that whites and blacks were employing different formal means for the same communicational function—that of cueing the approach of a LRRM in the next interactional moment. The black style consisted of relatively broad strokes of the marking pen. Not all pauses were marked as moments of listening-response relevance, but those that were so marked were given great emphasis. They were preceded by syntactically elaborated "windups," including antecedent filler phrases (e.g., "you know," in the immediately preceding phrase) and by steeply falling intonation contours. The white style consisted of marking relatively more pauses as LRRMs, and of doing so in ways that were syntactically less elaborated and intonationally more subtle.

The converse seems to be the case for the differences in ways *listening response* tended to be given by whites and by blacks. Listening response was given with rather broad behavioral emphasis by whites in our sample. It was given much more subtly by blacks. In the white cultural style listening response was often done verbally and nonverbally at the same time; a verbal back channel would often be accompanied by a head nod (see Table 5.3). While head nods may have appeared without back channels in the white cultural style, the verbal back channels never appeared except together with the nods. For blacks, however, the pattern was different. When black listeners were listening to black speakers the preferred response form was the verbal back channel alone, without head

Table 5.3
General Form of Listening Response by Social Identity of Listener and Speaker[a]

Form of listening response (LR)	Social identity of listener					
	Black			White		
	With black speaker (A)	With white speaker (B)	Total (C)	With black speaker (D)	With white speaker (E)	Total (F)
Verbal LR	12	4	16	—	0	0
Nonverbal LR[b]	5	26	31	—	4	4
Verbal and nonverbal LR[c]	2	13	15	—	8	8

[a] N for black–black films = 2; N for white–white films = 2; N for white–black films = 5.

[b] N = 34 instances of nodding response; 1 instance of gestural response.

[c] For this row all nonverbal LR's are nods.

nod. This is a more subtle way of providing listening response than to do so verbally and nonverbally at the same time.

Further evidence for the existence of two different patterns of providing listening response is shown in Table 5.3. Looking at Column (A), which indicates frequencies of response form when a black listener was listening to a white speaker rather than to a black one, one sees that the second most frequent LR form used by the black listener (13 responses) was the form most frequently used by white listeners listening to a white speaker (see Column [E]). A comparison of Columns (A), (B), and (E) shows that the black listeners listening to white speakers shifted their listening style adaptively in the direction of the frequency distribution typical for the white style.

A similarly adaptive direction of style-switching in listening behavior is apparent in Table 5.4, which shows white and black differences in the culturally conventional form of nodding. The typical nodding form for whites listening to whites was a kinesically emphasized nod, accentuated by acceleration at the change of direction at the "bottom" of the nod. The typical nodding form for blacks listening to blacks was not accentuated kinesically; there was no acceleration of motion in the kinesic "turnaround" at the bottom of the nod. Table 5.3 shows that not only were these different nodding forms preferred differently by blacks and whites (compare Column [A] with Column [E]), but that in no instance was an "accented" nod used by a black listener listening to a black speaker and in no instance was an "unaccented" nod used by a white listener listening to a white speaker. Despite the small numbers of instances in this table, the zeros in the opposite conditions (compare Columns [A] and [E]) provide clear evidence of cultural difference in listening

Table 5.4
Form of Nodding by Social Identity of Listener and Speaker[a]

	Social identity of listener				
	Black			White	
Behavioral form of nodding	With black speaker (A)	With white speaker (B)	Total (C)	With black speaker (D)	With white speaker (E)
Accented	0	14	14	—	4
Unaccented	5	12	17	—	0

[a] N of black–black interviews = 2; N of white–white interviews = 2; N of black–white interviews = 5.

response form. The same conclusion can be drawn from the data on style-switching by black listeners. When listening to whites (see Column [B]), the black listeners actually used the white culturally conventional listening response form more often than the black form, although the occurrence of either form was almost equal (compare Columns [A], [B], and [E]).

In short, the points of behavioral emphasis were opposite in the white and black cultural styles of *explaining* and of *listening while being explained to*. In the white cultural style it was listening response (LR) that received special emphasis; the cues for listening-response-relevant moments were relatively subtle. In the black cultural style it was the cues for listening-response relevance (LRRM) that were emphasized and the listening responses themselves were relatively subtle.

These differences in cue form might lead blacks and whites engaged in conversation to make the following kinds of errors in inference:

Type I error   Black listeners would tend to miss those LRRMs that were cued relatively subtly, and consequently in the absence of listening response the white speaker would persist at the point.

Type II error   White speakers would tend to miss those listening response cues that were provided relatively subtly by black listeners, and consequently the white speaker would persist at the point.

In both cases the inferential errors deriving from cultural differences in LRRM cueing and in listening response could be expected to lead to hyperexplanation by a white speaker talking to a black listener. This is in fact what happened in the instances studied (see Table 5.5).

Table 5.5
Form of LRRM Contexualization Cue, Listening Response, and Speaker's Next Move in Interracial Interviews[a]

| Form of LRRM cue feature (intonation contour) | Speaker's next move | | | | |
| | Raise next point | | Persist at point | | |
	+ LR	− LR	+ LR	− LR	Total
Sustained contour	6	6	14	37	63
Sharply falling contour	16	3	4	6	29

[a] *N* of interviews = 5 (speaker always white, listener always black); LR = listening response.

In talking to black listeners the white speakers used sustained intonation 63 times at a clause-terminal juncture and only 29 times used a steeply falling contour. But the black listeners seemed to have consistently missed the form of LRRM cue that was most frequently used by whites. When the white speaker used the cue whose form was closest to the form of the cue found in the black cultural style (steeply falling intonation), the black listener provided listening response in 20 out of 29 instances. When the white speaker used the LRRM cue form that is absent in the black cultural style (sustained intonation), the black listener provided listening response in only 20 out of 63 instances—a far different proportion of "hits" to "misses."

White speakers also tended to miss listening responses by black listeners when the form of those responses was that not present in the white cultural style—the unaccented form of head nod. This is apparent in Table 5.6.

When the black listener used the form of listening response present

Table 5.6
Form of Listening Response and Speaker's Next Move[a]

	Black listener			
White speaker's next move	Contextually most "correct" LR form (NV + VLR)	Contextually "correct" LR form (accented nod)	Contextually "incorrect" LR form (unaccented)	Total
Persist at point	5**[a]	1**	9	15
Raise next point	8	13	3**	24
Total	13	14	12	39

[a] It should be noted that the asterisked numbers in the table are all exceptional, "marked" instances, in which the speaker went on because he had already persisted at least twice previously at the same point—and then apparently moved ahead to the next discourse subtopic just to be able to continue the interview! It is curious that in these cases in which a long string of successive repetitions of the same point are made by the speaker, and indeed in all the instances of hyperexplanation examined, at no time did any one of the white interviewers stop and say explicitly, "I don't think you understand what I've been talking about." Rather, the interviewers persisted in hyperexplaining, occasionally making a clause into a tag-question that formulated speaker concern about listener comprehension— "You see?" "Understand?"—but doing so only rarely. This recalls the discussion (in Chapter 2) of the white counselor's tendency in those interviews characterized by low comembership to avoid talking explicitly about trouble the student is in, including face-to-face interactional trouble such as not appearing to be paying attention or to be understanding what the counselor is saying.

in the black cultural style but not in the white—the unaccented nod—
the white speaker persisted at the same point in 9 out of 12 instances.
When the black listener used the form of listening response that was
contextually correct when listening to a white speaker—the accented
nod—the proportions are reversed. Then the white speaker only persisted
at the same point in 1 instance out of 14. The same was true when the
black listener used the most preferred listening response form in the
white cultural style, the accented nod plus verbal back channel. When
the black listener provided both verbal and nonverbal listening response
together, the speaker went on to raise the next point in 8 out of 13
instances.

   Our final example, Example 5.10, is the one presented first in this
chapter as Example 5.1. In this example a black student had just told
a white counselor that he too wanted to be a counselor. Then the counselor hyperexplained, persisting at the first speaking point concerning
"state certification." The counselor repeated himself at successively
lower levels of abstraction until the black student provided a cluster of
relatively emphatic listening responses during a pause in the speaker's
speech. The cluster of responses included an "accented" head nod followed immediately by an "mhm" that was accompanied simultaneously
by a large movement of the arm as the student brought his hand to his
face. Then—and only then—did the counselor move on to the next speaking point in the explanation:

EXAMPLE 5.10

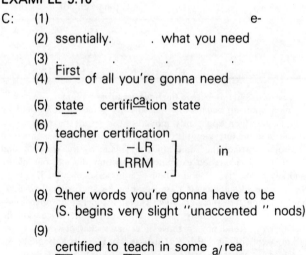

(10)
⌈ (slight unaccented nods by S.) ⌉
⌊ . LRRM . ⌋

(11) En̲g̲ lish . or Hi̲s̲ tᵒʳʸ . or

(12) whatever else happens to be your bag
(slight nods by S. continue →stop)

(13)
⌈ (S: says "mhm" and   ⌉   P::
  gives slight "accented"
  nod LRRM   E::
⌊   .   .   ⌋   (S and C both bring
                                   right arms to face in
                                   synchrony with each
                                   other)

(14) Se̲condly you're gonna have to have a

(15) Ma̲ster's degree.

(16)
⌈ (slight   (slight   ⌉
  "unaccented"   "unaccented"
  nod)   nod)
      LRRM
⌊   .   .   . ⌋

(17) which as youₖₙₒw .   .
                    is an ad-

(18) .   .   .

(19) va̲nced   de
                     gr̲e̲e̲

In the example the student apparently misread the counselor's initial LRRM cues, and then the counselor apparently misread the student's initial listening responses. The first pause in speaking occurred at (7) after the counselor had said "state teacher certification." That was the first LRRM, according to our criteria. The tone group just before that LRRM (6) had a relatively sustained intonational contour with a slight rise–fall followed by a slight rise on the final syllable (a rise too slight to be a question-intonation). At this first LRRM, signaled in the "white cultural" manner by a pause without a steep rise–fall intonationally, the black student failed to provide listening response, and the counselor persisted at the point.

Notice what happened next. At (8), as the counselor began to repeat the explanation again, saying "in other words, you're gonna," *the student began to provide active listening response. But the counselor continued to hyperexplain, as if no listening response had occurred.* The student's listening responses were given in the "black cultural" manner— slight, unaccented nods without accompanying vocal back channels. Yet the counselor continued to recycle the explanation of "state certification." The counselor was literally "talking down" to the student, until the student provided a more behaviorally gross set of listening responses, in a manner more similar to the "white cultural" style of listening behavior. The counselor's "talking down" continued from (8) through (12), all the while the student was continuously nodding, but in an "unaccented" way. The "talking down" only stopped at (13), when the student said "mhm," provided an "accented" nod, and gave another sort of kinesic emphasis by raising his hand to his face, a gesture that was mirrored in precise synchrony by the counselor.

At the moment they brought their hands to their faces and the counselor proceeded to begin the next point at (14), the counselor and student had reestablished conversational cooperation. But before that cooperation had broken down. The counselor and student were not interacting in a fully social way.

Each did not take action in full account of the actions of the other. The student apparently "misread" the counselor's first intonational LRRM cues. The counselor apparently "misread" the student's kinesic listening responses, and persisted in misreading the student's responses. In missing each other's transition relevance cues they took successive actions that conjointly produced a brief interactional "incident."

EVIDENCE FROM VIEWING SESSIONS

Not only was the moment of explanation in Example 5.1, turn *b* uncomfortable in the sense that it was behaviorally disorganized; it was also uncomfortable in terms of the interpretive reactions of the counselor and student in their viewing sessions. Generally this was true in viewing sessions; moments of behavioral disorganization were the ones at which the student and counselor stopped and reported negative reactions. Often at such moments the interpretations made by the counselor and by the student were discrepant. That was the case in Example 5.10. The student had stopped the tape in the viewing session and said, referring to the arhythmic hyperexplanation:

> Well, I couldn't really say, but I wasn't satisfied with what he wanted to push..I guess he didn't think I was qualified, you know. That's the way he sounded to me...This guy seems like

he was trying to knock me down, in a way, you know. Trying to say no...I don't think you can handle anything beside P.E., you know. He just said it in general terms, he just didn't go up and <u>pow</u> like they would in the old days, you know. This way they just try to use a little more psychology...they sugar coat it this way.

Viewing the tape a second time the student referred to this same moment and reported an even stronger reaction:

He insulted my manhood.

Although the counselor stopped the tape during his viewing session at exactly the same place as had the student, the counselor reported an interpretation of the meaning of what was being said that differed from that of the student:

Right now we both seem to be concentrating on giving information... He on the other hand is concentrating.. on accepting the information and putting it together... he's got aspirations for the future, P.E. and uh .. uh, counseling... he's a little bit ahead of himself as far as the counseling.. as the year progressed, I guess I got the question so often that it became one of my favorite topics an' I was ready to, uh, numerate.. essentially what he did was he started me off on my information.

Notice that neither the student nor the counselor reacted to the uncomfortable moment in terms of its behavioral organization. Rather, they reported interpretations of the "real" meaning—the social as well as referential meaning—of what was being said. The student inferred that what the counselor really meant, without saying it in so many words, was that the student was not qualified, and that was an insult. The counselor, however, showed no indication in his viewing session comments that his hyperexplanation might have been interpreted by the student as an insult.

Moreover, there is no evidence from the counselor's conduct during the interview itself that he was aware of the way in which the student was interpreting the counselor's explanation and advice. The counselor, apparently, was unaware that interactional *repair* was necessary at that point. Consequently, the counselor took no steps to remedy the damage to rapport.

This lack of rapport was not simply a matter of the counselor's lack of good intentions. It was a consequence of a breakdown in the social ecology of communication. In the viewing session the counselor had said that the student had been given bad advice by another advisor, and that the student had not so far taken the courses that would lead to majoring in counseling at a 4-year college. The counselor expressed the concern about the student's pattern of courses taken. *But he did so after the uncomfortable moment.* By then it was too late. After the counselor's arhythmic hyperexplanation had gone by without any attempt at repair by the counselor, the student had decided not to trust anything more the counselor might have to say.

A relationship between behavioral disorganization and interactional inference is illustrated further in Example 5.11. Again, the counselor is white and the student is black. Again, the counselor's explanation is marred by arhythmia and hyperexplanation, although the behavioral disorganization is not so extreme as that found in Example 5.1. Earlier in the interview the student had expressed interest in being a physician, and indicated indirectly what his preference for a medical specialty would be, by saying "pediatrician," in an offhand manner. (The student had spent a summer in a special internship program for minority students interested in becoming physicians, and he and the counselor had discussed the summer program briefly.) When the time came for the student to reveal his future career goal, however, he did so in an extremely indirect way. He said he was thinking of "something in the medical field." Then the counselor responded:

EXAMPLE 5.11

(a)   C: If you want to stay in the medical field have you examined what areas in the medical field you could go into...um, with a college degree?

(b)   S: No.

(c)   C: A sstr.. with a .. with a straight...h..college degree..what.... areas of medicine you could go into or what areas in the field of medicine you could go into?

(d)   S: Yeah.

(e)   C: Because wi..with a general degree...now with a college degree exclusive of the medical field..you're pretty much ending up in some aspect of business having to do with uh..um..m..with a hospital or a medical center probably.

Here the manifest referential content of the counselor's advice is that the student should consider getting a general academic degree rather than a "premed" program that would permit subsequent acceptance into a medical school. That is a redirection of the student's goal from that of physician to some ancillary and lower status position in health care, such as hospital administration. Later in the interview the counselor went even further down the prestige ladder and suggested that the student consider becoming a male nurse—a suggestion the student in his viewing session said he regarded as demeaning.

Although the referential content of the counselor's questioning and explaining could account all by itself for the character of this moment as uncomfortable, the sense of discomfort was apparently amplified by the behavioral disorganization that was also occurring. The counselor hesitated in speech and hyperexplained. During the counselor's explanation the student's listening behavior included the "black cultural" ways of nodding, and included also giving very subtle listening feedback, which may account for some of the counselor's hesitations. The hesitations in turn c were arhythmic.

As in the previous example, the student's viewing session reactions to the counselor's advice at this point were quite strong:

> See right there. Right there, that was it. He should've been
> saying' ... y'see something like that can really stifle a person.

This was the second time the student had stopped at this point during the viewing session. In his comment the student did not elaborate on what the counselor should have been saying because the student had already stated that the first time he stopped at this spot:

> I think that right there instead of tellin' me .. ah, askin' me
> had I checked into .. ah what kind of fields I could go into
> with a straight degree he shoulda' then maybe given me a
> few suggestions, like "Well, ah, you can go on to, ah, become
> a pediatrician or obstetrician"—things like this instead of askin'
> me had I checked into it and <u>tellin'</u> me that I should check
> into it.

This uncomfortable moment was the one that was the most prominent in the interview from the point of view of the student. This was not the case for the counselor. Although the counselor stopped during his viewing session and commented on the same moment in Example 5.11, that moment was not nearly so salient for him as it was for the student. And although the counselor noticed a shift in social relations occurring at that point, he misinterpreted the meaning of the shift:

He seems to be listening much more intently than he previously had been listening... so he seems to be paying some
attention to me, you know. Or at least he seems interested
in what I'm saying.

The student's change in ways of listening was actually an indication
of his disapproval of what the counselor was saying at that moment. But
neither the counselor's viewing session comment nor what he did in the
actual interview at that point suggests that he was aware of the salience
of that uncomfortable moment to the student nor the student's interpretation of the meaning of what was happening. The counselor's and the
student's interpretive procedures were mutually incongruent at the same
time that their interactional behavior was rhythmically irregular and the
counselor's way of speaking was that of hyperexplanation.

Discussion

Examples 5.5 and 5.11 are similar in that in each the counselor is
attempting to tell the student some *bad news* about the likely future
ahead. They are also similar in that the telling of the bad news is done
in a relatively implicit way, accompanied by behavioral irregularity—
arhythmia and hyperexplanation—which, as we have seen, appears to
be interactionally produced. These irregularities are neither person's
"fault." Yet in situations of intercultural contact, such as that between
a white counselor and a black student, there often seems to be inadequate
reciprocity and complementarity between the communicative action and
inference of the conversational partners, unless the partner who comes
from the minority speech community style switches to adapt to the ways
of acting and interpreting that are customary for the partner who is a
member of the majority speech community. In these ways cultural differences in communicative traditions seem to exacerbate the problems
that all communicative partners face constantly in maintaining together
an adequate level of cooperation in speaking and listening behavior.

Consider in contrast Example 5.12, in which the counselor had bad
news to tell the student, but in which cultural differences in communication style did not seem to make telling the bad news more difficult.
The counselor is the same as in Examples 5.5 and 5.11. He is white
(Irish–American). In this example he was talking to a white student
(Polish–American) who was in quite serious academic trouble, in that
some of the Data Processing courses he had taken as part of his major
field at the junior college might not transfer to the 4-year college the
student was thinking of attending:

EXAMPLE 5.12

(a) C: One of the things you can do is check.

(b) S: Yeah, I will .. I'm gonna get in on that.

(c) C: Please do that because the sooner you know the easier it's gonna be for you to make a decision as to whether you want to continue on here and get that 2-year A.A. (associate of arts degree) or whether you .. you know .. you're planning on transferring over to State.

(d) S: Oh, oh, oh, um, excuse me, I thought you meant that after, you know, my 2 years are done here (Counselor: Mhm) then go to State. (Counselor: Mhm) I wanna get my degree here first.

(e) C: Definitely wanna get your..

(f) S: Yeah.

(g) C: Awright, make sure though, that if you .. you plan on going on in Data Processing that it will be worth your while to stay here. See, there's the key.

This example differs from 5.5 and 5.11 in that during the telling of the bad news there was no arhythmia or hyperexplanation. In addition it differs from 5.5 and 5.11 in that the counselor told the bad news explicitly. There was a misrepresentation of meaning, but it was one with which both counselor and student dealt directly, rather than indirectly. In turn *d* it became apparent that the student had misunderstood the counselor's warning. The counselor had been saying that if the student continued to take Data Processing courses (at the junior college) that would not be accepted at the senior college, it would make sense for the student to transfer sooner rather than later. The student's misinterpretation was explicitly referred to by the student, and then corrected by the counselor. At every level of organization, from behavioral regularity to interpretive inference, the two conversational partners were taking account of each other's communicative actions and taking explicit steps to fix whatever communicative troubles they were in. They were able to repair a misinterpretation of explicit referential meaning without confusion over implicit social meaning, or disorientation at the level of the conversational steering devices of rhythmic regularity and contextualization cueing.

In Example 5.12 the counselor and student were *with* each other. In viewing sessions the counselor said that being *together* or *with* was important to him. What he meant by *with* became progressively clearer as he pointed out instances of *with* and *not-with* behavior during his viewing session.

In the following quotes from the first viewing session held with that counselor one can see how the theme emerged. The counselor had watched the whole interview without stopping the tape to comment on it. Then he made general comments about the interview as a whole. At one point he said:

C: There were a couple of times that I noticed that he and I were pretty much together .. There were a couple of times that I.. as I say I thought we were together and we were both pretty much agreeing, uh, we seemed to have established some type of mood...

R: Let's go back over the beginning of it and see if we can pinpoint some of the sections where, uh, you're especially together... (The videotape plays from the beginning of the interview. At a point early on the counselor is saying, "I went into the registrar's office a little earlier today and picked up your most current transcript, and ah..." The counselor and student have both leaned forward to look at the transcript on the interviewers desk. They mirror one another's posture.)

C: (signals to stop the tape) All right, right about this point I felt that both (student's name) and I were pretty much together, we were both concentrating on that transcript. (At other times later in that viewing session the counselor again pointed to his concern for the student's being *together* or *with* the counselor.)

C: OK—(Researcher: "Mhm." The tape stops.) (Student's name) again was following me. He apparently had been listening to what I was saying and digesting it, and then when it came time to, uh, interpret it, we both..he was with me.. (Researcher: "Mhm") We were both there. (The tape resumes.)

C: Right there. (Tape stops) (Name) was again with me as he has been in a number of points here that I haven't pointed out.. (Researcher: "Mhm.") where he just kind of reaffirms what I'm saying by shaking his head and indicating to me that he is with me. And I just continue along.

The distinction made by the counselor between *with* and *not-with* relations with the student is a distinction not unique to that counselor alone, although other counselors placed more emphasis on the counselor's side of the relationship as well—on the need for the counselor to be *with* the student as well as for the student to be *with* the counselor. Notice that in describing the *with* relationship this counselor referred to specific aspects of the communicative means by which the student's intentions are realized: "he... reaffirms what I'm saying by shaking his head." In commenting on another student the counselor said, "I think that when he was with me... he was pretty still and bent in kind of a listening posture." Apparently, it was the student's listening behavior that provided the grounds for the counselor's inferences of the student's intent.

Notice also that the behavioral evidence the counselor reports using as a ground for inference involves the performance of the right behavior *in the right time:* "He apparently had been listening to what I was saying and digesting it, and then when it came time to, uh, interpret it we both..he was with me. We were both there." For them both to *be there* involved congruity and complementarity, in communicative performance and in interactional inference. In being *with,* the student was "listening and digesting," and was anticipating the moment in which it would come time to "interpret" what the counselor had been saying. The student was also performing the listening behavior necessary to show that a congruent interpretation was being made.

CONCLUSION

While the dimension of *with–not with* was an expressed concern of the counselor in terms of the conduct of the interviews he was watching during viewing sessions, the same dimension can be applied at another level of analysis to the relationship of congruity or incongruity between the interpretive procedures of the counselor and the student. When the viewing session comments of counselors and students are compared, some of the most incongruent inferences—not "withness" at an overall, global level of interpretation and impression formation—occur at uncomfortable moments in the original interviews in which both hyper-explanation and interactional arhythmia are occurring. This is intriguing. There seems to be a relationship between inferential incongruity and lack of behavioral mutuality at both levels of the social organization of communication—at the specific, "micro" level (of which conversationalists are not usually consciously aware) and at the more general "macro" level of which conversationalists can be consciously aware.

What is suggested is that behavioral regularity, especially rhythmic regularity, may be prima facie evidence of shared interpretive frameworks among those engaged in interaction. The absence of such rhythmic regularity may be evidence that there is inadequate sharing of interpretive frameworks. People who interact by fits and starts may be showing through their jointly produced interactional arhythmia that they are not members of the same speech community. In their stumbling they may be revealing themselves as cultural strangers.

6

Contrasts in Ways of
Asking Questions and Telling Advice

In Chapter 2 it was noted that the counselor may exercise optional ways of performing his role to present himself alternatively as a person whose primary concern is for the student and his immediate welfare, or as a person whose primary concern is for the institution and its standard operating procedures.

This chapter considers some of the specific communicative choices the counselor made in enacting the optional aspects of his role—in acting as the student's advocate, or as his judge. At major turning points in the sequential structure of the interview the counselor has alternative ways of acting available by which he can make the student's role easier or harder to perform.[1] The counselor's exercise of alternative options at

[1] For discussion of the major sequential turning points of the interview, see Chapter 2, pp. 20–26. The optional ways of acting analyzed here involve what linguists refer to as *syntagmatic* and *paradigmatic* aspects of organization in speech. Whereas syntagmatic relations are not necessarily sequential, as we use the term here the *syntagmatic* refers to appropriate sequence relationships from one point in time to the next—in this case the relationship between a kind of question asked and a kind of answer that question summons. (Syntagmatic relations also obtain at the levels of sentence grammar and analysis reported here.) In contrast, *paradigmatic* aspects of order involve the range of appropriate alternative ways of acting that could be chosen for performance at any single point in the syntagmatic order—in this case, the range of kinds of questions that could be asked at any given point in the conversation, or the range of kinds of answers that could be given once

these sequential choice points seemed to be one of the main ways that the counselor could present himself as relatively more or less helpful and approving of the student. The choices were not consciously made, apparently. But whether intended or not, what the counselor did at major turning points seemed to have an affect on the interactional accomplishment of *rapport*.

At most of the major turning points in the interview, the counselor could choose from among a range of optional ways of asking a student something or of responding to the student's answering. Each of the sets of available choices came in a three-part sequence of interactional "slots," or "moves": (1) the counselor's *asking;* (2) the student's *answering;* (3) the counselor's *next move.* The first and second of these slots, and the second and third were tied together as *adjacency pairs,*[2] with the counselor's question functioning as the summons of an answer from the student, and the student's answer requiring a next move from the counselor. In the first slot the counselor formulated the topic of the question to be asked and then asked it. In the third slot the counselor responded to the student's answer either by evaluating its correctness, by giving advice, or by proceeding directly on to the next question. (See Figure 6.1.)

It is apparent from Figure 6.1 that the counselor's optional ways of eliciting a response from the student placed differing kinds of requirements on the student's response. The requirements differed in the terms of the level of difficulty in responding that was involved. Asking "What did you get in Math 101?" required only a single response, while asking "What grades did you get?" required multiple responses. In addition, the latter way of asking also required more complex recall from the student than did the former way of asking. For the student to answer by telling all his grades in a connected list required that the student remember the entire set of courses taken as well as each of the grades received.

Differences in the counselors' ways of asking questions and in responding to student answers were apparent at three major turning points

---

a certain kind of question had been asked. For discussion, see Lyons, 1968:70–79; Gumperz, 1972:16–20; Hymes, 1974:53. At issue is the organization of elements of style in appropriate cooccurrence relationships. The matter is discussed in terms of relationships of "horizontal" (sequential) and "vertical" (simultaneous) alternation and cooccurrence by Ervin-Tripp, 1972:213–250, 1973:302–373.

[2] This is a term used by conversational analysts to refer to what linguists term *syntagmatic* sequence relationships of *horizontal cooccurrence.* See Sacks, Schegloff, and Jefferson, 1974; Mehan and Wood, 1975:127, 131.

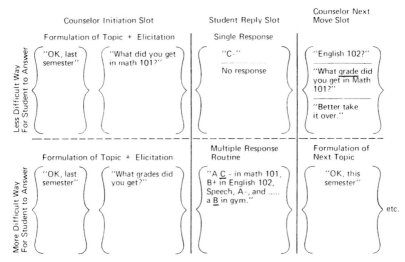

Figure 6.1.   Optional ways of eliciting response from student.

in the interviews: (1) the beginnings of elicitation rounds in which the counselor asked the student what grades and courses he had received; (2) the point at which the counselor elicited from the student a statement of his future goal; (3) the point at which the counselor gave advice about the student's goal. Two kinds of difference in interactional quality discourse structure and counselor–student role relationship were apparent at these points—differences involving the level of difficulty in responding that was required of the student, and differences involving the amount of approval and immediate usefulness in the counselor's advice to the student. The major turning points in discourse will be considered here in the same sequence in which they appeared in the interviews: grades and courses first, the student's future goal next, and the counselor's advice last.

TURNING POINT I—DISCUSSION OF GRADES AND COURSES

The whole first half of the interview consisted in the counselor's determining who the student was in official terms as a social person. Two aspects of social identity were considered, the student's current academic status and the student's current definition of a goal for the future. Only after these aspects of the student's status in the present were defined could the counselor give advice about future courses of action that might be taken.

Current academic status was established by the counselor's reviewing the student's academic transcript in the cumulative file and bringing it up to date first by asking the student what grades he received in courses taken during the previous semester and next by asking the student what courses he was taking in the present semester. Figure 6.2 illustrates the primary sequential slots in that discourse process. Figure 6.2 also shows the main optional ways of asking and responding that actually occurred in 15 interviews conducted by three different counselors.[3] The interviews done by the fourth counselor in our sample are omitted from this analysis because the sequential structure of those interviews differed from the rest. (See discussion in footnote 3.)

There were two differing ways in which the counselors elicited information about courses the students were taking and grades they had received the previous semester:

Strategy 1: The counselor read the course names aloud and asked the student to respond either yes or no, or with the grade he received.

Strategy 2: The counselor asked the student to list the courses and grades himself.

[3] It should be pointed out that Figure 6.2 does not include every option that could conceivably be available to the counselors, but rather only those options that actually were chosen, as evidenced by their performance in the encounters. There are many other possible options that the counselors could choose in their elicitation of students' grades and courses, but only those listed in the diagram actually occurred in the encounters. We do this here and throughout this chapter because our analysis focuses on the use by the counselor of variation in means within a quite narrow range of choice. The official, professional character of the gatekeeping encounter, occurring as it does among near or total strangers in a bureaucratic formal organization in the United States (with "American" limits placed on how overtly domineering a bureaucratic official can be), restricts the counselor's options. He cannot even say, "You ought to be ashamed of yourself!" or "You're black and poor; you can't ever be a physician, no matter how hard you try." On the other hand, he can't say "I'd have dropped calculus, too; the teacher is an idiot." So both extremes of the paradigmatic range of choices—from those that are most secular and high in interpersonal solidarity to those that are most officially sacral and low in interpersonal solidarity—are not available to the counselor. He must make use of slight variation around the center of the range. Our analysis attempts to illuminate the social meaning of these slight variations in ways of speaking.

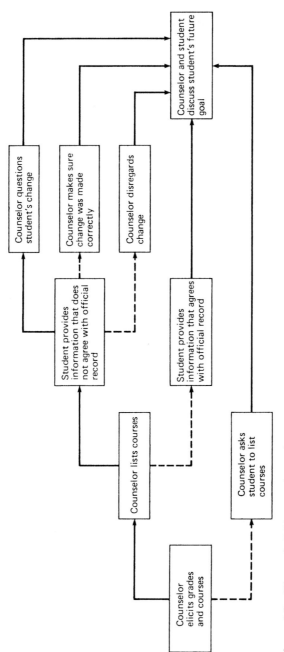

Figure 6.2. Ways of eliciting grades and courses.

The following is an example of Strategy 1:

EXAMPLE 6.1

C: All right, this semester you have Biology 102, English 101...
S: I have no English at all.

The following is an example of Strategy 2:

EXAMPLE 6.2

C: OK, would you tell me what you're taking, please?
S: I ha ... Electronics...
C: Mm Hmm. Which one?
S: Eh 130 .. Engineering 131 ... English 100... Reading 100... and m ... Mech Tech.

The elicitation strategies differ in the level of difficulty involved in producing a correct and socially appropriate answer. The individual counselors differed in the extent to which they used the two strategies. Table 6.1 contains the number of times each of the counselors used each elicitation strategy.

The table shows that, overall, the two strategies were used in about equal proportions. It can also be seen that each counselor had a preferred pattern of use. Counselor 9-1 usually read the course names as a list and had the student acknowledge each as it came along, while counselor 9-3 usually had the students list the courses themselves. Counselor 9-2 used the two strategies almost equally.

Counselor 9-3 used strategy 2 uniformly. All students received the same treatment from him. Counselors 9-1 and 9-2, on the other hand, each used strategy 2 with only one student. The two encounters in which the counselors used strategy 2 were the ones lowest in terms of the amount of particularistic comembership between the counselors and those students. (See the discussion of *comembership* in Chapter 2, p. 17.) These two counselors used strategy 2 with students with whom they had the least in common. This may have been a way of saying to the student that it was his responsibility to keep the encounter going, and a way of providing as little help to the student as possible. For counselors

Table 6.1
Frequency of Use of Two Alternative Course Elicitation Strategies

	Strategy 1: Counselor lists courses	Strategy 2: Counselor asks student to list courses
Counselor 9-1	6	1
Counselor 9-2	2	1
Counselor 9-3	0	5
Totals	8	7

9-1 and 9-2, strategy 2 may have functioned as a way of acting that distanced them from those students.

When counselors 9-1 and 9-2 were being easier on students by using strategy 1, they read aloud from the student's cumulative record card the courses that the student had presumably taken the previous semester and the courses that the student was presumably taking during the present semester. It was up to the student to confirm whether or not what appeared in the student's official record was accurate and up to date.

At this junior college, it was commonplace for a student to drop a class during the semester. In seven out of the eight encounters in which counselors 9-1 and 9-2 used strategy 1, the student had to correct the information that was in his official record. In all cases, the student had dropped a course he had previously registered for. The counselors had several options for dealing with this. In choosing any one of the options, the counselors set the tone for the next part of the encounter. Hence the form of discourse structure took shape out of the set of functions that were institutionally required of the interview.

In the information the student provided in his reply slot did not agree with the information that was in the student's official record, then the counselor could exercise one of several options for dealing with the discrepancy: (a) ask the student to justify the change; (b) check to be sure the student dropped the course in an officially appropriate manner; (c) let the matter pass and go on to the next question.

> Option (a):   Questioning the student's change by making him
>   justify why he dropped the course.

EXAMPLE 6.3

C: English 102, Engineering 131...

S: Yes.

C: Math 96...

S: No, I dropped that.

C: How come?

S: Well, 'cause it...the only time they had was at 6 to 7:15 and it was kind of late 'cause I start at 8 every morning.

C: Mech Tech 205?

> Option (*b*):   Making sure that the student dropped the course in a bureaucratically acceptable manner, so that the student will not be penalized for not attending a course. Here the counselor does not question the substance of the student's decision to drop the course, but rather makes sure that the student has followed the correct procedures.

EXAMPLE 6.4

C: Math?

S: Naw, I didn't take Math.

C: Did you register for it?

S: No...I registered for Speech instead of Math 'cause I...

C: Now we don't have to drop your Math class now. You're not registered. See, if you're registered in it, you're just gonna attend. You're gonna receive an "F" at the end of the semester.

S: Naw, I didn't even get a class card for it.

C: Okay, all right. Data Processing 112?

> Option (*c*):   Letting the issue pass, without either questioning the student's decision or making sure that the student has followed the correct procedures.

EXAMPLE 6.5

C: OK. This semester. English 101? That's what you've got now. Biology 102... Soc Sci 101...

S: I...I... I don't have Biology 102. I have, um, 112.

C: Soc Sci 101?

There is one major difference among the options with respect to the relationship of helpfulness between the counselor and the student. When a counselor used option (a), he was looking after the best interests of the institution by making sure that the student had a good reason for dropping the course. The counselor only checked to be sure that the student had an organizationally legitimate reason for doing what he did. The counselor did not make sure that the student was in any way harming his academic program by dropping the course. In contrast, when a counselor used option (b), he was attending to the best interests of the student, making sure that no harm of any kind would occur because of the decision to drop the course. Option (c) falls somewhere in the middle in terms of helpfulness, because the counselor was not questioning the student's judgment, but at the same time he was not taking care to protect the student from making a decision the student might later regret.

One would expect that the different options might be used differently by each counselor. There should be a relationship between the amount of particularistic comembership and the optional ways of asking chosen by the counselor. This is shown in Table 6.2, which reports the number of times each strategy was used with students with whom the counselor had different amounts of particularistic comembership.

Notice that options (b) and (c) tend to be used in high-comembership encounters, while option (a) is the only one used in low-comembership encounters. Even though the number of cases in each cell is very small, there still appears to be a clear pattern.

Option (a) was used only once, in one high-comembership encounter. This option was the one in which the counselor questioned the judgment of the student. That seems to be an unusual thing for the counselor to do in a high-comembership encounter. Given the amount of similarity in background between counselor and student in high-comembership encounters, it is not expected that the counselor would question the student's judgment.

Table 6.2
Number of Occurrences of Each Strategy for Dealing with Mismatch of Information with Students with High, Medium, and Low Comembership

	Option (a): Questioning student	Option (b): Looking after student	Option (c): Letting issue pass
High comembership	1	1	2
Medium comembership	1	0	1
Low comembership	2	0	0
Totals	4	1	3

To understand this it is necessary to drop down one level of generality in analysis, and look more closely at the counselor's way of questioning. The counselor did question the student's judgment, but did so in a very different way from the way in which he questioned the judgment of the student with whom he had a low-comembership relationship. That way was shown in Example 6.3. There the counselor reacted to the student's statement of the reason he dropped the course (it met too late in the evening) by simply going on to ask for the grade the student received in another course, doing so in a business-like, bureaucratically neutral tone of voice.

In the high-comembership encounter the counselor treated lightly the student's admission of difficulty in a course. The counselor did not preach a sermon on why the student should have persevered. Rather, the counselor reacted in a joking tone of voice, which functioned to maintain the previously existing atmosphere of fellow feeling and secular pragmatism in the encounter. The text of the high-comembership interview is given in Example 6.6.

EXAMPLE 6.6

S: I'm ready to drop another class.

C: How come?

S: I really can't handle this class. It's Speech. I didn't take calculus again.

C: (jokingly) You know we add three and you deduct two from here. (Prosodic and pitch register shift) Now, let's have some grades: Last semester, Data Processing 101, what did you get for a grade?

Here the contrast in social relationship between high and low co-membership is marked by voice pitch, tempo, and rhythm, signaling seriousness in the one case and joking in the other. The contrast between joking about a matter such as dropping a course and not commenting on the student's explanation (but doing so seriously, moving right along) provides a major qualitative difference between high-comembership encounters and low-comembership encounters.

The previous high-comembership encounter is also the only encounter in which that counselor used option (b), making sure that the student dropped the course in a bureaucratically acceptable manner, thereby looking after the best interest of the student. The counselor used option (b) at a point later in the elicitation round, when the student revealed he had also dropped a Math course. (See Example 6.4.) This is another use of a communicative option to indicate the high level of solidarity between the counselor and the student in this encounter. Not only did the counselor treat lightly the fact that the student had dropped a course, but he also showed concern for the best interests of the student by making sure that the student had dropped the course in a procedurally correct way.

TURNING POINT II—DISCUSSION OF THE STUDENT'S FUTURE GOALS

Following the elicitation of the student's current courses and past grades the conversation turned to a discussion of the student's goals. In so doing, the counselor and student were shifting time frames: from the past and the present (in the elicitation of courses and grades) to the future (in the discussion of the student's plans).

Just as the counselors used alternative strategies to elicit courses and grades from students, they also used several different approaches to open the discussion of the student's goals. The strategies for eliciting the student's future plans differed along two dimensions: *time* and *specificity*. There was variation in the point in future time the counselor referred to. The counselor could refer to the student's life at the junior college, or he could refer to the student's life after junior college. There was variation in how specifically focused the counselor was in his questioning of the student. The counselor could ask the student about a specific goal such as transferring to a 4-year college, or the counselor could ask the student a question about the future without specifying any particular academic or occupational goal.

This variation is illustrated in Figure 6.3, which shows the options chosen by three counselors in 15 different interviews.

In 12 of the 14 interviews in which the counselor introduced the topic of the student's future goal, the counselor asked the student about his life after leaving the junior college.[4] In these 12 encounters, the counselor initiated the discussion of the student's future goal by asking the student about his life after junior college. The main distinction among these encounters was in the specificity with which the counselor asked about the future goal. In some cases the question was asked very specifically: "Do you intend to transfer to a 4-year school?" In other cases, the

---

[4] In only two interviews did the counselor use the atypical strategy of asking the student about the student's life at the junior college. In one of these instances, the student's future plan discussed was the courses the student would take during summer school. In the other encounter in which the counselor asked the student about his life at the junior college, the goal that was discussed was the courses the student would take the following Fall semester.

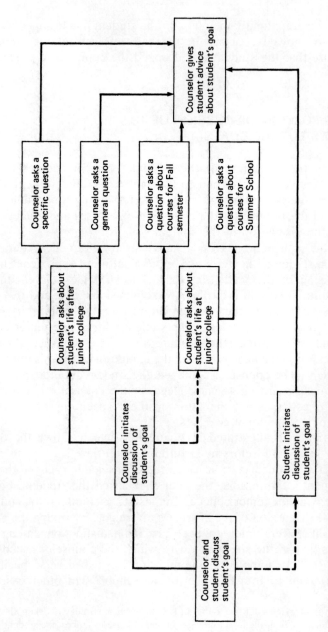

Figure 6.3. Ways of discussing student's future goal.

question was asked in a much more general way: "All right, now what are you going to do? What are your plans when you leave here...after you graduate?"

Three different strategies were used by the counselors to ask the students about their future goals:

Strategy 1:   Ask the student a specific question about his life at the junior college. In the two cases in which this occurred, the question referred to courses the student was planning to take in an up-coming semester.

Strategy 2:   Ask the student a specific question about his life after junior college.

Strategy 3:   Ask the student a general question about his life after junior college.

These three strategies were used differently. Table 6.3 contains the number of times each counselor used each of the three strategies to ask a student about his future.

There are two things of note in Table 6.3. First, specific questions (strategies 1 and 2) and general questions (strategy 3) were asked in almost equal proportions (8 to 6). Second, two of the counselors, 9-1 and 9-3, preferred one strategy of asking questions about the student's future goal over the others.

Counselor 9-1 preferred to ask specific questions (strategies 1 and 2), whereas counselor 9-3 preferred to ask general questions (strategy 3). Asking a general question places more answering responsibility upon the student than asking a specific question. It is a way of asking about the future which is analogous to the general way of asking the students about their courses and grades in the past and present semesters. Asking a general question places the responsibility upon the student to choose a

Table 6.3
Frequency of Use of Three Strategies for Eliciting the Student's Future Goal

	Strategy 1: Ask the student a specific question about life at junior college	Strategy 2: Ask the student a specific question about life after junior college	Strategy 3: Ask the student a general question about life after junior college
Counselor 9-1	2	3	2
Counselor 9-2	0	1	1
Counselor 9-3	0	2	3
Totals	2	6	6

goal for himself, rather than restricting the student to discussing the goal the counselor is asking about in his question. Remember that in the eliciting of grades and courses, counselor 9-1 chose to list the courses himself, whereas counselor 9-3 asked the student to list the courses. As with the elicitation of the student's goal, the strategy chosen by counselor 9-3 was the one that demanded more of the student, whereas the strategy chosen by counselor 9-1 was the one that demanded less of the student.

The next issue that arises involves the relationship between the three strategies for eliciting the student's future goal and the amount of particularistic comembership between the counselor and the student. Table 6.4 shows the number of encounters with high, medium, and low comembership in which each of the strategies was used.

There are two points of note in this table. First, low-comembership encounters were the only kinds of encounters in which the counselors most often asked general questions rather than specific ones. In two of the interviews the question asked was, "Why are you in school?" Such a question seems threatening to a student. The two encounters in which the counselor used this question were the two lowest in particularistic comembership for each of the two counselors involved. These two counselors were the same ones who had used in low-comembership encounters the "difficult to answer" strategy of asking the student to list all the courses he was taking. These counselors, then, had a way of differentiating encounters with low comembership from encounters with medium and high comembership by the elicitation strategies that they used. Students with whom they had less in common were given more difficult ways of answering than were students with whom the counselors had more in common.

Table 6.4
Number of Encounters with High, Medium, and Low Comembership in Which Each of the Student Goal Elicitation Strategies Was Used

	Strategy 1: Ask the student a specific question about life at junior college	Strategy 2: Ask the student a specific question about life after junior college	Strategy 3: Ask the student a general question about life after junior college
High comembership	0	3	2
Medium comembership	1	2	0
Low comembership	1	1	4
Totals	2	6	6

The second thing of note in Table 6.4 is that general questions (strategy 3) were used in encounters with high comembership as well as in those with low comembership. Similar questions were asked of students with whom the counselors had a great deal in common and students with whom the counselors had very little in common. One possible reason for this is that the asking of general questions can have at least two distinct social meanings. First, the asking of a general question can demonstrate trust in the student's ability to be able to specify what he wants to do in the future. By asking the student a general question, the counselor in this instance is allowing the student latitude to express himself freely.

In contrast, the asking of a general question can also be used to put the student on the spot. This is especially true of questions such as "Why are you in school?" By asking the student a general question in that way the counselor gave the student just enough rope to hang himself. In both instances in which the counselor asked this question, the students responded with very general answers. Since the counselor needed from the student a statement of a specific goal in order to give advice, the lack of specificity of the student's answer compounded the advising problem for the counselor. But it was the counselor's general way of asking that set the student up to answer in an inadequate way.

TURNING POINT III—ADVICE ABOUT THE STUDENT'S FUTURE GOAL

After determining who the student was in the present and what his future goal was, the counselor gave the student advice about that goal. In 12 of the interviews the counselor asked the student a question about goals after leaving junior college. Then the discussion of the student's future always turned to the topic of whether the student was going to transfer to a 4-year school, regardless of the question the counselor had previously asked. In all instances the student said he planned to transfer to a 4-year school. The counselor's subsequent advice invariably had to do with the courses the student should take in the following semester considering that the student was planning later to transfer to a 4-year school.

Just as there had been differences in the ways the counselors elicited the student's current academic status and future goal, so there were differences in the ways the counselors gave advice about what courses the student should take next. Three differing strategies were used for giving this advice:

1. Suggest courses likely to improve the student's choices of admission to a 4-year school.
2. Tell the student to consult the proposed 4-year school's catalog to be certain about the transferability of the courses taken at the junior college.
3. Give advice only in terms of the junior college's graduation requirements.

Strategy 1:   Tell the student outright what courses the student should take that would either transfer to a 4-year school, or would in some other way help the student to be admitted to a 4-year school.

EXAMPLE 6.7

C: Instead of taking a full-year Phy-Sci, take two courses in Home Ec, which is the equivalent. Now, if you're gonna go on to a 4-year college... I'd suggest taking a Phy-Sci.

S: I'll take the Phy-Sci.

Strategy 2:   Tell the student to check with the 4-year school in which he wants to enroll to be sure that the courses taken in junior college will transfer.

EXAMPLE 6.8

C: Where do you intend to go from here (name of student)? ——— as far as college or school... (——— means unintelligible)

S: Maybe (name of college) for a while.

C: Have you been checking any other catalogs up in our library?

S: No.

C: What you should start doing now is make sure we're hitting the ball on the head with the courses here, see what the freshmen and sophomores are taking at (name of college) so that if there is any change we could make it 'cause we still have a year to go...

S: Yeah.

C: Don't wait until the last semester to find out a lot of these courses are not accepted by them.

S: Yeah.

C: ...Understand?

S: Yeah.

> Strategy 3:   Tell the student what courses he should take in order to satisfy his 2-year junior college degree. In this strategy the counselor does not relate the course sequence to the student's plan to transfer to a 4-year school.

EXAMPLE 6.9

C: Right. How about finishing your English 102?

S: English 102.

C: Wanna get that out of the way? Or you can start a Biology.

S: I need a...do I need a Biology?

C: Yeah.

S: I do?

C: Are you gonna get...a degree in Liberal Arts...? You're gonna have to take everything here... everything that's on there (pointing to a list of requirements)...1 full year of all those courses.

Figure 6.4 shows the counselor's optional ways of giving advice, in the context of the goal the student has just previously stated. These three ways of giving the student advice about his goal fall along a continuum of helpfulness to the student in terms of whether or not the advice has a high "face value" of helpfulness relative to the student's future plans. In strategy 1, the advice the counselor gives the student is obviously helpful to the student's goal in that the counselor provides the "answers" about transferability. In strategy 3, however, the advice the counselor gives is not necessarily helpful in providing information about transferability. Strategy 2 falls somewhere in between in that it is somewhat helpful to the student but still leaves a great deal of information up to the student to seek.

For this set of options no individual differences were apparent across the three counselors. For all counselors there was a clear relationship between the strategy the counselors used and the amount of particularistic comembership between the counselor and the student. In Table 6.5 it can be seen that most instances of strategy 1 occurred in encounters with high comembership, while strategy 3 was never used in these encounters. Although there were two low-comembership encounters in

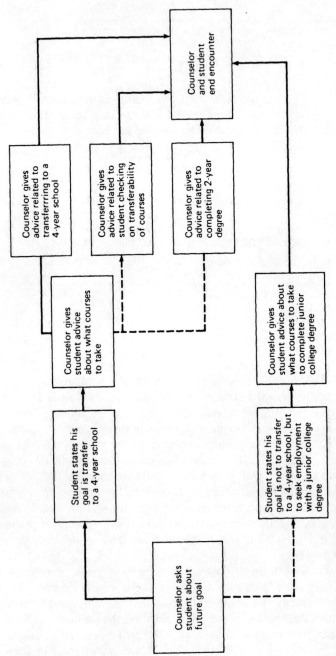

Figure 6.4. Ways of giving advice.

Table 6.5
Frequency of Use of Three Options for Giving Advice about Stated Goal

	Strategy 1: Advise about 4-year transfer requirements	Strategy 2: Tell student to check with 4-year school	Strategy 3: Advise about completing 2-year degree only	Totals
High comembership	5	0	0	5
Medium comembership	0	1	1	2
Low comembership	2	0	3	5
Totals	7	1	4	12

which strategy 1 was used, one of those involved the counselor giving the student advice about a goal that the *counselor* had chosen for the student, rather than giving the student advice about the goal that the student himself had chosen. If this aberrant instance is not counted, then the strategy that was used most often in low-comembership encounters was strategy 3, by a three-to-one margin.

These results demonstrate that the counselors were more likely to look more actively after the interests of the student in high comembership encounters, but that they were less likely to do so in low-comembership encounters. By choosing strategy 1 in all high-comembership encounters, the counselors seemed to be saying implicitly that they approved of the student's goals and that they were going to help them meet them. By choosing to use strategy 3 most often in low-comembership encounters, the counselors seemed to be saying implicitly that they wanted to be sure that the students made it through the junior college. That was of higher priority for the counselors apparently than was helping the student tranfser to a 4-year school. The use of the different advice-giving strategies seems to have conveyed subtly different meanings to the students. Since for a working-class student in a United States junior college being able or unable to transfer to a 4-year college or university opens up or virtually closes off the possibility of achieving middle-class occupational rank as an adult, the issue of transfer is an important one. It is a crucial mobility gate in the student's academic career. Consequently, the social meaning of the gatekeeping counselor's ways of giving advice about transfer to a 4-year school had salient social meaning. The counselor's choice of option 1 or option 3 as a way of giving advice enabled him to say implicitly either "For you the gate is open." or "For you the gate is likely to be closed."

CONCLUSION

The 14 interviews considered here, conducted by three counselors, were classed as low, medium or high in comembership relationship between the counselor and the student. High-comembership encounters tended to be encounters in which the counselor did not question changes the student had made in his program, in which the counselor asked the student specific questions about his future, and in which the advice the counselor gave the student was directly relevant to the student's attainment of a desired future goal. Low-comembership encounters tended to be encounters in which the counselor questioned the changes the student made in his program, in which the counselor asked the student general questions about why he was in school and what he planned to do in the future, and in which the advice the counselor gave the student was mainly concerned with making sure the student was meeting the requirements of his degree program, rather than taking directly into consideration the student's desired future goals. A direct contrast can be seen when the two kinds of encounters are compared. In the former case, the counselor is acting as the advocate of the student, while in the latter case the counselor appears to be the student's judge.

The two differing modes of social relationship, high and low comembership, appeared to provide differing contexts of situation. In the high-comembership context, solidarity with the student and distancing from the official role of counselor was appropriate. In the low-comembership context less solidarity with the student was found and the counselor embraced the official role of institutional gatekeeper. This role-distancing and role-embracement did not appear to happen randomly, although it seemed to be done by the counselor without conscious awareness. The different ways of relating to students are general patterns that resulted from specific choices among optional ways of acting that were available at major sequential points in the interviews. This chapter has considered some of those choice points and the options actually made use of at those points by three counselors.

This is not to say that the alternative ways of asking and of giving advice that have been identified were the only aspects of communicative means employed by the counselor to signal the social meanings of role-distancing (advocacy of the student) or role-embracement ("impartial" judgment of the student). Contrast in nonverbal communicative means—facial expression, tone of voice, continuity or discontinuity of interactional rhythm—in many instances cooccurred with the features of style in speaking that have been considered here, as did aspects of style in choice of vocabulary and pronunciation features that have been characterized by linguists as *careful* and *casual* speech, respectively.

What is most significant here is that in addition to all these other communicative means by which role-distancing and role-embracement by the counselors were signaled, the very ways of asking questions and of giving advice that on the surface would seem to be the most "business-like" kinds of talk in the interviews seemed to have been carrying subtle shadings of expressive meaning.

Optional ways of speaking were available even within what is ostensibly the most instrumental and affectively neutral core of the interview. Regular alternation by counselors in the choice of these options invested the workaday language of officially legitimate talk with implicit social meaning. By making use of this implicit system of meanings, the counselor as a gatekeeper could say "yes" or "no" to a student without having to say it in so many words.

7

Overall Patterns and
Summary Evidence[1]

In the previous chapters various aspects of the interaction process were considered separately. It is now appropriate to consider some of these aspects of the process together, and also to consider interaction process factors in relation to some of the gatekeeping outcomes of the counseling interviews. Accordingly, this chapter takes a much more broadly synoptic view of the interviews than did the previous chapters. It presents a statistical picture of the major patterns of relationship that were found between interactional processes and outcomes.

Data from 25 encounters, involving 4 male counselors and 25 male students from two United States junior colleges, are reported here. Two of the counselors were white; two were black. Although a few counselors and students had met previously, their acquaintance seemed to have had no systematic effect on the conduct of interaction in their interviews.

OVERVIEW OF THE VARIABLES

Three sets of variables are considered together: (1) those concerned with the social identity of the counselor and the student; (2) those con-

[1] This chapter, with the exception of the introductory paragraphs, is reprinted from F. Erickson, Gatekeeping and the melting pot, *Harvard Educational Review* 45(1), 44–70. Copyright © 1975 by President and Fellows of Harvard College.

cerned with the outcomes of the interviews; (3) those concerned with the interactional character of the interviews.

Social Identity Variables

The social identity variables were ethnicity or race, panethnicity, and comembership. Ethnicity—Italian–American, Polish–American, Irish–American, Chicano, Puerto Rican, and black—was determined by last name and skin color of the participants. Each encounter was then labeled: Intraethnic encounters were those in which the counselor and the student were of the same ethnic group and interethnic encounters were those in which counselor and student were of different ethnic groups. In addition, each encounter was labeled either intra-panethnic if the counselor and student were of the same panethnic group (white ethnic or Third World) or inter-panethnic if the counselor and student were of different panethnic groups. Each encounter also was categorized according to high, medium, or low comembership. (The comembership score was an index of situationally defined similarities including but not limited to ethnicity and panethnicity; cf. Chapter 2, pp. 17, 35–37.)

In the analyses and in the tables that follow, each encounter was counted and sorted according to each of these three categories of social identity, in order to determine the relationship between differing levels of inclusiveness in shared social identity and measures of interactional character and outcomes. (Note that each successive category in the series *ethnicity, panethnicity, comembership* is more inclusive than the previous one; for example, the category intra-panethnic includes all encounters in which the counselor and student were of the same ethnic or racial group as well as all those encounters in which the counselor and student were ethnically different but were members of the same panethnic category.)

Outcome Variable

One convenient way to evaluate the outcome of an interaction is to measure the special help each student receives from a counselor. Special help was defined as assistance that went beyond the counselor's regular routine or involved bending organizational rules.

Interactional Character Variables

Three aspects of interactional character were coded for each encounter: the overall behavioral smoothness, the smoothness of behavior during the most uncomfortable moment in an encounter, and the overall emotional tone of each encounter.

The overall smoothness was assessed by a summary score, the overall behavior symmetry coefficient (OBSC), which counted the total number of uncomfortable moments, asymmetric verbal interruptions, and symmetric verbal overlaps within each encounter. The frequency of uncomfortable moments in an interview turned out to be an appropriate and useful index of overall interactional symmetry. Raters trained to watch films of the interviews were able to identify uncomfortable moments with high agreement.

The second interactional character variable was the Arhythmia Code (AC). It was derived from a detailed analysis of the most uncomfortable of all the uncomfortable moments in the encounters. In all cases for which we had viewing session data (23 out of the 25 cases reported here), the uncomfortable moment our raters designated most uncomfortable was the one that the counselor, or the student, or both, had also identified as an uncomfortable moment. Films of these moments, usually between 45 seconds and 1.5 minutes in length, were then analyzed frame-by-frame in slow motion. Charts showing the timing of speech and body motion were prepared (see Chapter 4, pp. 90–91) and these charts were categorized according to high, medium, or low interactional arhythmia.

The third interactional character variable, overall emotional tone, was an indication of the degree of friendliness of an encounter, rated on a scale from hostile to very friendly. Rating turned out to be a complex decision process because the deviations from a business-like manner on the part of the interviewer were slight. Moreover, since each counselor had his own personal style, it was sometimes difficult for the raters to make comparable judgments. Generally, however, there was fairly good agreement among raters.

RESULTS

To test the working hypothesis that the social identities and communication styles of the counselor and student affect the character and outcome of the interaction, we looked first at the relationship between social identity and special help. The data in Table 7.1, despite individual differences among counselors, generally supported the working hypothesis. As can be seen from the overall means in the first two rows of the table, students of the same ethnic background as the counselor tended to receive more special help than students of different ethnic backgrounds (12.7 as opposed to 8.0). Similarly, intra-panethnic encounters resulted

Table 7.1
Mean Special Help by Different Social Identity Classifications

Social identity	Number of encounters	Counselors				Overall means
		A	B	C	D	
Intraethnic	9	13.0	12.7	—	12.0	12.7
Interethnic	16	12.7	6.8	5.8	8.0	8.0
Intra-panethnic	15	13.0	10.5	5.3	11.2	10.4
Inter-panethnic	10	11.7	—	6.2	7.4	8.6
High comembership	7	10.8	18.0	7.9	11.8	12.6
Med comembership	9	16.2	9.8	7.3	11.5	10.5
Low comembership	9	11.5	6.2	3.8	5.2	6.6

in somewhat more special help for the student than inter-panethnic encounters (10.4 to 8.6). Analyses of variance for each social identity category showed that the differences in the amount of special help received were statistically significant when the encounters were classified according to comembership (12.6 to 10.5, $p < .025$; see Table 7.7). This suggests that some shared attribute other than ethnicity can evoke advocacy from a counselor.

Since the character of the interaction conveys messages of encouragement or discouragement, even when no special help has been given, we were also interested in the relationship between social identity and interactional character. Looking first at the OBSC, the measure of the overall smoothness of the encounter, Table 7.2 shows that again the

Table 7.2
Mean OBSC by Different Social Identity Classifications

Social identity	Number of encounters	Counselors				Overall means
		A	B	C	D	
Intraethnic	9	16.2	14.7	—	8.0	14.4
Interethnic	16	11.8	11.5	14.4	15.2	13.6
Intra-panethnic	15	16.2	13.5	17.6	12.3	14.4
Inter-panethnic	10	11.8	—	12.3	14.8	13.2
High comembership	7	18.2	16.0	16.8	16.3	16.9
Med comembership	9	11.5	14.7	18.4	10.7	13.9
Low comembership	9	12.2	10.7	9.2	15.0	11.7

results generally supported the working hypothesis. Sharing particularistic attributes of social identity was associated with higher OBSC scores. This suggests that the social identity of the counselor and student is related to the relative ease and smoothness with which the encounter takes place. Interestingly, the differences between high and low comembership (16.9 to 11.7) were greater than between intra- and interethnicity (14.4 to 13.6). It was originally expected that the OBSC would be an index of shared cultural communication style: Encounters between people of the same ethnic group would have high OBSC scores whereas encounters with high comembership, including people who are ethnically and culturally different, would have lower OBSC scores. This was not the case. Table 7.2 suggests that factors of social identity independent from cultural style-sharing influenced the overall ease of the encounter.

The AC, the detailed measure of the level of rhythmic instability during the most uncomfortable moment in an encounter, confirmed our original expectation: Differences for ethnicity were greater than for comembership. Table 7.3 contrasts these two measures. Because the AC is categorical, contingency tables are presented instead of means; the OBSC is presented in a comparable form. The effect of shared social identity as measured by the AC is statistically significant only for ethnicity ($\chi^2 = 6.86$; $p < .05$), while the effect as measured by the OBSC approaches significance only for comembership ($\chi^2 = 9.10$; $p < .10$). These tables suggest that the AC is more sensitive to cultural influences on communication style than the OBSC.

The third indicator of interactional character is emotional tone. In Table 7.4, the overall means show a pattern similar to that found with the OBSC. There were some differences between intra- and interethnic (7.9 to 6.2) and intra- and inter-panethnic encounters (7.5 to 5.8), but the differences were far greatest for comembership (9.0 to 7.0 to 4.8): On the average, the most cordial encounters were those in which high comembership was established. These findings support the other analyses in showing both that social identity does influence gatekeeping encounters and that commonality in social identity can be established on grounds other than ethnicity.

Because the AC tapped the match of cultural communication styles between counselor and student, it seemed to measure social identity as well as general interactional character in a way that the OBSC and emotional tone measures did not. It was then decided to see whether the AC was related to the outcome of the encounter in the same way that our other measures of social identity were. The relation between AC and special help is shown in Table 7.5. Notice that for the "low arhythmia" column the most encounters (6) were characterized by *high*

Table 7.3
Arhythmia Levels and OBSC Levels by Different Social Identity Classifications[a]

Social identity	Overall behavior symmetry scores				Arhythmia levels			
	High	Med	Low		High	Med	Low	
Intraethnic	4	2	3	9	8	1	0	9
Interethnic	5	5	6	16	6	3	7	16
	9	7	9	25	14	4	7	25
	($x^2 = 0.47$; NS)				($x^2 = 6.86$; $p < .05$)			
Intra-panethnic	7	3	5	15	10	3	2	15
Inter-panethnic	2	4	4	10	4	1	5	10
	9	7	9	25	14	4	7	25
	($x^2 = 0.47$; NS)				($x^2 = 4.02$; NS)			
High comembership	5	2	0	7	5	1	1	7
Med comembership	3	3	3	9	6	1	2	9
Low comembership	1	2	6	9	3	2	4	9
	9	7	9	25	14	4	7	25
	($x^2 = 9.10$; $p < .10$)				($x^2 = 3.12$; NS)			

[a] Cell entries are the number of encounters in each category.

special help, and the least (3) had *low special help*, whereas the reverse is true for the "high arhythmia" column. There the fewest encounters (1) had *high special help*, whereas three encounters had *low special help*. The ratio of high to low special help is thus 6:3 under the low arhythmia condition, whereas it is 1:3 under the high arhythmia condition.

Although the relationships are not statistically significant, they do show a trend for low arhythmia to be associated with high or medium special help. This suggests that in some cases a match in cultural communication style may result in a counselor deciding that a student was someone to be advocated. But special help and arhythmia are not related in a mechanical way. Exceptions are possible. Looking again at Table 7.5, it

Table 7.4
Mean Emotional Tone by Different Social Identity Classifications

Social identity	Number of encounters	Counselors				Overall means
		A	B	C	D	
Intraethnic	9	8.6	7.8	—	—	7.9
Interethnic	16	6.8	7.0	5.6	7.1	6.2
Intra-panethnic	15	8.6	7.6	6.8	5.7	7.5
Inter-panethnic	10	6.3	—	2.7	7.3	5.8
High comembership	7	9.0	9.4	9.1	8.6	9.0
Med comembership	9	7.8	7.7	6.2	6.1	7.0
Low comembership	9	6.4	6.4	0.2	5.5	4.8

is apparent that in one instance high special help was received by a student in an encounter in which the most uncomfortable moment was highly arhythmic, and interaction then was proceeding by fits and starts. Conversely, in three instances in which there was low arhythmia at the most uncomfortable moment, the student nonetheless received low special help. Apparently other factors could in some cases override the negative effects of mismatch in cultural communication style, as indicated by arhythmia during uncomfortable moments.

Table 7.5
Incidence of Arhythmia Levels by Special Help Levels

Special help	Arhythmia[a]			
	Low	Medium	High	
High	6	2	1	9
Med	5	1	3	9
Low	3	1	3	7
	14	4	7	25

$(\chi^2 = 2.32; \text{NS})$

[a] Cell entries are the number of encounters in each category.

Differences among Counselors by Race

Even though our sample of counselors for this portion of the data is extremely small, some interesting differences are revealed in the relationship between special help and arhythmia according to the race of the counselor, as in Table 7.6.

If the arhythmia score is indeed a valid indicator of sharing or non-sharing of communicative traditions among speakers, what this table may suggest is that the black counselors, members of a culturally "different" group themselves, are more tolerant of differences in cultural communication style than are the white counselors, or are more willing to give special help despite the race and culture of the student. Whereas the numbers involved here are very small, the pattern of these results suggests that more extensive research on this issue could have important implications for institutional policy in schools.

A Broadly Synoptic View

Table 7.7 is a summary of the overall means in each social identity grouping for special help, OBSC, and emotional tone. (The AC is not included in this table because its analysis does not yield means.)

While the interethnic and inter-panethnic scores are interesting, in some ways the intra-panethnic scores are even more interesting. They suggest considerable ease and solidarity in those encounters despite the cultural differences between ethnic groups in the same panethnic category. It could be argued, for example, that the cultural differences in communication style between Italians and Polish–Americans are as great as those between Italians and Mexicans, yet our data suggest that, de-

Table 7.6
Arhythmia and Special Help by Race of Counselor

Special help	Arhythmia		
	Low	Middle	High
	White counselors (N = 2)		
Low	5	0	0
Middle	2	1	2
High	1	0	2
	Black counselors (N = 2)		
Low	3	0	1
Middle	3	0	1
High	3	0	1

Table 7.7
Mean Special Help, OBSC, and Emotional Tone by Different
Social Identity Classifications[a]

Social identity	Number of encounters	Special help	OBSC	Emotional tone
Intraethnic	9	12.7 (5.0)	14.4 (3.7)	7.9 (1.7) ⎤
Interethnic	16	8.0 (4.2)	13.6 (3.4)	6.2 (2.7) ⎦ *
Intra-panethnic	15	10.4 (5.0)	14.4 (3.5)	7.5 (1.6)
Inter-panethnic	10	8.6 (5.0)	13.2 (3.5)	5.8 (3.2)
High comembership	7	12.6 (4.2) ⎤	16.9 (1.8) ⎤	9.0 (0.7) ⎤
Med comembership	9	10.5 (5.0) ⎬**	13.9 (3.4) ⎬*	7.0 (1.3) ⎬***
Low comembership	9	6.6 (4.2) ⎦	11.7 (2.9) ⎦	4.8 (2.7) ⎦

* $p < .05$.
** $p < .025$.
*** $p < .005$.
[a] Standard deviations are shown in parentheses.

spite cultural differences between Italians and Polish–Americans, an Italian–Polish encounter is likely to be much more relaxed and friendly than an Italian–Mexican encounter.[2]

This does not mean that cultural differences in communication style have no influence on the course of face-to-face interaction, for even in an encounter between an Italian and a Polish–American that is comfortable overall, there may be moments of discomfort and misunderstanding that seem to be due to cultural differences in communication style. But despite these occasional moments at which interactional pratfalls occur, two intra-panethnic speakers tend to pick up the encounter and carry on again much more easily than do speakers from different panethnic groups.

[2] This is even more striking when we consider that, given differential acculturation within an American ethnic group, ethnicity does not necessarily predict gross features of cultural style in communication behavior.

Something more than cultural style seems to be at work here. There seem to be conditions under which cultural differences can be overridden in face-to-face interaction. These conditions are *situationally defined comembership* in a social category—a class of persons—other than the ethnic group. "Panethnicity" is one such social category. Sharing "member" status in this category, two speakers are able to signal their comembership by the topics they choose to talk about, by the manner in which they talk about the topic, or by nonverbal communication style.[3]

Comembership can, of course, extend beyond shared panethnic status. And indeed, looking at Table 7.7 as a whole, it is apparent that the differences in the scores are most statistically significant for comembership. Also, encounters characterized by high comembership have the highest overall means on all three measures—higher than those for either ethnicity or panethnicity. Under the condition of high comembership, encounters were the smoothest and most friendly, and students received the most special help. These findings suggest that neither ethnicity nor cultural communication style alone is a necessary condition for positive interactional character and outcomes. Whereas ethnicity usually made a big difference in how the counselor and student treated each other, sometimes it did not. This is consistent with the earlier theoretical discussion at the beginning of Chapter 6.

For each counselor studied, there were encounters in which a student who differed from the counselor in ethnicity and cultural communication style received as much friendliness and special help as did a student who was similar to the counselor. But these were exceptions, and in almost every one of them, situationally relevant, particularistic comembership was established between counselor and student. This suggests a fundamental principle underlying the data reported in Table 7.7. If a student is ethnically different from the counselor and wants special help and friendliness, he or she must make up for ethnic differences by establishing some other form of comembership. For example, if a student is Polish–American and the counselor is Italian–American, it helps if they both happen to be wrestlers and reveal themselves as such.

It also follows that, lacking comemberships, a student might make up for background differences in other situational ways, such as acting especially deferential or attentive toward the counselor. There were students in the sample who had extremely low comembership with their counselors but who displayed high deference and attention and received

[3] Just as cultural style can be used by ethnics as a "diacritical marker" signaling comembership in an ethnic group (cf. Barth, 1969:31) so "pancultural" diacritics can be used to signal panethnic comembership. Among these are dress, posture, hair style, and strategic use of nonstandard linguistic forms, joking, and small talk.

a moderate amount of special help. Conversely, there were cases in which students sharing ethnicity or panethnicity and additional co-memberships with the counselor (such as the Italian–American wrestler) received high special help with low deference. The number of instances showing these patterns is small but they suggest that in some cases, the more different the counselor and student are in social background, the more special help "costs" in deference. This can be expressed less formally as, "When you talk to the Man you sometimes have to Uncle Tom, but when you talk to a brother, you don't." Since for everyone, white ethnic, Latino, and black alike, there is always somebody who is the Man, the possibility of demonstrating differential deference costs according to social identity is intriguing. An *increments of deference* hypothesis should be framed and tested more systematically.

Alternative Interpretations

One could argue that the reported differences in interactional character and outcomes are attributable to factors other than social identity, such as other characteristics of the student, or to inadequacies of the research design. One such factor is social class. Admittedly there is some overlap between the panethnic categories, white ethnic and Third World, and social class categories. But there were intraethnic differences within and interethnic similarities across social class ranks; and when the cases were sorted by social class rather than by ethnicity, panethnicity, and co-membership, the relationship between social background on the one hand and interactional character and outcome on the other was not clearly patterned. Furthermore, the high degree of association between co-membership and interactional character and outcome suggests that, in face-to-face interaction, people use various combinations of ways of being alike, including social class, but also including nationality group, race, cultural sharing, panethnicity, and a host of other commonalities. No one index of social identity explains the data as well as combinations of indices do, and so an emphasis on social class by itself (or ethnicity or race by themselves) as the main factor would be misleading.

Another confounding variable might be student grades. The range of grade-point averages was small—most of the students in our sample were average in performance. Conceivably, some small differences in grades could have been important for particular counselors. We failed to interview them about this. But we doubt that it was true since in some cases students with the highest and lowest grades had AC and emotional tone scores that were inconsistent with their grade rank but consistent with their ethnic similarity to the counselor. Still, it is possible that, at the extremes of the grading scale, grades might be more important than social identity. For students in the middle of the grade range, however, ethnicity, panethnicity, and comembership were better predictors of interactional character and outcome than were student grades.

A third possible confounding factor is practice effects, here defined as the position of an encounter in the series that was filmed for each counselor and the number of times the counselor and student had met before they were filmed together. However, there were no systematic differences between encounters attributable to their position in the series. Although encounters in which the counselor and student were meeting for the first time did tend to receive lower scores on the OBSC and emotional tone measures than did encounters in which both parties had met before, there were still large differences according to ethnicity and panethnicity, and having met before seemed not to have any effect on the AC.

One possible methodological weakness is the sample size. Because there were 25 students but only four counselors, it could be argued that, even if our findings are correct, we should not generalize from them. One response to this is that the findings reported here are supported in our other work. We also studied a number of encounters involving participants other than male junior-college counselors: two high school counselors one female junior-college counselor, four job interviewers, and 25 pairs of students (Erickson *et al.*, 1973). Across many of these encounters there were sharp differences in behavior symmetry and emotional tone attributable to social identity and cultural communication style. This is not to say that a larger sample size is not desirable. We have discussed elsewhere procedures for doing a less intensive but more extensive study.[4]

Although the findings reported here must be considered tentative, they are not entirely so: Despite small sample size and somewhat nonstandard methods, a kind of collective reliability was apparent in the data. The diverse pieces of evidence fit together in patterns showing regularities not likely to be caused by chance or by repeated measuring of the same things in different ways. Our loosely defined working hypothesis was supported: Ethnicity and other forms of comembership and cultural communication style in some combination almost always predict the emotional tone of encounters and the amount of special help junior college students can expect to receive in academic counseling interviews.

[4] See Erickson, 1976.

8

Some Implications for
Practice and for Research

REVIEW OF FINDINGS AND INTERPRETATIONS

Three kinds of factors other than the student's formal academic status seemed to make a difference in the character and outcomes of the counseling interviews: (1) *cultural communication style;* (2) *normative social identity,* as defined along dimensions external to the situation at hand (i.e., the dimensions of ethnicity, race, and panethnicity); (3) *performed social identity,* as defined emergently in the local situation of the interview itself.

Each of these three kinds of factors seemed to influence different aspects of the interviews at differing levels of organization.

Cultural style sharing—the knowledge by counselor and student of similar communicative traditions of performance and interpretation—seemed to have the greatest influence at the temporally specific, moment-to-moment level of organization of interaction in the interviews. Some of the effects of sharing and nonsharing of interpretive frameworks between counselor and student were discussed in Chapters 4 and 5. *Listeners' ways of listening appear to have regulated speakers' ways of speaking.* Mismatch between the listener's cultural style in the performance of listening behavior and the speaker's cultural expectations for the kinds of listening behavior to be performed seems to have resulted

179

in hyperexplanation by the speaker. The maintenance of a stable pattern of interactional rhythm in the verbal and nonverbal behavior of both speaker and listener seems to have enabled interactional partners to predict strategically salient next moments in interaction (Chapter 4). Among counselors and students from culturally differing speech communities—people who did not share the same communicative traditions for ways of speaking and ways of listening—it seems to have been more difficult to maintain a stable rhythmic pattern in interaction than it was for those who came from the same speech community (i.e., among counselors and students of culturally differing backgrounds, interactional *arhythmia* was likely to occur during uncomfortable moments (Chapter 5). The counselor and student did not seem to understand each other well when arhythmia occurred, and they appeared to be unable to co-ordinate their actions together adequately.

Normative social identity, as defined extrasituationally along dimensions such as ethnicity, race, and panethnicity, seems to have had effects on the character of counseling interaction at a more general level of organization than did cultural style sharing or nonsharing. The relative similarity or dissimilarity in normative social identity between the counselor and student seems to have affected the overall *character* and *tone* of the whole counseling encounter.

More uncomfortable moments occurred if the counselor and student were ethnically dissimilar. In the case of encounters in which the counselor and student came from differing panethnic groups (white ethnic and Third World), a positive tone for the encounter as a whole may have overridden the negative effects of momentary interactional pratfalls (see Chapter 7), although the pratfalls themselves may have been due mainly to cultural differences in communication style (Chapter 5). Attributes of normative social identity other than student grades or test scores also seem to affect the overall outcomes of the counseling encounters—the interview's results in terms of gatekeeping decisions by the counselors, as measured by the level of special help given the student (Chapter 7).

Situational or *performed* social identity—all the aspects of similarity between student and counselor in *particularistic attributes of social identity,* including ethnicity and panethnicity, but also including anything else the student and counselor had in common—seems to have had an even stronger effect on the overall character and outcome of the encounter than did social identity defined solely in normative, extrasituational terms. Particularistic comembership was the variable most closely associated with levels of special help, overall behavioral smoothness (Chapter 7), and the counselor's choices among ways of asking and explaining that were more or less supportive of the student (Chapter 6).

Comembership seemed sometimes to have a powerfully overriding positive influence on the otherwise negative effects of cultural difference in communication style.

There might still be arhythmic uncomfortable moments (Chapter 5) in an interview in which the counselor and student experienced a mismatch in communicative traditions but had high comembership. In such an interview the counselor might hyperexplain (Chapter 5). But these kinds of social disorganization in interaction at the moment-to-moment level would not *count* so much as they would in an interview characterized by low comembership between counselor and student. In the high comembership encounter, despite things going wrong momentarily, overall the counselor would be supportive in ways of asking questions and telling advice (Chapter 6). Such an encounter would probably be characterized by high special help and high overall behavioral symmetry (Chapter 7).

THE INTERVIEW AS A PARTIALLY BOUNDED ENCOUNTER

The finding that *situationally emergent* rather than *normatively fixed* social identity had the strongest influence on the character and outcome of the interviews is consistent with the notion that encounters are *partially bounded* social settings.[1] Encounters occur within a general social system, and social and cultural influences affect to some extent what happens within the encounters. But encounters also seem to have a life of their own. Persons in encounters are able to make choices among optional general courses of action, and among optional specific ways of acting from moment to moment to accomplish those courses of action. Choice is possible among various attributes of status to be attended to or ignored. One person's communicative choices from moment to moment constrain the choices of others, and in this sense single individuals are not the sole cause of what happens; social interaction both constitutes and is constituted by the circumstances of enactment. Individuals are part of an ecosystem when they engage one another in interaction.

In gatekeeping encounters such as the counseling interviews considered here, face-to-face interaction has outcomes beyond the encounter itself. The "social fact" of an officially ratified status of the student is in part interactionally produced. The status in society of the student *as student* cannot be seen simply as a fixed property of that individual; rather, it can be seen as the result (in part) of practical decisions about

---

[1] See Goffman, 1961:19–30 and the discussion in Chapter 2, pp. 14–15.

action that are made in the real time of face-to-face interaction by school counselors, testers, and teachers—and by the student himself. Actual people make those decisions together, not some reified *society* or *culture*.

Because the gatekeeping encounter is partially bounded, there is leeway available to those engaged in interaction. Not only is it possible for ethnic and racial identity and cultural difference in communication style to produce differences in interview character and outcome (despite the organizational rules that mandate uniformly "fair" treatment). The leeway available also permits the effects of normative social identity and normative patterns of cultural communication style *to be overriden* by emergent, situationally defined social identity. Under the condition of high comembership, counselors and students seem to have been choosing to overlook things in one another's communicative performance that otherwise would have made a negative difference. Such choices would not be possible if encounters were not partially bounded.

Yet the findings also show that the counseling interview was only partially bounded; its life was not wholly its own. The larger world outside the encounter did seem to have influenced the microcosmic world within it. Normative status and normative culture did seem to provide customary channels or constraints within which ranges of optional communicative choice are usually confined. Difference in social identity and cultural style did increase the probability of things going wrong. Counselors did seem to avoid telling bad news explicitly to students whose ethnic and racial background differed from the counselor's own (Chapters 2 and 6). Hyperexplanation and arhythmia did seem related to cultural knowledge of how to perform and interpret communication (Chapter 5). This is conventional, shared knowledge. The counselor and student did not invent it on the spot. They brought it to the interview as life experience learned through participation in various speech communities in everyday life outside the particular encounter they happened to find themselves in at the moment. Usually they employed culturally conventional resources for their choice-making, even though they may have gone beyond the conventions occasionally to improvise new ways of making sense together.

In beginning this study we expected that cultural style in communication behavior would be the most powerful single factor affecting the outcomes of gatekeeping encounters. By the end of the study, that formulation of the research problem seemed too simple. Ethnicity and communication style influenced gatekeeping outcomes in many encounters, but had little influence in others. These findings help explain how social scientists as well as laymen can get into such bitter arguments in the field of educational policy—arguments about the importance of race, ethnicity, and cultural style compared to such factors as intelligence, social class, or temperament. Those who assert the alternative theories can always find instances to confirm their favored explanation of cause.

That the results are mixed is intriguing. It seems not a matter of *either* the conventional normative order *or* the situationally improvised order as main causal factors, but a matter of *both–and*. Overemphasis in interpretation on either side seems unwarranted, although this is what "order" theorists such as the older structural–functionalists in sociology and anthropology have done on the one hand, and what newer "spontaneity" theorists in phenomenology and ethnomethodology have sometimes done on the other.[2] The balanced position inherent in the notion of *partial boundedness* seems the most appropriate in the light of the data we have reported. It takes proper account of the influences of social and cultural norms in the conduct of face-to-face relations, but it also shows that people confronting the practical circumstances of immediate action are not entirely constrained by the norms.

SOCIAL ECOLOGY AND THE POLITICS OF COMMUNICATIVE KNOWLEDGE

In confronting the data it was necessary to rethink some usual assumptions about the ways that normative cultural knowledge is shared in human groups. It is usual among anthropologists and sociolinguists to assume that differing communicative "subcultures" exist in complex polyethnic societies such as the United States. These subcultures would involve knowledge of communicative traditions that would be shared within discrete segments of the population such as ethnic, racial, or social class aggregates. Within any given segment of the population ("Puerto Ricans," "blacks," "Italian–Americans") the communicative culture traits characteristically occurring together as an internally unified and coherent set (the "subculture") would be distributed fairly continuously among members of the population. Whereas some members of the population segment would be relatively assimilated to an American mainstream communicative culture, and others would be "assimilated" only minimally, most of the members of a given "subcultural group" would fall somewhere in the middle. There would be a unimodal distribution of shared cultural knowledge within the population segment (i.e., one and only one bell-shaped curve would account for the distribution of cultural knowledge within the population segment).

[2] It is unnecessary to refer here to the extensive literature on these controversies. The interested reader is referred to the notes of Chapter 2 for relevant citations.

Individuals who were "modal types" subculturally would act continually on the basis of their single set of shared knowledge of how to act. They would be, as it were, uniformly programmed into the subculture by socialization. They would act constantly on "automatic pilot" on the basis of their communicative socialization.

The relationship between the sets of communicative culture traits in the *mainstream* cultural pool (set) and the *subcultural* pool would be one of simple overlap. In some subcultural sets there would be more overlap with the mainstream set and in other subcultural sets there would be less overlap. In consequence, cultural difference in shared communicative traditions would be essentially a one-dimensional affair, in terms of the placement of individuals within a given subcultural group along a single continuum of relative assimilation. Cultural difference between groups would also be able to be contrasted unidimensionally. Various social groups could be distributed along a single continuum of "assimilation."

According to the usual anthropological and sociolinguistic view, by knowing the ethnic, racial, or social class "subcultural group" membership of two interactional partners one should be able to predict fairly accurately the degree of "interference" in communication style between those individuals. One could expect for example that (*a*) cultural differences in interactional performance and inference would be present in interviews between an Irish–American counselor and a black American student and would not be present between that same counselor and an Irish–American student. According to this view one could also expect that (*b*) the culture difference present in one Irish–American–black counselor–student pair would not only be (for analytic purposes, at least) *identical in amount* to that in another counselor–student pair of the same ethnic and racial combination, but that (*c*) *the same amount of communicative culture difference would always make the same kind of interactional difference* across differing interviews.

The findings reported in Chapter 7 suggest that expectation (*a*) is indeed generally the case; knowing the ethnic and racial group membership of the counselor–student pairs, one can usually predict the degree of similarity and dissimilarity in some aspects of cultural communication style that will exist between the counselor and the student in an actual interview. But expectations (*b*) and (*c*) were not clearly warranted by the data. While cultural differences in communication generally could be predicted if one knew the ethnicity of the conselor and the student, this was not always so. Though difference in communicative traditions did seem to make a difference in many of the interviews, in some interviews culture difference seemed to have made less difference than in other interviews.

In coming to understand why this should be so, two aspects of the usual assumptions about culture sharing and culture difference need to be modified: (1) assumptions about the distribution of culture sharing within a population; (2) assumptions about the social and political ecology of cultural difference.

Rethinking How Communicative Knowledge Is Shared

In complex polyethnic societies ethnic, racial, and social class populations do not live in total isolation from one another. Some members of those populations may live in relatively greater isolation from everyday contact with outsiders than other members of the same ethnic population. Because of this it is reasonable to expect differential effects of acculturation within a given population. The assumption that interactional knowledge (communicative competence) will be uniformly shared or even unimodally distributed within a given population can be seen to be unreasonable for any polyethnic society that does not have absolutely rigid patterns of social segregation. What this means for communication research is that a given *speech community* and a given *ethnic, racial, or social class population* are not necessarily one and the same.[3]

Moreover, the constant everyday contact of members of a given ethnic population with members of other ethnic populations, together with the acculturative influence of the mass media, provides individuals with constant exposure to the ways of speaking and listening of interaction communities "other than one's own." As a child acquires interactional competence during maturation one would expect to see the acquisition of knowledge of ways of speaking and listening that differ from the knowledge shared within the family or the ethnic group. These new aspects of communicative knowledge, once acquired, are also one's "own." They are not totally alien to the individual; it is just that they are not those used in intimate occasions in family and ethnic or racial community settings.

The process of learning ways of acting other than those appropriate in the home or close to home can be termed *second culture acquisition*,

[3] This recapitulates our discussion in Chapter 5, pp. 99–103. See also Moerman, 1965; Barth, 1969. While the *speech community* is defined in terms of shared communicative traditions, aggregates such as ethnic, racial, or social class groups are not so defined, necessarily.

analogous to *second language acquisition*. Exposure to the new ways of acting happens within acquaintance networks whose patterns may differ from individual to individual or from subgroup to subgroup within a given social class or ethnic or racial group. Some people's networks may include many people from different speech communities, and so those people encounter in their normal daily round a wide variety of interaction styles. Other people's acquaintance networks may involve mostly others from the same speech community. Acculturative influence would be much less in the latter sort of network.

Another way to think of this is to distinguish between *primary* and *secondary* membership in speech communities, following the sociologists' distinction between primary and secondary social relations. Primary membership would refer to relatively full-knowledge of ways of interacting that are appropriate across a broad range of intimate and nonintimate occasions inside and outside the family—the full set of such occasions encountered by members of a speech community in interaction with other members of that same community. Secondary membership would involve only partial knowledge of a range of ways of interacting. It would involve knowledge of those ways of acting appropriate across a selected set of *nonintimate occasions* outside the family—the knowledge necessary to conduct secondary rather than primary relations with members of interaction communities other than one's own.

By having acquaintance networks that included persons with primary membership in speech communities other than one's own, one would acquire secondary membership in diverse interaction communities. One would acquire multicultural communicative knowledge.

It is reasonable to assume that multicultural communicative knowledge is usual, not unusual, for individuals in complex modern societies. Individuals are likely to possess repertoires of knowledge that include knowing ways of dealing with members of varying speech communities. Because this knowledge is for the most part learned and held outside conscious awareness, use of the various parts of one's communicative repertoire is not done reflectively. Individuals could switch from one cultural style to another without being aware they were doing so.

In Chapter 5 we noted that black listeners switched cultural styles in listening behavior occasionally when interacting with white speakers. This sort of style switching, verbally as well as nonverbally, makes great interactional sense, given the radical nature of the interpersonal coordination necessary to conduct conversation face-to-face. Notice, however, that in the case of the behavioral form of nodding used by black listeners, the "white" cultural form of nodding was used only half the time by the black listeners. Apparently they alternated randomly between using the "black" cultural form—the unaccented nod—and the "white" form. The response of the white speakers was not random, however. In almost every instance, when the black listener used the unaccented form of nod as a listening response, the white speaker hyperexplained. The white speakers seemed to have no knowledge of a form of nodding other than the one appropriate in their own speech community. The black listeners seemed to "know" the form of nodding customary in the white speech community, but made use of that (presumably implicit) knowledge inconsistently. Consequently, the multicultural knowledge of the black listeners was only partially adaptive, in the context of dealing with white speakers who seemed to know little or nothing of the "black" cultural patterns for listening response.

Individuals whose communicative repertoires include knowledge of ways of acting appropriate in a variety of speech communities can put their knowledge of alternative ways of acting to effective use by style switching. But in order to do this in an entirely effective way, the knowledge of the other system must be quite complete. The constraints placed on acquaintance networks by patterns of racial and social class segregation make it difficult, although not impossible, to acquire the level of knowledge of other speech communities' ways of acting that is necessary to style-switch effectively.

Given patterns of residence, occupational stratification, and religious identification it is likely that acquaintance networks are likely to overlap more among some sets of ethnic and racial groups than among others. In the large city in which our study was done, Italian–Americans, Polish–Americans, and Irish–Americans were more likely to participate in acquaintance networks that overlap those ethnic categories than they were to participate in networks that included blacks and Latinos. Moreover, the contacts the "white ethnics" had with "Third World" people were likely to be limited to a narrow range of social situations characterized by secondary rather than primary social relations. This meant that the opportunities for white ethnics to develop communicative competence in "Third World" ways of interacting were, speaking generally, quite limited.

Similarly, blacks and Latinos were likely to encounter one another in a wider range of social circumstances than they were likely to encounter lower-middle-class white ethnics, or upper-middle-class whites from the suburbs. Blacks and Latinos encountered one another in school and work settings, and now and then in life on the "street," which provided opportunities to acquire a panethnic "street culture." Blacks and Latinos were also relatively open to exposure to culturally "mainstream" communicative styles through the mass media and the schools. Consequently, while their *comprehension* of the "mainstream" ways of acting may have been great, their *performance* of ways of speaking and ways of listening was often different enough from that of the mainstream to be maladaptive. Blacks and Latinos lacked opportunities to practice "mainstream" performance skills.

In addition, within the metropolitan area there was not simply a pattern of difference in the distribution of *knowledge* of the various interaction styles; there was a difference in the *allocation of prestige* among the various styles and among the various social groups who use the styles. Consequently there may have been differential motivation for learning some of the styles—the acquisition of Third World panethnic styles by white ethnics may have little adaptive value, since the white ethnics were dominant in the institutions of the city.

In short, there was a political dimension to the acquisition of interactional competence. All this leads one to revise expectations in the following way:

1. Intraethnic (and intraracial) encounters will usually proceed more felicitously than interethnic ones, but this will not always be the case—partly because of the possibility of intraethnic cultural difference, and because of the possibility of adaptive style switching in interethnic encounters.
2. Intra-panethnic (and intraracial) encounters will usually proceed more felicitously than inter-panethnic ones, because adaptive mutual style switching is more likely because of prior acculturative contact within panethnic boundaries.

These revised expectations account for much of what our data revealed. In addition, we found that whereas intra-panethnic encounters were usually more felicitous than inter-panethnic ones, in some exceptional cases this was not so.

Somehow, in a way we cannot claim to understand very well yet, the apparent tendency of particularistic comembership to override culture difference seems to have influenced the differential distribution of *the social costs of cultural difference across different kinds of encounters.*

Sharing high comembership, the counselor and student sometimes managed to communicate effectively despite their difference in shared communicative traditions. Conversely, under conditions of low comembership in aspects of social identity other than ethnic or racial background, what cultural similarity in communication style there was between counselor and student was not invariably an asset. Without much comembership, counselors and students who shared similar communication style patterns still managed to miscommunicate. Thus, neither cultural style sharing nor commonality of social identity were by themselves both necessary and sufficient conditions for effective communication and cordial relations in the interviews. Only some combination of both factors made for that, and of the two the comembership factor seemed to be the most consistently influential one. High and low comembership seemed to provide different micropolitical contexts of interaction for the counselor and the student.

An alternative explanation is possible. Under high-comembership conditions the conversational partners may have style-switched to accommodate to one another more than they did under conditions of low comembership.[4] In that case the cultural differences in communication style would not have been *overridden* but *erased*.

This possibility was considered in our analysis, but it did not seem to hold. Perhaps adaptive style switching might have been apparent if we had looked even more closely than we did at features of linguistic and kinesic style. But at the most fine-grained analytic level we used—in the analysis of interactional arhythmia—troubles in conversational cooperation were *present* under conditions of high comembership. It was just that they didn't seem to "count" as much as similar troubles did under conditions of low comembership.

Under the differing conditions of comembership differing thresholds of tolerance for communicative troubles seemed to obtain. It is not clear how or why this happened, but three analogies may be relevant. First, the apparent willingness of adults, especially parents, to disregard performance errors in the speech of young children. As children grow older, the same kinds of "mistakes" in speech that were previously ignored or tolerated are noticed and tolerated no longer.

Second is the apparent variation in thresholds of tolerance for mistakes in situations of serious play, such as artistic performances and athletic events. The parents of junior high school musicians or athletes, for example, may overlook performance errors in a student orchestra concert or football game that the same audiences would notice and criticize harshly if committed by professional musicians or athletes.

Third, at the level of the general society, are the processes of developing ethnic and national identity. Under conditions of conquest or immigration, cultural differences in communication style between social groups that may formerly have been very salient may become much less salient as the political context of intergroup relations changes.[5] Among

---

[4] Interactional style switching here is analogous to linguistic code switching and dialect switching. See Blom and Gumperz, 1972.
[5] See Fanon, 1970:53–54, 67.

Italians in the nineteenth century, after the unification begun by Garibaldi, it was by broadening categories of social inclusion and by overlooking cultural differences of dialect and demeanor that groups of people who had thought of themselves primarily as Calabrians, Tuscans, or Lombards came to regard themselves as *Italians*. After immigration to the United States these tendencies were even greater. As the political context of culture difference changed there were changes in the definition of boundaries of inclusion, alliance, and cultural style sharing within the ethnic group.[6]

All this seems to involve influences of attitudes on the definition of situation, or influences of attitudes on perception of interactional mistakes. These are factors and processes that our research design was not able to address. It does seem, however, that the interviews that were high in comembership and the ones that were low in comembership were differing political contexts for performance, within which differing thresholds of toleration for interactional troubles applied.

Further work on this issue is necessary. The importance of the co-membership relationship and its apparent influence on the immediate and "local" politics of cultural differences in communication style will continue to be considered as we discuss the implications of this research for the practice of counseling and for the development of theory in sociolinguistics and the ethnography of communication.

IMPLICATIONS FOR COUNSELING PRACTICE

The presence of interactional leeway in the interview provided opportunities for mutual accommodation between counselor and student, despite difference in normative social identity and cultural performance style. That is a hopeful sign. It leaves open possibilities for change. But it would be unwise to be too optimistic, for the factors inhibiting change seem to be profound at the levels of the general society, the institution, and the individual.

In the following sections we will suggest lines along which some change could take place, through organizational rearrangements and through the education of individuals. It should be noted that neither of the authors is a professional counselor. We are not close enough to daily issues of practice to attempt specific recommendations. That is up to the counseling profession itself. As we said at the outset, what may be most useful here is a way of thinking about the fundamental nature of the problem of *rapport* in interethnic and interracial counseling situations.

---

[6] See Zorbaugh, 1928; Nelli, 1970:156–170.

What is said about that may also apply to face-to-face interaction in other kinds of gatekeeping interviews, to more therapeutic forms of counseling, and to interpersonal relationships in social work, medicine, law, industry, and government.

The Social and Cultural Ecology of Rapport

The kinds of interactional troubles that have been described here do not seem to have causes simply within individuals, nor simply in face-to-face situations, nor simply in social-structural and cultural influences beyond the specific individual and situation. All these levels of organization often seem to be involved when interactional troubles, misunderstandings, and uncomfortable moments take place in a school counseling interview. This means that failure of rapport in an interview does not seem to be solely (or even primarily, necessarily) a function of the internal states of the counselor and student—of their intelligence quotients, or their states of motivation, cognitive development, temperament, or emotional maturity and mental health. These characteristics of individuals, which are studied by social, clinical, and educational psychologists, have been shown to have effects on what happens in counseling interviews. They are not, however, the only factors relevant to the conduct of interviewing. There seem to be additional factors at work in and through the processes of engagement in interaction itself.

Rapport can be thought of as an issue of immediate social ecology, in which factors external to the individual provide an environmental surround. An important aspect of this ecology for the counselor and student in the interview is the communicative choices the other person is making.

The interface between person and environment involves characteristics of the persons as well as of the environment, however. The contexts of action that present themselves to the individual are those as they are *perceived* there in the scene, not just as they are physically present. The way this is most clearly shown in the work reported here is in the evidence on hyperexplanation (Chapter 5). There it seemed as if white counselors, employing a white American cultural mainstream perceptual set for the interpretation of the social meaning of head nods, did not *see* kinesically unaccented head nods by black listeners as constituting listening response. The nods were ("objectively") present, but apparently they were not ("phenomenologically") perceived. Only the listener's kinesically accented head nods seem to have been perceived by the white speakers as constituting listening response. It was usually only when the listeners nodded in that way that the white counselors did not persist at explaining the same point, but went on to the next point instead.

External communicative behavior is available as potentially meaningful cues, and internal perception apparently assigns meaning—cue function—to some aspects of the behavior and not the others.[7] For interaction to proceed smoothly and reciprocally in so interdependent a set of social–ecological relationships as we claim existed between the counselor and the student, each of the two interactional partners must possess not only the ability to perform communicative behavior in ways that are meaningful—cue-relevant—to the other, but must also possess the ability to interpret the other's communicative behavior in ways that are consonant with the other's intentions. In the hyperexplanation sequence the white speakers and black listeners were apparently using different *emic* standards of interpretation (see the discussion in Chapter 3). In consequence they were systematically *not seeing* and *not hearing* one another.

Given so finely tuned a system of interpersonal coordination required for communication face-to-face, it is a wonder that any two people are ever able to interact meaningfully and felicitously. It is certainly no wonder that communication is often more difficult in an intercultural, interethnic, or interracial situation. When counselors and students of particular social and cultural backgrounds consistently find that others of a particular sociocultural background act "unreasonably" face-to-face, then part of the problem, we would contend, may lie in inadequate sharing between counselor and student of *cultural traditions governing how to act communicatively and how to perceive and interpret the communicative actions of others*. It is not that the recurrent behavior of a given student or counselor is unreasonable or bizarre, in itself. It is rather that the joint action of a pair of interactional partners is not adequately social—not adequately reciprocal and complementary. Neither partner is consciously aware of this, because interpersonal coordination in interaction takes place usually entirely outside conscious awareness, just as the grammar and sound system of a language is transparent to a speaker while speaking. When the interactional ecosystem is out of joint, both partners are actively engaged in *not making sense together,* each thwarting the other's actions while neither of them may be consciously intending to do so.

SOME OPTIONS FOR INSTITUTIONAL CHANGE

If our analysis is correct, what are some reasonable steps to be taken? There seems to be no short list of easy answers, if rapport and meaningful

[7] See the discussion of the emic–etic distinction in Chapter 3, pp. 56–59, and the citations accompanying that discussion.

communication in face-to-face interaction are, as we have claimed, parts of an ecological process. Ecosystem relationships are complex. There are no one-way causal relationships to manipulate. If parts of the system involve factors inhibiting change, then those factors are continually present to be dealt with. Perhaps they cannot simply be "eliminated" or "solved." Rather, as enduring and intrinsic problems of practice, perhaps they must be continually confronted and worked at. Yet the systems of communicative choice and action we have described are not simply operating through blind determinism. Critically reflective deliberation about the outside-awareness choices made in face-to-face interaction can still be done, at various levels. There are genuine choices to be made at the level of the general society, at the level of people-sorting institutions such as schools and work settings, and at the level of the individual. Fundamentally, all the various kinds of choices involve value decisions about the nature of gatekeeping as it is performed by institutions and individuals.

The General Societal Level

At the general societal level, what is involved is the allocation of large numbers of people to the various occupational slots and social class strata of the society. If one were seriously to consider changing the gatekeeping practices of individual academic advisors or job interviewers, it would be appropriate to redefine the purposes of gatekeeping at the level of society at large.

What our close look at the actual conduct of gatekeeping interviews suggests is that gatekeeping encounters are not a neutral and "objective" meritocratic sorting process. On the contrary, our analysis suggests that the game is rigged, albeit not deliberately, in favor of those individuals whose communication style and social background are most similar to those of the interviewer with whom they talk. One result is that in gatekeeping encounters the "gates" of encouragement and special help are opened wider for some individuals than for others. Another result is that some individuals will experience gatekeeping encounters in which both the interviewer and interviewee seem reasonable and interactionally competent together, while other individuals will not have that positive experience in their gatekeeping encounters.

The influence of cultural communication style and social background over gatekeeping processes and outcomes seems to place constraints on the social mobility of the people who are least similar to the gatekeeping interviewers. In our study of junior college academic advisors, the students who were least similar to their advisors usually were members of the ethnic, racial, and social class categories which were lowest ranked in the society. Upper-middle-class students typically did not attend urban junior colleges, so the sorting that took place was within a student population consisting of "white ethnic" students (Polish–American, Italian–American, Irish–American) on the one hand and "Third World" students (black and Latin) on the other. Given the predominance of white ethnic counselors in those junior colleges, the social mobility that was being limited—not in every case, but more often than not—was that of the Third World students. Since at the general societal level there is a scarcity of desired occupational slots, this kind of gatekeeping practice is "functional." But is it societally desirable? Perhaps yes, perhaps no. The most fundamental value issue to be addressed is whether such de facto constraints on the educational and economic opportunity of members of the least privileged groups in the society are desirable or not.

The Institutional Level

What is involved at this level is not only the work of the individual gatekeeper, but the functions of the institution within which the gatekeeper operates. In the case of the junior college, various sociologists have maintained[8] that a major unstated purpose of that sort of school is to discourage students, to lower their expectations for the future. Counselors, it is argued, serve to accomplish the discouragement of students in the "one-on-one" situation of contact with the institution.

One study bases its argument on Erving Goffman's notion of "cooling out the mark"—the con man's practice of convincing the sucker that what happened was the sucker's own fault. In the junior college, it is argued, those students organizationally designated as unworthy must come to believe that the failure is their fault, not the school's. The junior college is attended by students whom society defines as marginal—lower-class, ethnic, and Third World students being heavily overrepresented in this category. A few are allowed access to 4-year college and to the upper middle class, but at least two-thirds are redirected toward alternative occupational goals, usually of lower social rank.

In our data we saw a few instances of cooling out in intraethnic encounters, more instances in interethnic encounters, and even more instances in encounters with low comembership between the academic advisor and the student. Cooling out rarely occurred in encounters characterized by high comembership. Even though official school policy may have said that counselors should attend only to universalistic criteria in making gatekeeping decisions, some particularistic criteria were appar-

[8] See, for example, Clark (1960) and Karabel (1972) on the junior college.

ently attended to in each encounter. In further discussion we will argue that it is possible that without the "leakage" of ethnicity, race, and other particularistic factors within the universalistic frame of the gatekeeping encounter, face-to-face interaction simply could not proceed. It follows then that if particularistic factors cannot be removed from a gatekeeping encounter, a policy dilemma arises: Counselors are required to be fair to students (as fairness is defined by the 1964 Civil Rights Act prohibiting discriminatory treatment because of race, color, religion, or national origin). But they are being asked to be "fair" in ways that may be interactionally impossible. In response to this dilemma, two kinds of organizational changes seem warranted. One kind of change involves rearrangements in the organizational routes by which students get access to counselors. The other kind of change involves redefining the constraints placed by the school on the counselor's official role. Specifically, this means changing amounts of special help counselors are officially allowed to give individual students.

If cultural differences in communication patterns and differences in social identity are a common source of interactional trouble in interethnic and interracial counseling, then one way to reduce these negative effects is to give students regularly available access to counselors who come from the same speech community and the same ethnic, panethnic, or racial group as the student. In the schools we studied, access to a counselor whose background was similar to one's own was available to white ethnic students as a matter of course, given the metropolitan area's existing patterns of ethnic succession into occupational niches. This was not so for the students of ethnic and racial minority background. They were Third World students, whereas most of the counselors were white ethnic.

One way to increase the access of minority students to counselors who share similar communicative traditions with them is for schools and colleges to hire substantially larger numbers of counselors of ethnic and racial minority background. Under the currently tight employment conditions in schools and colleges this may be difficult to do, but our findings suggest that it is very desirable nonetheless. Our data show that cultural communication style and ethnic and racial identity do make a difference in the character and outcome of school counseling interviews. Changes in hiring patterns are an obvious organizational response to a need that clearly exists.

Another way to increase the access of students to counselors whose social identity and cultural style is congruent with that of the students lies in changing the procedures by which students are assigned to counselors. In one of the junior colleges we studied most closely, assignment of students to counselors was random and mandatory. In the other junior college studied closely, students were required to see a counselor each term, but each student could choose the counselor he or she wanted to talk with.

One procedural option would be for a school to allow students to choose their own counselors, and to make public the ethnicity, race, and other background attributes of the counselors. The *Bakke* v. *University of California* decision is relevant here. In it the Supreme Court did not declare unconstitutional the *consideration* of particularistic attributes such as ethnicity or race, just the *sole or mandatory use* of them as a basis of organizational decisions by schools. That distinction is useful in terms of the implications of our study. Our data do not suggest that intraethnic and intraracial encounters are invariably trouble-free, nor that interethnic and interracial encounters are invariably troublesome. One would expect that under "free market" conditions of access to an ethnically and racially diverse pool of counselors, students would not always find it in their interest to pick a counselor of their own ethnicity or race. Third World students might occasionally want practice in "talking to 'the Man.'" Moreover, a growing body of evidence, including the evidence reported here, suggests that ethnic, racial, and linguistic minority students have a tremendous adaptive capacity for multicultural communicative knowledge. It appears that it is normal for humans, especially those who live in complex multiethnic societies, to be primary and secondary members of more than one *speech* or *interaction* community.

Mandatory assignment of students to counselors would fail to take into account multicultural communicative knowledge and it would deny choice to minority and majority students alike. Voluntary self-selection by students, with knowledge of the counselors' ethnic and cultural backgrounds available, would not necessarily lead to resegregation of students. But this option would make it possible for a student who expected to be ill at ease with a counselor who was a non-comember (however the student defined that term) to avoid that sort of encounter by selecting a comember as counselor. Obviously, the option of voluntary self-selection is related to the option of hiring more counselors of Third World ethnicity and race. Any rearrangement of organizational procedures so as to increase access of students to counselors of their own ethnic or racial background requires that the proportional distribution of ethnicity and race in the student body be matched by proportional distribution within the counseling staff. The practical organizational need for a functional match between counselors and client populations has not been changed by the *Bakke* decision, only the legal means for addressing that need has been changed, and that only slightly.

Another kind of organizational change would be for schools to allow counselors to give more special help to all students. Greater advocacy by counselors across the board might increase the likelihood that a higher percentage of both Third World and white ethnic students would be let through the school mobility gates into the middle and upper occupational strata of the society.

At the institutional level just as at the societal level, the basic decisions on such matters must be made on other than empirical grounds—is greater flexibility in the procedures regarding the social selection process regarded as desirable? That value issue must be resolved first. Only then the question of whether to alter the channels of access to counselors should be addressed. Otherwise one places the gatekeeper in a new double bind. In everyday life in counseling the counselor's available stock of special help is limited. If the range and amount of special help the counselor can offer is narrow and small, and if because of an organizational change in patterns of access to counselors, a given counselor is dealing with more "same-ethnics" than before, that counselor may have less special help to give than is situationally appropriate.

The school gatekeeper is still liable to be in a double bind because of his or her dual functions of acting on behalf of the student as advocate and on behalf of the organization as the student's judge. This is why it is especially important in the case of educational and other human-service institutions that a change in the routine procedures of gatekeeping in counseling be preceded by serious consideration of the consequences and by change in other aspects of the institutional rules governing the organization's delivery of human services. Influencing what happens face-to-face in the counselor's office by exercising such options as changing the ethnicity of the participants, while yet leaving unchanged the organizational context in which counselor and client or student must operate, may do a disservice to all parties involved. Moreover, in the wider society, unless more occupational slots are created than presently exist one would, by opening the mobility gates wider in schools, have little effect on increasing equality in society at large. One would only shift the white ethnic–Third World conflict over scarce resources from the school to the employment office.

OPTIONS FOR COUNSELOR EDUCATION

In the absence of widespread social change the gatekeeping functions of school counselors are not going to be eliminated entirely. Whereas there seem to be serious limits on the possibilities for rearranging institutional procedures that influence the conduct of gatekeeping, some rearrangements at the institutional level seem both badly needed and actually possible. We turn now to consider options for promoting change at the level of the individual through programs of initial and continuing professional education of counselors and other kinds of interviewers.

There are at least two possible types of educational approaches whose aim is the improvement of the interethnic and intercultural communication abilities of counselors and other interviewers. The first type involves training in specific discrete communication skills. The second type involves a more broadly educative approach to the development of critical awareness. We see the latter approach as more appropriate than the former. The discussion that follows presents our reasons for this.

Training in Specific Communication Skills

By *skills* we do not mean what that term usually means in the field of counselor education.[9] From our microecological perspective toward the complexity of interactional cooperation that is involved in face-to-face interaction, such "skills" of the counselor as *active listening, reflecting feelings,* and *self-disclosure* do not appear to be discrete skills at all. Rather, they seem to be complex packages of sets of discrete skills. The labels on those "skill" packages are far more abstract and global than are any of the component behavioral skills inside the package.

Moreover, we have shown in the preceding chapters that such "skills" as *active listening* (Chapters 4 and 5) and *self-disclosure* in the establishment of comembership through small talk (Chapter 2) are not just actions done by one party alone. Rather, they appear to be cooperative activities done in reciprocal and complementary ways by the counselor and student together as they alternate in exchanging the roles of listener and speaker in their conversation during the interview. Finally, we have also shown that such "skills" as active listening and self-disclosure are socially and culturally situated. Speaking activities such as self-disclosure and active listening are *culturally* situated in that they are culturally specific in appropriateness of use (i.e., they are not considered universally appropriate across all speech communities, even across all speech communities within a given society in which all people speak the same "language"). For example, recent research in the United States and Canada suggests that the specific behaviors usually employed in doing

[9] For the literature of counseling and clinical psychology as skills *reflecting feelings,* see Rogers, 1951:8; on *active listening,* Carkhuff and Berenson, 1967; on *self-disclosure,* Jourard, 1971.

so-called active listening in an attempt to communicate empathy are considered inappropriate and unnecessary by many native Americans who speak English as their first language.[10] In many Native American speech communities it is not necessary to nod or vocalize to show attention and concern in listening. In consequence, well-meaning attempts by counselors to be "supportive" towards their clients by performing active listening may be perceived by the clients as inappropriate interactional activity—indeed as a kind of conversational "hyperactivity," from the point of view of the Native American client.

Speaking activities such as active listening and self-disclosure are *socially* situated in that their appropriate enactment is affected by the relative social identity of the interactional partners, as well as by the cultural conventions regarding politeness that were discussed in the previous paragraph. For example, the sheer *amount* of nonverbal and verbal behavior required to respond appropriately as a listener not only may vary from one speech community to the next, but may vary depending upon the amount of familiarity or comembership between the interactional partners. Among people who have known one another a long time, such as spouses and lifelong friends, only small amounts of listening response may be necessary to show attention and concern for what the other interactional partner is saying. Counselors often may feel they need to be very active behaviorally in doing active listening simply because they are talking to strangers with whom one must "work harder" conversationally.

Self-disclosure can also be seen to vary in style and amount depending upon the social identities of the interactional partners. Among partners high in potential comembership (sharing similar sex, ethnic and racial, social class, educational, and other kinds of group or category membership), very little conversational "work" may be necessary to reveal shared comemberships, and hence to accomplish self-disclosure. Among interactional partners whose positions in the social world outside the encounter are very dissimilar (in terms of ethnicity, race, social class, and other kinds of potential comembership categories) it may be necessary to spend more time in small talk to establish comembership, and to do such self-disclosing talk about more universally shared commonalities among people (e.g., whereas an Irish–American Catholic male counselor is unlikely to be able to establish comembership with a black American Protestant female student on the basis of talk about Catholic high school league sports scores, such a counselor could establish co-

---

[10] See Basso, 1970; Phillips, 1972; Van Ness, 1977; Scollon and Scollon, 1979; Erickson and Mohatt, in press.

membership with the student in terms of their both having been the oldest children in their families, or some other more universally shareable category of similarity). In short, the speaking activity "self-disclosure" is socially as well as culturally relative, in that different interviewer–interviewee pairs must discuss different kinds of topics and use differing kinds of discourse strategies in order to establish comembership through small talk.

In our opinion, the lack of a sense of *social and cultural relativity* in the appropriateness of enacting such professional communicative "skills" as active listening and self-disclosure is a serious limitation in the education of counselors and other interviewers. These "skills" are actually communicative *styles* whose appropriate use is specific to certain interview situations and certain speech community backgrounds of conversational partners. Without an awareness of this an interviewer can come away from an interview with a person from a different speech community saying, "I tried to be supportive and empathetic with him/her, but he/she just wouldn't let me." The result is that the professionally trained interviewer blames the interviewee as an individual for what went wrong, or perhaps the interviewer blames himself or herself.

In the approach to the education of counselors and other interviewers that we are about to advocate, a fundamental principle is that when things go wrong interactionally, that is not considered the sole responsibility of either conversational partner, whether interviewer or interviewee. We assume that relatively "troublesome" and relatively "trouble-free" interaction are both jointly produced by the interactional partners. A corollary of this principle is that since the interviewer is not the sole causal agent in the interview (even though he or she does play the primary leadership role), changing the counselor's behavior alone would not be enough to eliminate the interactional stumbles that may be occurring. Since the stumbles are interactionally accomplished, their complete elimination requires the collaboration of both interactional partners.

It follows that one should not just train counselors to feel solely responsible for what they do with clients. It also follows that even a behavioral definition of communicative skills much more specific than the definitions of "active listening" and "self-disclosure" would not be likely to eliminate interactional troubles experienced by interviewers in interethnic encounters. The notion of "skill," even when properly specified and considered in a properly relativized sense, culturally and socially, is still *too individualistic a notion* to be useful in improving the conduct of interaction, if conversation is indeed so interdependent a process of cooperation between conversational partners as we have been claiming it to be.

We have been asked occasionally to give advice on the teaching and use of specific intercultural communication skills. These requests have sometimes been stated quite directly by English–American middle-class professionals: "Can you tell us what nonverbal behaviors we should use in giving appropriate listening responses to black Americans?" "What is the best way to say *explanations* to Chicano teenagers?" "Quite frankly, I'm a WASP and I get uncomfortable talking with Italian–American clients. Would it help if I *nodded more* during those interviews?"

This seems to be the wrong way to think about how to improve intercultural communication. It is possible to identify specific verbal and nonverbal behaviors whose appropriate use differs from one speech community to the next, as in the difference we think we have found between American white and American black cultural conventions for appropriate nodding behavior (see Chapter 5). But to try to apply such knowledge generally would be to ignore within-group speech community differences and other cultural differences within racial, ethnic, and social class groups. Specific skill training in "How to talk effectively with a *black or Chicano or Italian–American* client" done just as skill training alone would probably reinforce or reinvent racial, ethnic, and social class stereotypes. It would probably be ineffective since what an actual interviewer confronts daily is not a list of ideal types of interviewees, but a succession of actual, particular persons with distinctive characteristics, including those of distinctive patterns of social network and speech community membership.

Another reason such skill training by itself would be unlikely to be effective is that it would ignore the *partialness* of the boundaries of gatekeeping encounters, failing to take account of the influence of factors outside the encounter on the conduct of interaction within it. A case in point is the maxims for how to handle "bad news" that were discussed in Chapter 2 (pp. 40–48). In the absence of the establishment of situational comembership it seems to be inappropriate (in encounters in which the counselor and student are panethnically or racially different) (*a*) for the counselor to state explicit bad news about the student's situation, or (*b*) for the student to tell the counselor explicit bad news about the student's situation. Our empirical findings show that inter-panethnically and interracially, counselors and students avoided telling one another various kinds of bad news directly, in the absence of high comembership. We infer from this a general sociocultural pattern. If that inference is correct—if there does exist at the level of United States society and culture as a whole an ambivalence toward the exercise of authority in gatekeeping encounters, and if that ambivalence is manifested communicatively by the counselor and student because of the influence of the wider society on what they are choosing to do together face-to-face— then simply to train counselor or student in a discrete set of communication skills is likely to have little effect on their joint negotiation of role together. What they would need would not be specific skills. Rather, they would need a change of insight and a change of will, an awareness of the interactional double bind they are likely to be in and a commitment to redefine what they are doing interactionally. Once a counselor became aware of this and became committed to change, one thing that could be done would be to *search actively for situational comembership with the student*. This follows from our findings, which suggest that the higher the level of comembership, the more appropriately the bad news maxims can be set aside. The counselor might decide to spend more time doing small talk with students at the beginning of the interview. But the counselor's actions in asking and telling so as to reveal greater comembership with the student are not a single specifiable skill, as would be the ability to recognize that an unaccented head nod is a listening response. It is easier to imagine designing training to teach unaccented head nod recognition than it is to envision teaching a counselor how to do comembership revelation through small talk in a situationally appropriate way.

Finally, there is one other danger in simplistic attempts to do "skill training." This danger lies in attempts to teach gatekeeping interviewers the "skill" of being able to avoid making judgments about, or even attending to in any way, such factors as the communication style or social identity of the interviewee. From our point of view it seems that in order to conduct everyday interaction from moment to moment people must size each other up according to all sorts of cues. Interactional partners seem to be making assumptions *based on the full range of cues available* about the causes of the other's past and present actions, and about the likelihood of future actions. There seems to be no way in which one sort of cues along that range—the particularistic ones—can be fully eliminated from attention face-to-face. Skin color, linguistic accent, dress, listening behavior—all these and more can function as communication media for cues that point to particularistic attributes of social identity. These cue media are present to perception in the counseling interview. It may be that they must be noticed in some ways, for they seem to play a fundamental role in the coordination of action among interactional partners. The futility of trying to train interviewers to ignore particularistic factors in making gatekeeping decisions is illustrated by the following example.

A Negative Instance of Training

During the study reported here, two of the researchers participated as observers in a training course for job interviewers conducted by a large regional telephone company. A few years previously the parent company had made a major change in hiring policy. Before the change, telephone operators were required to speak *telephonese,* an artificial dialect of Standard English in which vowels and consonants that might be misheard over the telephone were pronounced in an exaggerated way. In those days, the everyday dialect spoken face-to-face by applicants for the job of telephone operator was a highly salient factor in the job interview. It was assumed that native speakers of "nonstandard" dialects could not be trained easily to speak telephonese. Persons who spoke such dialects of American English—especially southern American and Spanish–American dialects—were eliminated from consideration for hiring. This elimination occurred instantly. The style of ordinary language spoken by a job applicant was apparent to the job interviewer during the first few seconds of contact with the applicant. One of the main functions of the interview was to assess the applicant's speech style.

Then the company's policy changed. It was no longer permissible to eliminate applicants on the basis of dialect because that criterion "discriminated against" job applicants who were black, white Appalachian, and Hispanic. Other decisions to departicularize the job criteria followed—hair style and dress were ruled irrelevant to the gatekeeping decision process. One consequence of these policy changes was a retraining program for experienced job interviewers, designed at the national level of the company for implementation by all regional systems. Every interviewer in the region was to have completed training by a certain date.

The researchers attended the training program with eight other trainees and two trainers. All the company employees present were women. Three of the trainees were black. All but one of the trainees had begun working for the company as an operator under the old system of formal rules and informal customs governing ways of speaking and ways of making hiring decisions.

The training workshop lasted 5 days. On each day the issue of what an interviewer *should not* attend to was raised by the trainers. Each time the issue was raised the trainers remarked that "in the old days" it had been permissible to attend to language style, eye contact, dress, and hair style of applicants (as well as to body odors, biological and cosmetic, and to unmarried pregnancy). Now under the new system it was very important that one *not attend to or ask about these things*. Only universalistic "objective information" about school achievement and previous work record was now relevant to the hiring decision.

In discussing specific case examples, however, the trainers observed that it was legitimate to use particularistic information as the basis for inference about universalistic attributes—for example, one could infer from "how the applicant answers questions" an estimate of the applicant's intelligence, or one could infer from information about the applicant's unmarried pregnancy an estimate about probable reliability on the last job held. When an experienced interviewer–trainee who was black pointed out the logical inconsistency in this position and further maintained that one could not ignore such features as skin color, she received strong negative sanctions from the trainers.

In this instance a gatekeeping double bind was being *trained for*. Through a well-intentioned staff development process, in the name of objectivity and fairness gatekeepers were being taught to deny an awareness of how particularistic cues influenced them, thus making it even more difficult for them to be in touch with the ways they actually made gatekeeping decisions than it had been under the old system, in which the formal rules and informal customs regarding judgment on the basis of particularistic criteria were explicit and were attended to consciously by the job interviewers.

Education for Critical Awareness

From our point of view, the fallacy in the telephone company's training lay in the attempt to eliminate awareness of the influence of particularistic factors in the interviewing process—factors we contend are always attended to, whether consciously or not. A more appropriate aim for training would be to help interviewers recognize the ways in which they are influenced by particularistic factors during an interview, and to teach the interviewer how to "bracket" their inferences occasionally and make them momentarily problematic and hypothetical during the course of the interview itself. This would be educating counselors in critical awareness of their clinical practice, rather than in a set of specific behavioral skills.

The essential feature of the approach would involve learning to be able to take a critical or hypothetical stance toward one's own habitual processes of inferring social meaning and intent from the communicative form of verbal and nonverbal speaking and listening behavior that is occurring at any given moment in an interview. This requires learning to be able deliberately to avoid at certain moments an ordinary tendency of people interacting face-to-face—the practical tendency to infer intent directly from implicit cues in the other person's verbal and nonverbal communicative behavior. Eye contact, gesticulation, posture shifts, pitch register and pitch shifts in speech, interactional rhythm, alternative ways of asking and answering questions—all these can provide the counselor and the student with cues pointing to how to interpret the implicit social meaning of what the other person is saying and doing at the moment. But as we saw in the case of the two qualitatively different types of head nods used to signal active listening response (Chapter 5), *the cue lies in the eye of the beholder*. Not all communicative behavior at any given moment apparently is perceived as carrying cue meaning, only certain aspects of it. Learning to recognize those aspects (and not to recognize other aspects) is a crucial aspect of socialization into competent membership in a speech community. The aspects of verbal and nonverbal communication form that *make a difference in meaning* differ from one speech community to the next. But people tend not to recognize this, because in the split-second decision making necessary to steer oneself through interaction from moment to moment, there is no time in which to reflect consciously on the perceptual and inferential processes by which one assigns cue value to some aspect of verbal or nonverbal communicative form and then interpret the meaning of that cue in the context of that moment. Everything happens too fast for reflection.

In face-to-face contact with members of one's own speech community it is not necessary to think about all this. Shared communicative traditions enable interaction to proceed smoothly without conscious reflection by the interactional partners. But this is not usually the case when people come from speech communities whose communicative traditions differ enough that there is inadequate overlap between interactional partners in knowledge of how to act and how to interpret the actions of others. Under those conditions face-to-face, the automatic, unexamined inference from *what is perceived as a cue to what is inferred as intent* is likely to be wrong. One is likely to infer intentions other than those the other person actually has, or at the very least, one is likely to feel confused and out of touch with what is going on in the conversation. Such impressions were what counselors occasionally reported while viewing videotapes of their interviews with students who were members of an interaction community different from the counselor's own.

The *with–not with* distinction made by one of the counselors (Chapter 5, pp. 141–143) is relevant here. The counselor said that at some of the uncomfortable moments in his interviews he had a sense that the student was *not with* him. Usually this counselor, and the others interviewed, did not point to specific behavioral features of communication and their interpersonal articulation as the source of such impressions of their counselor–student relationship. The counselor's impressions were usually global and undifferentiated. Impressions such as the following were expressed much more often when referring to interethnic and interracial interviews than to interviews in which the student was of the same ethnicity or race as the counselor: (*a*) the impression of something like the *not with* state; (*b*) the sense that the counselor was not quite sure what was happening—whether or not the student was paying full attention; (*c*) the sense on the part of the counselor that the student did not understand what was happening. At some points in the interethnic encounters, students reported feelings that something had gone wrong that the counselor didn't realize had gone wrong: The counselor did not seem to realize that the student had understood a hyperexplained point the first time around in the explanation, or the counselor did not realize the student felt put off by something the counselor was saying.

What seems appropriate as an educational strategy for counselors is to teach *ways of reflecting on uncomfortable moments as they occur during an interview*. This would not be specific skill training in "how to talk to a black student," or to an Italian–American or Chicano one. As we have suggested earlier, such training is likely to be stereotypic. Given the routinized way that communication skills so construed would be taught, those "skills" would be likely to be artificial and inapplicable to the particular circumstances of an actual interview.

It is a more flexible general insight rather than a fixed set of specific skills that seems called for. It might be useful for counselors to have an awareness that attribution of intent is a process of inference from actual communicative cues, that culturally conventional patterns for the use and interpretation of such cues vary from one speech community to the next, that the cues are communicated by various behavioral means (e.g., posture, speech prosody, syntactic junctures) on both the verbal and nonverbal channels, that the simultaneous, functionally interdependent speaking and listening behavior of counselor and student is involved in the smoothly fluent interactional production of socially and referentially meaningful and appropriate communication (i.e., the speaking and listening behavior of both parties is temporally synchronized and rhythmically patterned in form, and mutually regulative in function), and that when uncomfortable moments occur in which either party's, or both parties', actions seem not fully meaningful or appropriate, something may be going wrong with interpersonal coordination at the very basic level of the behavioral steering mechanisms of interaction.

Understanding the workings of the processes of interpersonal coordination in interaction, understanding the sorts of troubles that may be occurring when coordination is inadequate, and knowing that these coordination processes differ from one cultural group to the next, a counselor could do momentary clinical diagnosis of the interaction process in the midst of an uncomfortable moment as it is happening. Such a clinical stance would put an intermediate step of reflection between (a) the counselor's perception of the student's behavior and (b) the counselor's inferences about the intent behind the behavior. Reflection would focus not just on what the student was doing, but on the interdependent relationship between what the student and counselor were doing together. It would be the interactional ecosystem—ways of speaking in relation to reciprocal and complementary ways of listening—that would be subjected to momentary analysis rather than the communicative "faults" of one party or the other, considered in isolation and out of the context of joint interactional production. Such a microecological frame for clinical analysis might reduce blame and/or guilt in the counselor and still be a source of insight into the interactional dynamics of uncomfortable moments in which he or she is a participant.

To ask how one's ways of speaking or listening articulate with those of one's interactional partner or partners stops for a moment the ordinary interpretive process of leaping instantly and unreflectively from the intuitive perception of a communicative cue (or the intuitive perception of the *absence* of an expected one) to an inference of communicative intent. Such a momentary check on one's interpretive procedures and emotional reactions makes them for the instant problematic. The clinical mode of response during an uncomfortable moment may not only provide an insight through learning, but may help to reduce the negative emotional reaction one is experiencing.

The telephone company was teaching interviewers to ignore all this particularistic messiness and "subjectivity." In contrast, the approach we are recommending involves focusing on the particularistic factors, on the behavioral organization of communication, on the lack of predictability when things go wrong, and on the counselor's own feelings of frustration, anger, or puzzlement during an uncomfortable moment. Such a focus of attention can be a means of gaining insight into what, if anything, is going wrong in the behavioral ecosystem of interaction to produce the discomfort and potential misunderstanding. This is insight on the basis of which the counselor can gradually learn to take more adaptive next steps than he or she otherwise might take when that kind of breakdown in interpersonal coordination is occurring.

The approach is a kind of learning by doing. Basic orientation and background understandings could be taught didactically, through films and written materials. Counselors could be assisted in their learning through clinical supervision. But the fundamental learning by the counselor would occur individually, through clinical reflection on his or her own clinical practice. That would require both an awareness of the need for change and a willingness to undertake change through a process of self-diagnosis and trial-and-error learning within the activity of clinical practice itself.

At this writing we have no evidence from systematic attempts to apply this method of clinical learning in school counseling practice. Recent experience in working along similar lines with teachers, however, suggests that this approach may be useful for counselors in combination with analytic viewing of videotapes of their counseling.[11] The process of clinical investigation of clinical practice in teaching has involved a combination of (*a*) learning about the complexity of interaction process, verbal and nonverbal, from the perspective of a social–ecological theory of its organization, and (*b*) investigating one's own clinical practice in teaching from that point of view. Teachers have learned to reflect on interaction processes in their classrooms by watching videotapes of naturally occurring events in their own and in other teachers' classrooms. They view the tapes, looking first of all not to see what teacher or student did "wrong," but to see how the teacher's and student's joint production of classroom events is organized. Then they become able to diagnose problems of interactional organization in the classroom, sometimes through viewing videotapes after the fact, but also by momentary clinical reflection on the organization of interaction as it is happening.

The experience of Gumperz in recent applied research on interethnic communication patterns in London is also instructive:

> In a staff cafeteria at a major London airport, newly hired Indian and Pakistani women were perceived as surly and uncooperative by their supervisors as well as by the cargo handlers whom they served. Observation revealed that while relatively few words were exchanged, the intonation and manner in which these words were pronounced were interpreted negatively. For example, a person who had chosen meat would have to be asked whether he wanted gravy. A British attendant would ask by saying, "Gravy?" using rising intonation. The Indian women, on the other hand, would say the word using falling intonation: "Gravy." We taped relevant sequences, including interchanges like these and asked the employees to paraphrase what was meant in each case. At first the Indian workers saw no difference. However, the English teacher and the supervisor could point out that "Gravy," said with a falling intonation, means "This is gravy," and is not interpreted as an offer but rather as an announcement. When the Indian women heard this, they began to understand the reactions they had been getting all along which

[11] See Florio and Walsh, 1980.

had until then seemed incomprehensible. They then spontaneously recalled intonation patterns which had seemed strange to them when spoken by native English speakers. At the same time, supervisors learned that the Indian women's falling intonation was their normal way of asking questions in that situation, and that no rudeness or indifference was intended.

After several discussion/teaching sessions of this sort, both the teacher and the supervisor reported a distinct improvement in the attitude of the Indian workers both to their work and their customers. It seemed that the Indian workers had long sensed they had been misunderstood but, having no way of talking about this in objective terms, they had felt they were being discriminated against. We had not taught the cafeteria workers to speak appropriate English, rather, by discussing the result of our analysis in mixed sessions and focusing on context-bound interpretive preferences rather than on attitudes and stereotypes, we had suggested a strategy for self-diagnosis of communication difficulties. In short, they regained confidence in their own innate ability to learn [Gumperz, 1977, pp. 208–209].[12]

Teaching counselors about cultural patterns in communication style will not eliminate all problems of interethnic communication in academic advising interviews and other sorts of counseling and interviewing. That knowledge cannot change the general societal conditions that seem to impinge on the interethnic encounter and seem to contribute to interactional troubles within it. But knowing that differences in customary patterns of action is sometimes the cause of troubles (rather than individual malevolence or indifference) may well be of some use in the conduct of interviewing.

The approach of situation-specific diagnosis of intercultural communication problems through clinical inquiry into clinical practice is yet to be tested in counselor education. Its fundamental assumption seems reasonable. That assumption is demonstrated in what is already known about how human interaction is possible. People seem to be actively making sense in interaction face-to-face. They do not seem to be robots who are blindly and uniformly following culturally preprogrammed communicative rules and maxims. Rather, they seem to be using the normative, culturally conventional rules and maxims purposely. They are engaged from moment to moment in actively constructing perceptions of cues, definitions of situation, and inferences of intent. Employing their innate capacity to learn by doing was how they became socialized into speech communities as children and young people. For adults that kind of learning is more difficult, but it is possible. It seems appropriate as a way of learning how to communicate more effectively interculturally.

---

[12] From John J. Gumperz. 1977. Social cultural knowledge in conversational inference. In: Georgetown University Round Table on Languages and Linguistics 1977. Edited by Muriel Saville-Troike. Washington, D.C.: Georgetown University Press. See also Gumperz, Jupp, and Roberts, 1979.

Situational Comembership and the Politics of
Interaction Face-to-Face

In addition to education about differences in cultural communication style, education about differences in the politics of culture difference in the interviews seems appropriate. The latter kind of education is even more difficult to envision than the former because we do not understand yet how comembership actually *works* in interethnic and interracial contact situations. It is not clear how under different micropolitical conditions, apparently similar amounts and kinds of cultural difference in communicative traditions have differing effects on interactional character and outcomes. Yet such differing effects are what our data suggest. The condition that seemed to account for this was the level of situationally defined comembership between the counselor and the student.

Perhaps the comembership level should be thought of as an index of the micropolitics of the counselor–student relationship. High comembership covaries with the tendency of the counselor to act more as the student's advocate than as his or her judge. The causal relationship between the two factors is not necessarily one way; they both may influence each other.

Further research is clearly necessary on this point, as it is to confirm or modify the other recommendations for educational strategies that have been made in this section. But if interactional mistakes seem to count less for the student and for the counselor in those encounters characterized by high comembership, then something in their authority and rank relationship may be different from that found in the encounters characterized by low comembership. That would be a matter of micropolitics within the frame of the encounter. The association between (*a*) small talk, (*b*) relating to one another on the grounds of shared particularistic attributes of status (including ethnicity and race, but not limited to it), and (*c*) the tendency of the counselor to act as the student's advocate seems to be a relationship of mutually reinforcing influence that produces a qualitative difference in the politics of the helping relationship between the counselor and the student. How to increase the possibility of this relationship occurring more often between counselor and student seems a desirable aim for counselor education.

First of all, it would seem valuable for counselors to develop a critical awareness of the importance of comembership. Next, trying so simple a thing as *taking more time to engage in small talk with students,* in an active search for comembership with them, might have a good effect. Interestingly, Shultz found that searching for comembership was a very common occurrence in encounters between pairs of students who were strangers.[13] That search may be characteristic of relationships among persons relatively equal in rank. If so, the counselor's active search for comembership with a student could help to establish a definition of situation in the interview in which it was appropriate for the student and counselor to interact on a relatively equal footing. There are limits to the extent to which leveling of rank relationships can take place in such hierarchical organizations as schools. But the boundedness of the face-to-face encounter, however partial, does allow some room for change. The counselor can learn not to view the time taken in such "maintenance" activities as doing small talk to establish comembership as *wasted time* spent in matters irrelevant to the accomplishment of "task" activities. Given limited time available, spending some time in a search for comembership would seem a wise investment of effort.

To conclude, what has been said here of counselors who are academic advisors applies not to them alone, but also to more therapeutic counselors, to other kinds of interviewers, and to supervisors and managers in formal organizations. Moreover, what has been said here about the effects of ethnic and racial group differences in communication style and in probable opportunities for establishing shared comembership could also be said for cross-national differences, for social class differences, and for sex differences. The issue of stylistic and comembership network differences between men and women and their effects on gatekeeping and therapeutic encounters between members of the opposite sex clearly deserves further research, reflection, and application in education.

Interviewers and supervisors are persons who, as ordinary human communicators, are perhaps best thought of not as following conventional rules and routines for action uniformly, but as constantly and actively making sense and making value choices on each occasion of face-to-face interaction. Counselors, advisors, interviewers, and supervisors can learn to develop a critical awareness of their own processes of making sense and enacting values in communication. But there are personal costs for such commitments. Constant awareness can be immobilizing. Fortunately for the individual psyche, constant awareness seems to be impossible. But even intermittent critical awareness can be exhausting, even in institutional settings in which there is a shared commitment to change. In the absence of institutional supports for maintaining critical awareness, those individuals who become so committed should be realistic about the personal costs involved. They would be wise to seek support from whatever colleagues can be found who share those commitments. In the final analysis, even in the absence of formal organi-

---

[13] See Shultz, 1975.

zational supports, having discovered the kinds of social relationships one is constructing through communicative choice in interaction, the individual can decide to change.

IMPLICATIONS FOR RESEARCH IN INTERACTIONAL SOCIOLINGUISTICS

Four issues bear brief mention here: (1) the relationship between situational comembership and the politics of culture difference in communication; (2) the processes of interpersonal coordination in face-to-face interaction; (3) the need for simultaneous analysis of verbal and nonverbal channels; (4) the special character of professional encounters—in this instance, gatekeeping encounters—as speech occasions.

Situational Comembership and the Politics of Culture Differences

One of the most important findings of the study was that under conditions of high comembership, cultural differences between the counselor and student in ways of speaking and listening seemed to make less of a difference than they did in encounters in which the comembership level was low. This suggests that differences in communicative competence between interactional partners should be considered in the context of both small-scale and large-scale political relations. On a small scale, the politics of face-to-face relations between individuals need to be considered.

At the level of face-to-face interaction, one would expect the sharing or nonsharing of communicative traditions, as manifested in communicative performance, to symbolize relationships among interactional partners that mirror the social and political relationships among the speech communities to which the individuals belong. Inclusion and exclusion, solidarity or separation between individuals, could be signaled by the match or mismatch in communication style face-to-face. Superordination or subordination between individuals could be signaled by the relative prestige value of the interaction styles employed. "Mixed messages" of social rank could be communicated through interactional style if the rank relationship between the interactional partners in the encounter were contrary to the rank relationship between the speech communities to which the partners belong—for example, a counseling interview in which the counselor (who is superordinate to the student as rank is defined in organizational terms) uses a verbal and nonverbal interaction style of lower prestige than that used by the student, thus symbolizing communicatively the counselor's membership in a social group that ranks lower in the status hierarchy of the larger society than the group to which the student belongs.[14] We found within the counseling interviews both communicative mirroring of social rank held outside the encounter and "mixed messages" due to discrepancy in rank held inside and outside the encounters.

Yet differences in communication style did not seem so salient in some interviews as they seemed in others. This continues to puzzle us, and it warrants further research.

Interpersonal Coordination in Face-to-Face Interaction

Here the importance of interactional rhythm seems paramount. While temporal synchrony between listening and speaking behavior among interactional partners has been well documented in the literature (see the notes for Chapters 4 and 5), what has not been noted until quite recently is that regularity in the underlying rhythmic patterns of interaction may function among international partners to coordinate communicative choice from moment to moment.

Participation by all members of an encounter in a shared framework of timing (see Chapter 4) may increase the predictability of crucial next moments in the sequential structure of interaction. This would provide the common ground that makes possible the high degree of interpersonal complementarity in communicative choice that seems necessary if face-to-face communication is to proceed smoothly and intelligibly. The correlation in our data (Chapter 5) between *probable speech community membership* (as indicated by ethnic status) and *interactional arhythmia* is instructive, since it suggests that lack of shared communicative traditions may produce hesitant and arhythmic interactional stumbling. If our interpretation is correct, interactional arhythmia may be a useful clinical indicator of cultural mismatch in communicative competence among persons who meet face-to-face. Interactional arhythmia may also be useful as a general index of fairly serious interactional trouble in an encounter, whatever the causes of the trouble may be.

Another basic aspect of interpersonal coordination in interaction is the contextualization cueing process. Our findings suggest that discourse structure varies with participation structure (Chapters 2 and 4). If communicative rights and obligations are allocated differently across the boundaries between major discourse units (topics, routines, sequences of routines), then the clear marking of those boundaries is crucial for

---

[14] On the interactional opportunities (provided by social styles of differing prestige rank) for mutual adaptation on the one hand and one-upmanship on the other, see Giles and Powesland, 1975.

interpersonal coordination. A key aspect of communicative competence, we have argued elsewhere,[15] may involve the interpretive capacity to assess correctly the communicative cues that indicate that participants' role relationships are changing within an interactional event. We have speculated that contextualization cues at the junctures among primary constituent units in discourse structure may have strategically important salience and contrastive relevance. This speculation seems to be borne out in the data presented in Chapters 2 and 4. They showed that in clusters of contextualization cues occurring across the verbal and non-verbal channels simultaneously, *modality redundancy* (as indicated by the relative frequency of cooccurring cues on both channels) was highest for the clusters of cues occurring at the boundaries between major interactional segments. This was true for all ethnic and racial combinations of counselors and students in our sample. Since a shift in interpersonal distance always occurred in the clusters of cues at major segment boundaries, this suggests that posture and proxemics may have fundamental importance in signaling renegotiation of communicative role and status among interactional partners. The salience of postural and proxemic cues in communicating these relational "metamessages" in interaction may be a human universal, and may hold true across species as well. Cross-cultural and ethological research could shed light on this.

In addition, there may very well be culture-specific differences in ways of cueing the onset of major and minor segments of action. These would involve differences in the form and function of contextualization cues that our synoptic data analysis was too general to identify. Further research on this is necessary.

Our attempt and the attempts being made by other researchers currently to study the complementarity of speaking and listening behavior together are only beginning attempts. Knowledge about the relationships between conversational inference, behavioral rhythm, and contextualizational cueing needs to be advanced by combining insights from cross-cultural research, neurolinguistics, and information processing research in cognitive psychology, together with insights from interactional sociolinguistics, kinesics, and other approaches to the study of nonverbal behavior.

The Need for a Unified Approach to the Study of Communicative Competence

There is a problem with the notion of *speaking* as an object of study. Perhaps it comes simply from taking the term *speech* too literally as a

[15] See Erickson and Shultz, 1977.

label, since theorists in sociolinguistics have pointed out that the term *speech* should be taken metaphorically as standing for nonverbal as well as verbal communication.[16] A tendency remains to think of speech as talk only, or as talk primarily and centrally, viewing other aspects of social action and social context in communication as secondary or peripheral to talk. This has serious limiting consequences for developing a comprehensive theory of communicative or interactional competence.

There are at least three ways in which theories of communicative competence are limited by construing speaking as mainly talking: (1) by underemphasizing nonverbal and paralinguistic behavior at the expense of the verbal; (2) by fostering an analytic separation between speakers and their hearers that obscures the social organization of the face-to-face interaction within which talk occurs; (3) by focusing research attention on social situations in which talk is the central, "foregrounded" aspect of the activity, and consequently diverting empirical research and theory development away from considering interactional occasions in which talk is a secondary, "backgrounded" accompaniment to other action.

The seriousness of the first limitation, that of underemphasis on nonverbal behavior, becomes apparent in the context of the second and third limitations. If nonverbal behavior cooccurring with speech plays crucial regulatory functions in the production of speech, then to ignore nonverbal behavior in the study of speaking is to misconstrue the phenomenon of interest. The relationship between what the hearers are doing and what the speakers are doing is crucial, we would argue, for the study of speaking itself.

Moreover, much talk among humans occurs on occasions in which talk itself is not the main event. To relegate such talk to the residual category of *phatic communion*[17] and then leave it uninvestigated insures that the full range of ways of speaking extant in a community will not be identified. Neither will the full range of functions those ways of speaking serve be identified, nor will anything be learned about speaker–audience coordination processes on occasions in which talking and attending to talk is not the primary medium of participation in social intercourse.

Study of occasions in which speaking is an accompaniment to the interactional main event can shed considerable light on processes of speech comprehension and speech acquisition. Recent studies through naturalistic observation and audiovisual documentation of young children's speech at play[18] are instructive in this regard. Recent parallel

---

[16] This point is made in Hymes 1964 and in subsequent discussions by Hymes.

[17] The term is that of Malinowski, 1923:315.

[18] See, for example, Cook-Gumperz, 1977; Keenan, 1977; Boggs and Watson-Gegeo, 1979; Corsaro, 1979.

experimental work[19] is beginning to suggest that for young children, speech itself may not be the primarily medium for the communication of meaning, but rather that the presence of physical objects and nonverbal actions in an event may provide the primary redundancy on the basis of which children infer referential meaning.

Even in interaction among adults, the full context of situation may be semantically prior to language itself. People in interaction are not just inferring meaning by listening to each other through a keyhole. They can see one another as well as hear one another. Focus by linguists, psychologists, anthropologists, sociologists, and philosophers of language on linguistic features as semantically central leads to a tendency to dismiss as "surface phenomena" context of situation, kinesics, proxemics, and speech prosody, when actually these may be part of the semantic core, referentially and socially. Consequently there is a danger of "linguocentrism" in the study of speaking.[20] What is needed is a more comprehensive theoretical view and empirical approaches that not only do not separate social meaning from referential meaning, but that also do not separate the verbal from the nonverbal, and the speaker from the listener.

The research presented here was an attempt at a unified analysis. Our methods were crude. Much finer analytic distinctions are made by kinesicists and by linguists than were the ones we made in our attempt to analyze nonverbal and verbal phenomena together. But what was lost in the precision of analysis may have been compensated for by its scope. By putting the behavior of listeners together with that of speakers empirically as well as theoretically, one gains a dynamic view of communicative behavior as socially and culturally organized communicative action.

Talking to "The Man" in Professional Encounters

The very narrowness of the communicative constraints imposed in professional encounters makes them interesting settings for the study of the negotiation of status and role through communicative choice. The presence of role conflict and official and unofficial agendas, and the partial boundedness of the encounter frame provide interactional resources that can be drawn upon by the professional helper and the client for the implicit (or only partially explicit) communication of social meaning. It is by means of subtle choices among optional ways of acting in

---

[19] See Ervin-Tripp, 1979.
[20] On this point see Bauman and Sherzer, 1975; Sherzer, 1977.

relatively more or less interpersonally coordinated ways that ostensibly routine professional encounters come to have distinctive differences in quality and tone.

"Talking to The Man" is a phrase used by some speakers of Black English in the United States. Traditionally, "The Man" meant the white man in authority—the boss. In encounters with "The Man" (also known as "Mr. Charlie"), the relationship of superordination and subordination is more masked than it used to be before the Civil Rights movement of the 1960s. Yet that rank relationship is still there, as reflected in a joke that was told in one American city in 1966, in the middle of the Civil Rights movement era:

> Used to call "The Man" "Mr. Charlie."
> Now you call him "Chuck," but he's still "The Man."

Experience with "The Man" is not limited to black people. In a complex polyethnic society everyone must at some time talk to "The Man." When "The Man" is an institutional gatekeeper, a fundamental issue at stake is whether the gatekeeper will act as if he were "The Man" or not.

In the academic counseling interview and in other gatekeeping encounters there is room for role choice. Those choices seem to be manifested communicatively and negotiated interactionally. Which choices are made, and how and when they are acted on in real time, is of importance to the counselor and student in the practical matter of getting the encounter done. What the counselor and student choose and how they act together has theoretical and practical consequences beyond the gatekeeping encounter as well—consequences for the social scientist and for the society in which the encounters take place.

Scoring Comembership Levels
for the Interviews

As it became apparent that student race and ethnicity as "situation-free" attributes of social identity were by themselves an inappropriate way to classify the interviews for comparative purposes, the notion of comembership and a method of scoring it were developed. The theoretical basis for the notion is described at length in Chapter 2. Procedures for determining comembership level are outlined below. Because comembership is a person-specific as well as situation-specific way of identifying commonality of status between individuals, the scoring procedure involved two steps: (1) surveying the complete set of interviews for each counselor in order to determine the salience of various comembership attributes for that particular counselor; (2) coding each interview according to the comembership salience profile for the counselor conducting the interview.

STEP I. DETERMINING THE COMEMBERSHIP
SALIENCE PROFILE FOR EACH COUNSELOR

The particularistic attributes of students necessary to establish comembership with a counselor varied from one counselor to the next. Specific sets of attributes of students that appeared to have special salience for each counselor were identified by the three members of the research team who had viewed films and studied transcripts of all the interviews most thoroughly. What follows in Table A.1 are the sets of comembership attributes identified by the three coders as most salient for each of the counselors. Often attributes of student background such as neighborhood and interest in athletics were revealed in small talk during the interview, and so the coders kept small talk topics in mind as they developed the comembership saliency profiles for each counselor. Other attributes of students, such as race and ethnicity, were apparent without recourse to small talk. Race was visually apparent during the first seconds of the interview. Ethnicity was often clearly apparent, even before the interview began, from the student's last name as it appeared in the student's cumulative folder.

STEP II. DETERMINING THE COMEMBERSHIP SCORE FOR EACH INTERVIEW

Once the comembership salience profile for each counselor was identified, each interview was scored on the relative presence or absence of each of the attributes in each of the students, depending upon which counselor he interacted with. Based on these scores, the interviews were divided into high, medium, and low comembership. Following are two examples that demonstrate the manner in which the level of comembership for each encounter was determined. While reading through the examples, keep in mind the attributes of students necessary for establishing comembership listed in Table A.1.

Example 1: An Italian–American student comes to see the Italian–American counselor at the public junior college. Although he is of the same ethnic background as the counselor, he is overweight and a music major. (An excerpt from the transcript of this encounter can be found in Appendix C, pp. 239–241.)

a. The counselor, having been a high school wrestling coach and being a close follower of parochial school basketball, uses these interests in establishing comembership with students. The fact that this student is overweight and a music major makes it highly unlikely that he would share the counselor's interests in athletics. Even though the counselor discusses athletics in many of the other encounters, he does not do so in this one.

Table A.1
Comembership Salience Profile

Institution	Counselor	Attributes of students
Private junior college	Black American	1. Has a particular ethnic or racial background. 2. Acts in an appropriately subordinate manner.
Public junior college	Italian–American	1. Has a particular background or interests including but not limited to the following: attended parochial schools, lived in certain neighborhoods, is interested in high school and college athletics. 2. Appropriately reports official information related to being a student (e.g., grades, major). 3. Acts in an appropriately subordinate manner.
	Irish–American	1. Has a particular ethnic or racial background. 2. Is a good student (e.g., has good grades, has taken the right courses). 3. Acts in an appropriately subordinate manner.
	Black American	1. Is a good student (e.g., has good grades, right courses). 2. Appropriately reports official information related to being a student (e.g., grades, major). 3. Has a particular ethnic or racial background.

b. This counselor places a high premium on a student's ability to report the grades he has received, the courses he has taken, and the courses he is currently taking. This student is not sure of the courses he is currently taking and is vague about much of the information the counselor requests from him.

c. This counselor expects a certain amount of subordination and respect from students. He does not get it from this student, in that the counselor suggests that the student take a summer school course and the student refuses.

In evaluating this encounter, it was decided that, based on the student's physical appearance, his apparent lack of interest in certain areas, and his inability to perform in a manner the counselor would consider appropriate, this student scored poorly relative to the criteria for establishing comembership for this counselor. Consequently, it was determined that the level of comembership for this encounter was low.

Example 2: A Polish–American student is interviewed by the Irish–American counselor. The student has an easy manner, and the two appear quite comfortable in the interaction. They joke about mutual acquaintances and other topics. (An excerpt from the transcript of this encounter can be found in Appendix C, pp. 230–231.)

a. This counselor is more comfortable interacting with students who are from the same panethnic group that he is from (white ethnic) than he is when interacting with students from other panethnic groups. The fact that this student is Polish–American works in his favor in terms of facilitating the establishment of comembership.

b. This counselor places a great deal of emphasis on the student's ability as a student. Even though this student's grades are mediocre, he is well aware of what courses he is taking and the reasons he is taking them. He also has some definite plans about what he wants to do when he leaves the junior college, and is planning his academic career appropriately. All of this is apparent in the conversation the student has with the counselor.

c. Like the counselor in Example 1, this counselor expects a certain amount of respect and deference from the students he advises. This student responds appropriately by taking the counselor's advice very seriously, laughing at the counselor's jokes, and in general participating in the interaction in a manner that would not offend the counselor.

In this encounter, the counselor responds to the student with offers of special help to help him along in his academic career. It was quite evident, from the information provided above, that the level of comembership between this counselor and this student was high.

Table A.2 contains the comembership levels and ethnicity of each of the students seen by the four counselors in the study. Notice that in rank ordering the interviews according to comembership, ethnicity and race are distributed in a differentiated way that points up discrepant cases for the Italian–American counselor; whereas most of the interviews with fellow Italian–Americans rank high in comembership, one ranks low. For the black American counselor in the private junior college, whereas

Table A.2
Comembership Level and Ethnicity of Students Seen by the Four Counselors

Site	Counselor	Comembership level	Ethnicity–race of student
Private junior college	Black American	High	Black American Black American
		Medium	Black American White American
		Low	White American White American
Public junior college	Italian–American	High	Italian–American Italian–American
		Medium	Italian–American Italian–American Polish–American
		Low	Italian–American Polish–American Polish–American
	Irish–American	High	Polish–American
		Medium	Polish–American Black American
		Low	Black American Black American
	Black American	High	Polish–American Polish–American
		Medium	Polish–American Black American
		Low	Polish–American Puerto Rican

two interviews with fellow black Americans rank high in comembership, one interview with a black American ranked medium. For the Irish–American counselor, two interviews with black Americans ranked low in comembership but one ranked medium. For the black American in the public junior college, interviews with Polish–American students ranked higher (in two instances) in comembership than did the interview with a fellow black American and an interview with another Polish–American. The presence of these patterns suggests that the use of situation-free categories of social identity alone (e.g., ethnicity and race alone, considered by themselves) is an inappropriate way to classify interethnic encounters for comparative purposes because it does not take account of the "local" meanings to actors on the scene, nor does it take account of the labile character of ethnicity and race or social identity construction during the conduct of social relations face-to-face. From one perspective, social identity is a matter of interactional achievement rather than a matter of ascription; whereas ascription may play an important part in the achievement, it is not the whole story, at least in the encounters reported on here.

Equipment and Its Use
in Filming and Recording

If the participants in the gatekeeping encounters were not very camera-conscious while being filmed, this was due in part to the way in which the actual filming was done, as well as to the nature of the gatekeeping situation and to the development of rapport with the counselors. At the beginning of the project we collected behavior records by simultaneously videotaping and shooting silent 16 mm cinema film. It soon became apparent that sound rather than silent cinema would be necessary for the detailed analyses we intended to conduct of face-to-face interaction.

The system for simultaneous sound cinema and videotape recording consisted of a Bolex cinema camera with a 12.5 mm (moderate wide-angle) lens and 400 foot magazine mounted on a stationary tripod in a soundproof box (termed a "blimp"). The motor of the camera was connected by pilot-tone synchronization cable to the motor of a Nagra IV tape recorder (to enable the preparation of a synchronized cinema sound track). A directional "shotgun" microphone on a stand was used with the tape recorder. (An Electro-Voice EV642 was used first and later a Sennheizer MKH804 was used because of problems of background noise.) The audio signal from the microphone was connected through the tape recorder by line output to a video recorder, and the video camera (also equipped with a 12.5 mm wide-angle lens) was placed on top of the box in which the cinema camera was housed. The two cameras on one tripod and the microphone on its tripod were the only pieces of equipment in the interviewer's office. Outside the office, in a hallway or adjoining office, the video recording and playback deck, the video monitor, and the Nagra audio recorder were set up, usually on a projection cart, as a remote control monitoring station. (A switch on an extension cord made it possible to turn the cinema camera on and off from the monitoring station.) Since the interviews took place across a desk, it was possible to document them at an angle just above "eye level" on film and videotape using such a stationary camera setup. We were not able to document all the initial greetings and final leave-takings with the stationary cameras because the speakers usually stepped out of frame or cut off their heads by standing up. We felt that for the purposes of our study, the advantages of remote operation outweighed the disadvantage of a rigid visual frame.

The camera and microphone tripods were placed next to each other in a corner of the interviewer's office at right angles to the line of sight of the two interlocutors as they oriented themselves full-face toward each other across the desk. Even in a small office this meant that the stationary cameras and microphone were just at the edge of the interlocutors' peripheral vision, or just outside it. Since the cameras did not make any noise in being turned on or off and did not move during operation, the system was quite unobtrusive although clearly visible to the participants in the interviews.

The filming routine was as follows. When the interviewee arrived for his appointment he was asked if he was willing to participate in the study. If so, he then entered the interviewer's office, and as he did so, the operator of the camera and sound system turned the system on from the remote-control station. The 400-foot magazine on the cinema camera permitted 10 minutes of continuous filming, and the videotape reel lasted 1 hour. We always recorded the entire interview on video. At the beginning of the study we also did this with cinema, simply turning the camera on at the beginning of the interview and letting it run for a full 10 minutes. (Some of the interviews lasted less than 10 minutes.) After filming about 15 interviews in this way, we began to have a sense of the natural segments of the interview, and from then on we turned the cinema camera off to save film time during external interruptions (such as a phone call that had nothing to do with the interview taking place) or during moments in which the interviewer left the office to get a file. With this exception, there was no "camera editing" of the material we collected. The audio recorder was also left on throughout the interview.

Examples of Summary Tables and Corresponding Examples of Transcripts

Six examples of summary tables are presented along with the corresponding parts of the verbal transcript of the interaction. The reader is urged to read through the examples of the verbal text and simultaneously follow the corresponding summary table. While reading, note the points at which changes in discourse topic (to be seen in the transcript of speech) are accompanied by changes in other aspects of verbal and nonverbal behavior. These additional aspects are *time reference* (talk about the past, the present, or the future), *proxemics* (shift in interpersonal distance, which also entails a change of postural position), *pitch* (major shifts in pitch and in overall pitch level), *eye contact* (person A looks at person B, B looks at A, mutual gaze), and *viewing session comment* (made by counselor, or student, or both at this point). The summary table, then, is a synopsis of cooccurring changes across various dimensions of discourse organization and nonverbal behavior.

EXAMPLE 1
Black American Counselor, Polish–American
Student, High Comembership

(35)   C: You didn't pick up any other course to _____ it. 13 hours?
       (A line _____ means unintelligible.)
(36)   S: Yeah. (P)

Juncture—Discourse Topic: Summer School

(37)   C: OK. [Name of student] (P) How about summer school...? Plan-
             ning on summer school?

(38)   S: No.

Juncture—Discourse Topic: Major

(39)   C: OK. Working? (P) (1: Yeah.) So we'll figure out what you've got
             going for September....You're gonna stay in the Mech Tech
             Program?

(40)   S: Yeah. (P)

(41)   C: All right, English..sh..sh.sh Engineering 131 you've got now,
             Mech Tech 101 you've had, OK, English is outta the way...
             Mech Tech 205, Mech Tech 203. (P) OK. for September ...
             (P) Let's get back to that Math 96. (1: OK.) (P) Sure ya don't
             wanna go to summer school and pick that up ...?

(42)   S: No. . . I don't think I can make it, the summer after, but not
             this one.

(43)   C: All right, so figure a Math, Math 96, (P) Engineering 132, (P)
             all right, you're gonna have to take a typing class also.

(44)   S: I have to?

(45)   C: Yeah _____ type and use it for your term papers and so on..
             you intend to don't you?

(46)   S: Yes.. you want the back filled out then?

(47)   C: Just your name.

(48)   S: OK. (P)

(49)   C: Engineering 140, and a three, six, nine, twelve we'll give you
             one more... _____ Business 111.. that's organization and
             management. (P) All right, now, here's what we're doing'.
             These are all your required courses (1: mmhmm) all right, so
             we're gonna have to check mark so that the courses you've
             had or I'm giving you now.. OK. So next semester will finish
             your Math 96, this Engineering 132... Business 117, which is
             your typing.. um.. Engineering 140 and your Business 111.
             The reason why I'm not givin' you some of these other Mech
             Tech courses is they're offered in the evenings in the fall. You
             don't want to come evenings, do you, now? So we'll work this
             in and then the following semester we're gonna go heavy on
             Mech Tech again.

(50)   S: OK.

Table C.1

Example 1: Black American Counselor, Polish–American Student, High Comembership

Line number	Topic	Time reference	Overlap	Proxemics 1	Proxemics 2	Pitch 1	Pitch 2	Eye contact	Viewing session comment
35	1		1						
36	1				1				
37	11	1							
38	1		1			1	11	1	
39	11					1	1	1 1	
40	1							1	
41	11	11	1	1	1	111	1	1	1
42	1				11				
43	1				1	1	11		
44	1				1	1	1		
45	1	1	1	1	1	11	11	1	1
46	11							1	
47	1						1	1	
48	11	1	1	1				1	
49				1	11	11	11		
50	11					11			
51	11	11		111	11111	11		1	
52	1		(1)				1	1	
53						1	1		

Juncture—Discourse Topic: Registration for Fall
Semester, Transferring to Four-Year School

(51) C: OK. Now here's what I want you to do . . . on this stub, copy down all your courses and numbers, this way you've got a record of what you _____ comes September. (P) Where do you intend to go from here [Name of student] _____ as far as college or school.

(52) S: Maybe State Tech . . . for a while.

(53) C: Have you been checkin' any other catalogs up in our library?

EXAMPLE 2
Irish–American Counselor, Polish–American
Student, High Comembership

(65) C: Beautiful, unbelievable!

(66) S: I...I even (2 D) I never. . I ne. . never had anythin' like that. It was really funny.

(67) C: Yeah, I know what you mean. . . .Well, (2L) OK . . . um. . (noise/ tongue) How about these other courses?

(68) S: English, "C" - "B". . .

(69) C: And, uh, Business 111?

(70) S: I'm trying for the "A" in there. . I'm trying, I'm bustin' for it.

Juncture—Discourse Topic: Transferring to
Four-Year School

(71) C: OK, please do me one favor and check with State University.

(72) S: I will. I got State College's catalog, I got their _____ .

(73) C: Do they have. . Data Processing there?

(74) S: They're carrying graduate courses and they're startin' to get down into it a little more on a lower level...undergraduate courses.

(75) C: Check and see whether a...check them out a little bit more thoroughly. I think you're gonna find that it's gonna be difficult to find a school. . . uh, . that offers Data Processing and I think that a.. (S: or I'll go right, .) that you should find that.

(76) S: I'll go right into Programming then.. Computer Programming. There's the courses.

                                                          (C: Where?)

C: Well, Computer Programming is a little different from Data Processing and the courses I'm takin' now are leading right into Programming. These are, well, 111 is a program course . . . and I think, uh, well, 112 was one but they're not offerin' that.

Juncture—Discourse Topic: Major

(77) S: The courses as we list em here, we're, we're offering degrees simply in Data Processing, right?

(78) C: Yeah, the 2-year degree? (S: Yeah.) We have the 1-year course, too.

(79) S: Yeah. . ah. .   I don't think we in fact, well, 112, yeah. . . .
              (that ain't that hard)

C: We do. . ah. . but it's a very minimal, ah. . . offering. The Data Processing is of. . .well, the technical offered isn't offered at all. The business programmers, that 2-year degree, and you're pretty well on your way to that. Okay, so yo. . . so that's, when you say you're going into programmer that's what you're talking about, right?

(80) S: Yeah, and from there I can work my way. .

Juncture—Discourse Topic: Transferring to
Four-Year School

(81) C: OK, I want you to check that out, Where can you go from here with the courses that you've had. . Remember when I. . . remember when I transferred you over here? The one thing. I.. the one thing I told you about this? Whadd I tell ya?

(82) S: Just check it all out and everything. Make sure what I want to get into. . You know, make sure I don't get burned or anything if I decide to transfer.

(83) C: OK, but what did I tell you this course was specifically geared to, the transfer student or the stu..student who wasn't gonna transfer?

(84) S: Wasn't.

(85) C: OK, remember that,   it hasn't changed

(86) S: I realize that.

Table C.2

Example 2: Irish–American Counselor, Polish–American Student, High Comembership

Line number	Topic	Time reference	Overlap	Proxemics 1	Proxemics 2	Pitch 1	Pitch 2	Eye contact	Viewing session comment
65	—					—	—		
66	—					—	—		
67	—					—	—		
68	—						—		
69	—					—	—	—	
70	—							—	
71	—							—	
72	—		(1)(1)					—	
73	—							—	
74	—						—	11	
75	—		1 (1)					11	
76	1111	11	1 (1)			—	—	—	
77	—			1	1	—	—		
78	11		1	11		—	—		
79	—		(1) 1	11	111	11	—		
80	—	—				—	—	—	
81	11	—					—	—	
82	11	11					—	—	—
83	11	—					—	—	
84	—					—	—	—	
85	—	—				—		—	
86	—						—	—	

EXAMPLE 3
Black American Counselor, Polish–American
Student, High Comembership

(10)   C: Mechanical Technology.

(11)   S: 103.

Juncture—Discourse Topic: Major¹

(12)   C: ...Mm hmm. And what is your major?

(13)   S: Uh...my major is electronics.

(14)   C: Electronics, OK, so that's the uh. . 2-year program? . . In elec-
       tronics* . . mm hmm . . . How do you like your courses so
       far?

(15)   S: Yeah, I like them.

(16)   C: You like them. Are you learning anythin?

(17)   S: Yes sir.

Juncture—Discourse Topic: Courses for
Next Semester

(18)   C: Mm hmm, (P) and you're working on the 2-year degree* . . OK
       . . Now are you familiar with the requirements of that 2-year
       degree? [4 yes sir.] OK . . so you need (P) another English
       course. . English 101*. . so I'll put that down for you (P) aaand.
       let's see, your Engineering is OK. . . you're taking the elec-
       tronics. . 130. . which. . I think is. . the same as. . 103. I think
       it's just a new name. . _____ that I'll have to trip that off for
       you. . very quickly. (P) Mm hmm. (P) Yeah, they're about the
       same. . . so I guess you ought to go up to the next electronics
       course which would be . . 131* (P) Now . . . these are the
       courses that you have to take. . if you want to look through
       there we can pick out. . . a few other courses. Have you had
       a math placement test yet?

(19)   S: Uh, yes, I did. . one I, uh. . took for a fall semester*. . s..so I
       took the placement test a. . and on the. . I have a. . an I found
       out....

(20)   C: You have ma. . you placed in Math 111*. . OK, do you know
       what Math 111 is?

(21)   S: Uhh. . no.

(22)   C: Oh. . OK. Math 111 is a. . course that includes. . College Al-

---

¹ An asterisk indicates *mhm* said by listener with no pause or overlap.

gebra. . Trigonometry. . and Analytic Geometry. . . Uh, how much Math did you have in high school?

(23) S: In high school? Uh, I had uh. . I had it 4 years but uh. . on each uh. . . well, I'm ..from Poland, you know,* I graduated in Poland and uh. . . we had, you know, different, you know. . . kind of, you know. . classes. We had like, uh. . . I had 4 year..uh, 4, uh. . 4, uh. . 4 days a week we had math. . And, uh, every day we had 2 hours of math*. And on 1 hour we took Algebra and the second hour we took Geometry and then you know the next day we took Trigonom..trig and you know. . . and again Algebra so, uh. . I have 3 years . . of those of . . of each. . um, you know

(24) C: ...Three years of Algebra and Trig?

(25) S: And geometry.

(26) C: And geometry. . OK, in that case the only thing new would be the an..Did you have Analytic Geometry?* OK, so there won't be very much new coming in . . (S) The reason I ask is that sometimes our students, uh, are not prepared to take this course. If you have a good Math background in 111 it'll be..it'll be fairly easy. .

(27) S: You see, uh. . I didn't get a good grade on it but, uh. . I really liked it you know?*. . So, uh. . I think I..I..I know Math pretty good, you know. The only..my problem is, uh, you know, is. . Geometry and Trigonometry because uh. . some of those words I still don't know, you know, so uh*. . . all I gotta do is uh. . uh you know, just look up many of them but uh . . . it..it the Algegra is. . when I took the test out of the 40 I. . or 50 questions I had uh. . 37. . good. .*so. .

(28) C: But, uh, you feel that this score. . Yeah, I would recommend then that you take uh. . Math 111. . . and that will give you. . . a good background and also that's a. . good course. That's a 5-hour course. . that's a good transfer course.at. . OK. . . Now. . how's the, uh, English course coming?

(29) S: N..yeahuh, it's good. It n..uh um. . getting a little help from uh. . . from the reading department and, uh, help you know. . *you know. And it's coming along good,* most of it.

(30) C: Do you feel that uh. . . 101 will be difficult for you after the 100?

Table C.3
Example 3: Black American Counselor, Polish–American Student, High Comembership

Line number	Topic	Time reference	Overlap	Proxemics 1	Proxemics 2	Pitch 1	Pitch 2	Eye contact	Viewing session comment
10							1		
11	1						1		
12	1			1			1		
13				1	1		1		
14	11						1		
15	1						1		
16	1						1		
17	1						1		
18	11111111 111111	11111111	1	111111	111		1		1
19	1						1		
20	11	1					1		
21									
22	11	1		1	111		11		
23	111		1	1	1		1		
24	1						1		
25	1								
26	11	1		1	1		1		1
27	111	1					1		1
28	111	111					1		111
29	11						1		
30	1	1							

EXAMPLE 4
**Black American Counselor, Black American Student,
Medium Comembership**

*Juncture—Discourse Topic: Applying to
Junior College*

(13) C: So that was a vocational–technical program. And, uh, have you talked to them, uh, to see t..i..uh, you could get in on their transfer program this year?

(14) S: Naw.

(15) C: Well, that would be the first step. In case you can't, then you can come in as a vocational-technical student...and, uh.. you can uh..switch over later.* Uh, so you're interested in History. Have you thought about uh.. grade three, six, seven, eight, nine....

Juncture—Discourse Topic: Career in Teaching

(16) S: Well, yeah..I thought about that, I thought that, uh..because, like, as I've been informed by some people who have degrees though _____ they say that..have to have a Master's before I start teaching high school an' a Bachelor's while I teach un...uh, sixth seventh an' eighth grade

(17) C: That's right, that's what I was just getting ready to bring out. Um.. usually if you get a uh...B.A. in, say, the teaching of Social Studies with an education minor..then you are able to go an' teach in the, uh, elementary schools. The, uh..teaching History in the senior high schools usually, uh, takes a little more work in History. (S) But, uh..again it's up to you s..you know you set your goals _____

(18) S: Was it possible to uh..like I wanta teach a specific history, Afro-American

(19) C: You wanta teach Afro-American History? Yeah.*

(20) S: And so like I .. I could teach that in the, uh, sixth and seventh grades so forth*, you know.

(21) C: Uh..yes. . it depends on the school system you're in, uh..sometimes uh..uh, this..a teacher has to teach two or three different subjects so you'd probably be teaching Language Arts and History, uh, Math and History, uh.. uh, Math and a Language if you had..you know if you had a language that you s..uhspoke, uh, something else..Art, maybe, and uh..then, uh, you would

concentrate on .. your major field. Maybe you'd teach three classes of, uh, Afro-American History..couple classes of uh, art _____ Reading, English (S).. depending on what you..really want to do.

(22) S: What I feel like I really want to do is to teach History and to teach a language, also, like Swahili.* And like, uh, that would be like getting.. I'd have to get n..a Bachelor's in one an' the other to do that wouldn't I?

(23) C: No, what you do is..in a case like that you take, un...so many hours of History* and then you take, uh, another minor which w'd probably be 16 hours in Swahili or..an' this would be 16 or 20 hours over the basic courses so that you'd have a fairly..good knowledge of the language...But, uh, again those, uh, y'know two _____ yeah and, uh, languages are very difficult. Have you taken any Swahili already?

(24) S: No, but I've taken German. I wasn't too hot in that. (SL, IL)

(25) C: Yeah..well i..if you develop a skill for languages..I..think that you might be able to do, uh, fairly well in that. (P) Do you plan to teach in (Name of city) or outside of (Name of city)..

(26) S: Well, like I intend to, uh, teach, uh, about..my plans are to teach about 5 or 6 years in (Name of city) an' then move to a hotter climate because I can't take (Name of city)'s weather (SL) not too much longer the way it's going now. 'Cause it kind of gets me down in the wintertime. (laugh)*

Juncture—Discourse Topic: Applying to
Junior College

(27) C: _____ Have you always lived in (Name of city)? (P) (S) OK..so let's..let's review, we'll say that first of all you gotta check with the admissions office.* Are you free during the day?* OK.. so you can check with them between 9 and 4 any day. They're open every day. They're open on Monday and Thursday evenings*...And then, uh, if you can't get into the transfer program then you better try an' get in...to the Voc-Tech office and talk to Mr. (Name of counselor) and Mr. (Name of counselor), to see if you can squeeze in for next Saturday's late registration for Voc-Tech Students.* Uh. . . it is kind of late an' I wish I had known, y'know, wishh..when you made the appointment with me I had known that you hadn't been admitted.* But either way you're going to go through Freshman group counseling so I won't be making out a card like this for you now..You'll do

Table C.4
Example 4: Black American Counselor, Black American Student, Medium Comembership

Line number	Topic	Time reference	Overlap	Proxemics 1	Proxemics 2	Pitch 1	Pitch 2	Eye contact	Viewing session comment
13	11	1							-
14									-
15	111	1111			11				
16	11	11	(1)						
17	111	11	(1)(1)						
18	1								
19									
20	11	-		1	11				-
21	111	-	(1)		11				-
22	111	1			-				
23	111				11				
24	11	11		11	-				-
25	111	11	(1)		-				-
26	11								
27	1111	11			-	11			-
28			1 (1)						
29	1		(1)	1					
30	-		(1)(1)						
31	1111	11111							

that when you come in and take your English placement test an' your Math placement test an' then we'll have someone there to talk to you then. If you do have any problems, though, you can feel free to come in..talk with me.

(28)   S: _____(unintelligible).

Juncture—Discourse Topic: Leave-Taking

(29)   C: OK, an'..good luck on your, uh. . . chosen major. (3L)#

(30)   S: An' I'm 'a need a lot of it. (SL)

(31)   C: Yeah, well, y'know there aren't really that many courses offered in Afro-American History at our school. I think we offer one course in Literature and one course in, uh, Afro-American History. . but you c'n get the..uh required courses that you'll need when you go to the University an' (I coughs) excuse me.. an' then you can . . . .

EXAMPLE 5
Italian–American Counselor, Italian–American Student, Low Comembership

(61)   C: Anything else?

(62)   S: No, that's it.

Juncture—Discourse Topic: Courses for
Next Semester

(63)   C: Three, 6, 9, 12 hours. .right? OK, so next semester. .you'll be takin' this Music 113, (P) Music 134, which is Orchestra, again, (P) Music 101. .which is your Fundamentals. .and Music 121. . .That's your Introduction to Music. All right, so that's 3, 6, 7, 8 hours of Music now. .Let's get an English class in.

(64)   S: Yeah, that's what I wanted, it's an E..English class. .it's. .uhhh, I want the Basic English to start with cause I'll need it.

(65)   C: All right. We'll give you English 100. It's a remedial course but if you feel you need it. OK. All right. . .no sense second-guessing yourself. (1: I need it. .I need it.) (laugh) English 100. .that's 3 hours. . .awright. . .as far as. .your future. .what do you foresee, in the future what do you. . .why are you coming to school?

(66)   S: Basically I want to get a music major, I want to, uh. .either play or teach music.

Table C.5
Example 5: Italian–American Counselor, Italian–American Student, Low Comembership

Line number	Topic	Time reference	Overlap	Proxemics 1	Proxemics 2	Pitch 1	Pitch 2	Eye contact	Viewing session comment
61							1		
62									
63	111111	111	(1)(1)						
64				1		1	1		
65	111	11	1	1		111	111	1	
66	1								
67	1								
68	1			1		11	1	1	
69	111	11			1			1	
70	11	1						1	
71									
72									
73									
74	1		1						
75	11	11	(1)(1)			11	11	1	
76	1						1		
77	1								
78	1								

240

Juncture—Discourse Topic: Transferring to
Four-Year School

(67) C: Do you intend to go on to a 4-year college from here?

(68) S: Yes, I was planning to take two w..well, four semesters and
          then. . probably the easiest way to get into a. . 4-year college
          uh. . you know? Wouldn't it be?

Juncture—Discourse Topic: Courses for
Next Semester

(69) C: Y'know. . depends upon your grades now...they're gonna be
          the determining factor there. Your grades..All right, now, give
          me a class.. from here. Anything on here. (P) Anything on there..
          or an option could be your continuation of Business Law..but
          I don't see if..how that's gonna help you. (P)

(70) S: Got the English all right. How about Physical Science?

(71) C: Physical Science? Phy Sci? Just reading.

(72) S: Hmm?

(73) C: It's reading.

(74) S: Reading, huh? It don't hurt anybody. Physical Education, what'sss
          that, uh?

(75) C: That's gym. I'm gonna..enroll you in there. (P) Three, 6, 9, 12,
          15 hours...OK? How about summer school.. or are you gonna
          take off this summer?

(76) S: Well, I..I..planning to go to Canada for a..couple weeks I don't
          know...uh exactly I

(77) C: If you change your mind..an' you wanna pick up a course this
          summer..come and see me.. and we can make the change.

(78) S: All right, so we continue is if I..if I..if I don't..well, what if s..uh,
          one of my friends bought a lodge up there.

EXAMPLE 6
Black American Counselor, Polish–American
Student, Low Comembership

(Discussion of Courses for Next Semester
in Progress)

(31) C: How did you do?

(32) S: I had a "B" in it. I'm good in sciences.

(33)   C: You're very good in sciences. . Yes, I. . can see that because your grades in the science courses are pretty good. Um. . . but I still think you ought to have a little more Math before you go into the regular. . but if you've had the. . 131. . well if you've had the. . high school course that would take the place of the 131 course and so I would wait on that until after you get some more Math. . so you did the Math 95 so you are now ready for Math. . one. . oh, no, you didn't complete that course. . so you need that Math 95 again.

(34)   S: Do you think I'd be able to take another placement test because I feel that I..I have improved my math abilities somewhat.

(35)   C: Mm hmm. Who was your Math teacher for Math 95?

(36)   C: Mr. (Name of teacher)

(37)   C: What did he say?

(38)   S: I don't know (laugh). . I don't know, I guess it was my just. . inability in class I just was bored with it. . It seems so boring. . I just didn't want to come

(39)   C: When you took the Math 89 you got a "C."

(40)   S: So? (P) Yeah, just Math was never my forte.

(41)   C: Yeah, well, I think that you would probably. . .do better taking the (S: That's. .) 95 over again and getting a background. Because a "C" in 89 really is. . . (S: Yeah. __ good, huh?) too _____ no. . So I think that maybe what we can do it. . . (S) You know, uh, even though it's not a transferrable course it's giving you some knowledge that might. . enable you to do better. . in a college level course.

(42)   S: Then I have to go. . 89 to. . 100.

(43)   C: No, uh, 95. . and. . Did you have Geometry in high school?
            (S: 95)

(44)   S: Yes. I had a "B" in that.

(45)   C: Yeah, well, you can go from Math 95 to Math 101.

(46)   S: I think that would be good.

(47)   C: Yeah, so we'll put you down first of all for the Math course. The Math 95 . . . You still have the book?

(48)   S: Mm, hmm, yes. (laugh) Don't throw away the book.

(49)   C: That'll save you some money and um. .

(50)   S: Engineering?

Table C.6
Example 6: Black American Counselor, Polish–American Student, Low Comembership

Line number	Topic	Time reference	Overlap	Proxemics 1	Proxemics 2	Pitch 1	Pitch 2	Eye contact	Viewing session comment
31	1								
32									
33	11111	11111	?	11111	1111	1			1
34	1				1				
35	1	1							
36	1								
37									
38	1			1	1	1	1		
39	1				1	1	1		1
40	1								
41	111	111	1 (1)			1	1		1
42	11	1				1	1		
43	11	11	1						
44	1	1			1		1		1
45	1								
46	1	1		1	1	1	1		1
47	11	1		1	1	1	1		
48	1	1		1	1	1	1		1
49	1	1		1	1	1			
50	1	1		1		1			
51	111	1		1		1	1		
52	11	1		1	111	1	1		11
53	11111111	11111	?1			1	11		1
54	11111111111		(1)(1)				11		
55	1						1		
56	1								
57	11						1		1

243

(51) C: Yeah, the Engineering 131. (P) It's a 3-hour course, that's 6 hours. How do you like the Humanities course you're taking?

(52) S: Mm, I'm enjoying it, it's fun. But I'd like to have an elective instead of. . taking 202. . I think from, it's, uh. . from what I heard people say it's real hard. . and. . I don't know if I should jump into something like that.

(53) C: Yeah, w..well, the substitutes for um. . 202 are all pretty difficult. Philosophy 215..World Lit. . .Well at Private U. they would probably accept un/ a literature course for a Humanities and so maybe you can postpone that. And we'll put you down for the uh. . English 102 which is. . I don't see. . it on your program. And that is something that they usually want you to (1: 102) have at any 4-year school. A year of English 102. . the Math 95, the Engineering 131.. How many hours do you plan to take?

(54) S: Well, if I. . when I come back I want to take about 15 hours and s..

      C: You want to take. .15 hours next September. OK, so that means that we'll have to get another. . . course up above the line.

(55) S: What about that Soc Sci course?

(56) C: OK, that's a good one. 101 course, it has a lot of Psychology in it, you'll like that. . your PE. . . Now we've got the Math and we've got the Engineering. . and. . you intend to. .

(57) S: Well, I... wanted to go on after this and maybe even major in Engineering. . . like I'm just probing into it to see if I like it. . .But since my Math is bad I don't know if I should. . 'cause it has a lot of Math.

Descriptions of "Uncomfortable Moments" and "Asymmetry Segments" Coding and Procedures

Although the encounter participants commented on "uncomfortable moments" in viewing sessions, they did not identify beginning and end points for each segment thus labeled. It was also not clear to what extent the informants were using idiosyncratic criteria for defining discomfort.

Accordingly, we decided to code the 25 cases for "uncomfortable moments," using independent judges. We used two behavior raters, trained them for interrater reliability, and set them to watching the films. Their task was to identify the moments at which the interviewer and interviewee seemed uncomfortable, and to distinguish between three levels of discomfort—considerable, moderate, and minimal. Having identified the "moments," the raters then specified the beginning and ending of that section, using an L. W. Athena projector to view the section over a few times at regular speed with sound. Since the raters were working with frame-numbered film, they were able to locate the sections quite precisely, even at regular speed.

The raters were able to identify the "uncomfortable moments" with considerable consistency. There was one major discrepancy, however. Occasionally one rater would identify a moderately long section as uncomfortable and the other rater would identify the same material but would designate it as two separate "moments" rather than as one continuous "moment."[1] This kind of discrepancy was paralleled in the viewing session data. The example in Table D.1 demonstrates the discrepancy between the raters.

To resolve the discrepancy and to get at what aspects of behavioral form the raters (and the original participants) had been attending to differently, we set a *behavior coder* to examine in greater detail the sections identified by the *raters*. The coder was told to view the films in slow motion forward and backward without sound, and at regular speed forward without sound and backward with sound. By this means we prevented the coder from attending to the content of talk and focused attention entirely on the form of nonverbal behavior.

Viewing the film in this way and identifying subsegments within the "uncomfortable moments" defined impressionistically by the raters (who also were attending to the speech of the participants), the coder resolved all the discrepancies of section labeling that had occurred between the two raters.

What the behavior coder was attending to was *behavioral asymmetry*, operationally defined (in terms of the complementarity of speaking–listening behavior) as a *discrepancy between rates of kinesic activity or of proxemic relationship between both speaker–listeners*. The coder watched the film, attending to what the listener was doing while the speaker was talking—how wide the listener's "listening motions" were, how frequently they occurred. The coder looked at the listening style of the other "speaker" when the person who had been listening began to speak. Then the coder looked at the *relationship between listening style and speaking style* during each "turn" for speaking–listening. If the person doing "speaking" was using much kinesic activity and the listener was also moving considerably, this was defined as "kinesic symmetry" (complementarity). If, as the speaker moved forward the listener also moved forward or backward and both then *continued in that proxemic set* without shifting back and forth, this was defined as "proxemic symmetry." Deviations from symmetric relations between the speaker–listeners (often the result of a sharp change in speaking or listening style within a single "turn" by one of the participants but not by the other participant) marked the beginning of a segment of relatively greater asymmetry, and a return toward the symmetry marked the end of that segment.

The coder began 700 frames ahead of the section designated "uncomfortable" by the raters, and coded 200 frames past the end of that section, to get a sense of the behavioral form of "comfortable discourse"—the norm from which the behaviors of uncomfortableness deviated.

[1] This discrepancy may be due to the fact that the two raters were attending to different sorts of behavior areas in selecting the uncomfortable moments. Given all of the information available to a viewer of a film of the encounter, this is very likely to happen.

Table D.1
Discrepancy between Raters for Uncomfortable Moments

	Rater 1	Rater 2	Comments
Uncomfortable moment[a]			
1.	2165–2400	2120–3220	Rater 1's coding is contained within Rater 2's coding.
	4820–4848 Smooth		
	4848–5020 Slightly rough		
	5020–6000 Fairly rough		
	6000–6350 Slightly rough		Rater 2's coding
	6350–3820 Smooth		is contained
		6059–6104 Smooth	within Rater 1's coding, and
		6104–6182 Rough	also the relative smoothness
		6182–6353 Smooth	of sections is
		6353–6440 Rough	different for the two raters.
		6440–6582 Smooth	

[a] Using frame numbers from the films.

The result was that the "uncomfortable" section was placed in context and shorter segments within the whole "uncomfortable moments" section were identified.

The charts for asymmetry segments show that, within the larger section "uncomfortable moment," all the speaking–listening is not uniformly asymmetric. Segments of relative symmetry alternate with segments of asymmetry. The charts show visually that "uncomfortable" discourse proceeds by fits and starts; it is characterized by instability of behavioral form, verbal and nonverbal.

We wanted to know more specifically *how* the counselor responded asymmetrically at these uncomfortable moments, what was involved behaviorally in conducting interaction by fits and starts. The "asymmetry segments chart" shed light on the process of conducting discourse uncomfortably, but still provided only general outlines. Coding at this level of abstraction was useful for comparative purposes but was not close enough to the actual behavior to provide a clear picture of its structure. For this purpose, the kinesic and speech rhythm chart coding procedures described in Chapters 4 and 5 were developed.

References

Austin, John L.
  1962 *How to Do Things with Words*. Cambridge, Mass.: Harvard University Press.
Bar-Hillel, Yehoshua
  1952 Mr. Geach on rigour in semantics. *Mind 61*: 261–264.
Barth, Fredrik
  1969 *Ethnic Groups and Boundaries: The Social Organization of Culture Difference.*
        Boston: Little, Brown.
Basso, Keith
  1970 To give up on words: Silence in western Apache culture. *Southwestern Journal
        of Anthropology 26*: 213–230.
Bateson, Gregory
  1972 The message "This is play." In *Steps toward an Ecology of Mind*. New York:
        Ballantine Books.
Bateson, Gregory, Roy Birdwhistell, Norman McKeown, Margaret Mead, H. W. Brasen,
  and G. F. Hockett.
  n.d. *The Natural History of an Interview*. Chicago: University of Chicago, unpub-
        lished. (A ms. is available at the University of Chicago Library.)
Bauman, Richard, and Joel Sherzer
  1975 The ethnography of speaking. In *Annual Review of Anthropology 4*: 95–119.
        Palo Alto, Calif.: Annual Reviews, Inc.
Beebe, Beatrice, Daniel Stern, and Joseph Jaffe
  1980 The kinesic rhythm of mother–infant interactions. In A. Siegman and S. Feld-
        stein (eds.), *Of Speech and Time: Temporal Patterns in Interpersonal Contexts*.
        Hillsdale, N.J.: Lawrence Erlbaum.

Bennett, Adrian
  1977 Everybody got rhythm: The coordination of verbal and nonverbal channels in conversation. In Walburger von Raffler-Engel and Bates Hoffer (eds.), *Aspects of Non-verbal Communication*. San Antonio, Tex.: Trinity University Press.

Birdwhistell, R. L.
  1970 *Kinesics and Context: Essays on Body Motion Communication*. Philadelphia: University of Pennsylvania Press.

Blom, Jan-Petter and John J. Gumperz
  1972 Social meaning in linguistic structure: Code switching in Norway. In J. J. Gumperz and D. H. Hymes (eds.), *Directions in Sociolinguistics*. New York: Holt, Rinehart and Winston.

Boggs, Steven and Karen Watson-Gegeo
  1979 Interweaving routines: Strategies for encompassing a social situation. *Language and Society 7:* 375–392.

Bowles, Samuel, and Herbert Gintis
  1976 *Schooling in Capitalistic America: Educational Reform and the Contradictions of Economic Life*. New York: Basic Books.

Brazelton, T. Berry, Barbara Koslowski, and Mary Main
  1974 The origins of reciprocity: The early mother-infant interaction. In M. Lewis and L. Rosenblaum (eds.), *The Effects of the Infant on its Caregiver*. New York: John Wiley.

Byers, Paul
  1976 Biological rhythms as information channels in communication behavior. In P. P. G. Bateson and P. H. Klopfer (eds.), *Perspectives in Ethology (Vol. 2)*. New York: Plenum Press.
  n.d. *From Biological Rhythm to Cultural Pattern: A Study of Minimal Units*. Unpublished dissertation, Columbia University. Ann Arbor, Michigan: University Microfilms, No. 73-9004.

Carkhuff, R., and B. Berenson
  1967 *Beyond Counseling and Therapy*. New York: Holt, Rinehart and Winston.

Cazden, Courtney, Dell Hymes, and Vera John
  1972 *Functions of Language in the Classroom*. New York: Teachers College Press.

Chapple, Eliot D.
  1979 *The Biological Foundations of Individual and Cultural Forms*. Huntington, N.Y.: Robert Krieger.

Chomsky, Noam
  1965 *Aspects of the Theory of Syntax*. Cambridge, Mass.: M.I.T. Press.

Cicourel, Aaron V.
  1973 *Cognitive Sociology*. London: Macmillan.
  1968 *The Social Organization of Juvenile Justice*. New York: John Wiley.

Cicourel, Aaron V., and J. Kitsuse
  1963 *The Educational Decision-Makers*. Indianapolis: Bobbs-Merrill.

Clark, Burton
  1960 *The Open Door College*. New York: McGraw-Hill.

Condon, William
  1974 Neonate movement is synchronized with adult speech: Interactional participation and language acquisition. *Science 183:* 99–101.

Condon, W. S., and W. D. Ogston
  1967 A segmentation of behavior. *Journal of Psychiatric Research 5:* 221–235.

Cook-Gumperz, Jenny
  1977   Situated instructions. In S. Ervin-Tripp and C. Mitchell-Kernon (eds.), *Child Discourse*. New York: Academic Press.
Corsaro, William
  1979   "We're friends, right?": Children's use of access rituals in a nursery school. *Language in Society 3:* 315–336.
Dreeben, Robert
  1968   *On What Is Learned in School*. Reading, Mass.: Addison-Wesley.
Duncan, Starkey
  1972   Some signals and rules for taking speaking turns in conversations. *Journal of Personality and Social Psychology 6:* 341–349.
Duncan, Starkey, and Donald W. Fiske
  1977   *Face to Face Interaction: Research, Methods, and Theory*. Hillsdale, N. J.: L. Erlbaum Associates.
Durkheim, Emile
  1960   (1893) *The Division of Labor in Society*, George Simpson (trans.) Glencoe, Ill.: The Free Press.
Erickson, Frederick
  1979   Talking down: Some cultural sources of miscommunication in inter-racial interviews. In A. Wolfgang (ed.), *Research in Nonverbal Communication*. New York: Academic Press.
  1977   Some approaches to inquiry in school/community ethnography. *Anthropology and Education Quarterly 8*(3): 58–69.
  1976   Gatekeeping encounters: A social selection process. In P. R. Sanday (ed.), *Anthropology and the Public Interest*. New York: Academic Press.
  1975a   Gatekeeping and the melting pot: Interaction in counseling encounters. *Harvard Educational Review 45*(1): 44–70.
  1975b   One function of proxemic shifts in face-to-face interaction. In A. Kendon, R. M. Harris and M. R. Key (eds.) *Organization of Behavior in Face-to-Face Interaction*. The Hague: Mouton. Pp. 175–187.
Erickson, Frederick, and Gerald Mohatt
  In press.   Cultural organization of participation structures in two classrooms of Indian students. In G. D. Spindler (ed.), *Doing the Ethnography of Schooling*.
Erickson, Frederick, and Jeffrey Shultz
  1977   When is a context?: Some issues and methods in the Analysis of social competence. *Quarterly Newsletter of the Institute for Comparative Human Development 1*(2): 5–10; reprinted in J. Green and C. Wallat (eds.), *Ethnography and Language in Educational Settings*. Norwood, N. J.: Ablex Press, 1981.
Erickson, Frederick, with Jeffrey Shultz, Carolyn Leonard-Dolan, David Pariser, Clinton Jean, and Joseph Marchese
  1973   *Inter-ethnic Relations in Urban Institutional Settings*. Final Technical Report for Projects MH 18230 and MH 21460, submitted to the Center for Studies of Metropolitan Problems, National Institute of Mental Health.
Ervin-Tripp, Susan
  1979   Whatever happened to communicative competence? In *Studies in the Linguistic Sciences 3:2*. Champaign, Ill.: University of Illinois Press.
  1973   The structure of communicative choice. In Anwar S. Dil (ed.), *Language Acquisition and Communicative Choice: Essays by Susan M. Ervin-Tripp*. Stanford, Calif.: Stanford University Press.

1972   On sociolinguistic rules: Alternation and co-occurrence. In J. J. Gumperz and
       D. H. Hymes (eds.), *Directions in Sociolinguistics*. New York: Holt, Rinehart
       and Winston.

Fanon, Franz
1970   *A Dying Colonialism*. Harmondsworth, Middlesex: Penguin Books.

Fitzgerald, D. K.
1975   The language of ritual events among the *Ga* of Southern Ghana. In M. Sanches
       and B. Blount (eds.), *Sociocultural Dimensions of Language Use*. New York:
       Academic Press.

Florio, Susan, and Martha Walsh
1980   The teacher as colleague in classroom research. In H. Trueba, G. Guthrie, and
       K. Au (eds.), *Culture in the Bilingual Classroom: Studies in Classroom Eth-
       nography*. Rowley, Mass.: Newbury House.

Garfinkel, Harold
1967   *Studies in Ethnomethodology*. Englewood Cliffs, N.J.: Prentice-Hall.

Garfinkel, Harold, and Harvey Sacks
1970   The formal properties of practical actions. In J. C. McKinney and E. A. Tir-
       yakian (eds.), *Theoretical Sociology*. New York: Appleton-Century-Crofts.

Giles, Howard, and Peter F. Powesland
1975   *Speech Style and Social Evaluation*. London: Academic Press.

Goffman, Erving
1976   Replies and responses. In *Language and Society 5:* 257–313.
1974   *Frame Analysis*. New York: Harper & Row.
1961   *Encounters: Two Studies in the Sociology of Interaction*. Indianapolis: Bobbs-
       Merrill.

Goodenough, Ward
1976   Multiculturalism as the normal human experience. *Anthropology and Education
       Quarterly 7* (4): 4–7.
1971   Culture, language and society. Reading, Mass.: Addison-Wesley Modular Pub-
       lications, No. 7.
1965   Rethinking status and role: Toward a general model of the cultural organization
       of social relationships. In M. Banton (ed.), *The Relevance of Models in An-
       thropology*. London: Tavistock.

Gumperz, John J.
1977   Sociocultural knowledge in conversational inference. *Georgetown University
       Roundtable on Languages and Linguistics 1977*. Washington, D.C.: Georgetown
       University Press.
1972   Introduction. In J. Gumperz and D. Hymes (eds.), *Directions in Sociolinguistics:
       The Ethnography of Communication*. New York: Holt, Rinehart and Winston.
1968   The speech community. In David L. Sills (ed.), *The International Encyclopedia
       of the Social Sciences* (Vol. 9, pp. 381–386). New York: Macmillan Co. and
       The Free Press.
1962   Types of linguistic communities. In *Anthropological Linguistics*, 4(1): 28–40.

Gumperz, John, and Jenny Cook-Gumperz
1980   Ethnic differences in communicative styles. In C. A. Ferguson and S. B. Heath
       (eds.), *Language in the U.S.A.* New York: Cambridge University Press.

Gumperz, John J., T. C. Jupp, and Celia Roberts
1979   *Crosstalk: A Study of Cross-Cultural Communication*. Southall, Middlesex:
       The National Center for Industrial Language Training and B.B.C. Continuing
       Education Department.

Gumperz, John, and Deborah Tannen
  1979   Individual and social differences in language use. In C. Fillmore, D. Kempler, and W. S. Y. Wong (eds.), *Individual Differences in Language Ability and Language Behavior*. New York: Academic Press.
Hall, Edward T.
  1969   Listening behavior: Some cultural differences. *Phi Delta Kappan, 50*(7): 379–380.
  1966   *The Hidden Dimension*. Garden City, N. J.: Doubleday.
  1964   Adumbration in intercultural commmunication: The ethnography of communication. Special Issue, *American Anthropologist 66* (6,pt. II): 154–163.
Handelman, D.
  1973   Gossip in encounters: The transmission of information in a bounded social setting. *Man 8*(2): 210–227.
Hymes, Dell
  1977   Qualitative/quantitative research methodologies in education: A linguistic perspective. *Anthropology and Education Quarterly 8*(3): 165–176.
  1974   *Foundations in Sociolinguistics: An Ethnographic Approach*. Philadelphia: University of Pennsylvania Press.
  1964   Introduction: Toward ethnographies of communication. In J. Gumperz and D. Hymes (eds.), *Ethnography of Communication. American Anthropologist 66*(5, pt. II): 1–34.
Jenks, Christopher, and Marsha D. Brown
  1975   Effects of high schools on their students, *Harvard Educational Review 45*(3): 273–324.
Jenks, Christopher *et al.*
  1979   *Who Gets Ahead? The Determinants of Economic Success in America*. New York: Basic Books.
Jourard, Sidney M.
  1971   *The Transparent Self*. New York: D. Van Nostrand.
Karabel, Jerome
  1972   Community colleges and social stratification, *Harvard Educational Review 42*(4): 521–562.
Keenan, Elinor Ochs
  1977   Making it last: Repetition in children's discourse. In S. Ervin-Tripp and C. Mitchell-Kernon (eds.), *Child Discourse*. New York: Academic Press.
Keenan, Elinor, and Bambi Schieffelin
  1976   Topic as a Discourse Notion. In C. Liz (ed.), *Subject and Topic*. New York: Academic Press.
Keiser, R. Lincoln
  1969   *Vice Lords: Warriors of the Streets*. New York: Holt, Rinehart and Winston.
Kendon, Adam
  1977   *Studies in the Behavior of Social Interaction*. Bloomington: Indiana University Press.
Lyons, John
  1968   *Introduction to Theoretical Linguistics*. Cambridge: Cambridge University Press.
Maine, Henry Sumner
  1963 (1860)   *Ancient Law*. Boston: Beacon Press.
Malinowski, Bronislaw
  1923   The Problem of meaning in primitive languages. In C. K. Ogden and I. A. Richards, *The Meaning of Meaning*. New York: Harcourt, Brace & World.

Mayo, Clara, and Marianne LaFrance
1978   *Moving Bodies: Nonverbal Communication in Social Relationships.* Monterey, Calif.: Brooks/Cole.

McDermott, Raymond P.
1976   *Kids Make Sense: An Ethnographic Account of the Interactional Management of Success and Failure in One First Grade Classroom.* Unpublished dissertation, Stanford University.

McDermott, Raymond P., and Kenneth Gospodinoff
1979   Social contexts for ethnic borders and school failure. In A. Wolfgang (ed.), *Nonverbal Behavior.* New York: Academic Press.

McDermott, Raymond P., Kenneth Gospodinoff, and Jeffrey Aron
1978   Criteria for ethnographically adequate description of concerted activities and their contexts. *Semiotica 24*(3–4): 245–275.

Mehan, Hugh
1979   *Learning Lessons: Social Organization in the Classroom.* Cambridge, Mass.: Harvard University Press.
1978   Structuring school structure. *Harvard Educational Review 48*(1): 32–64.

Mehan, Hugh, and Houston Wood
1975   *The Reality of Ethnomethodology.* New York: Wiley Interscience.

Meyer, Leonard B.
1956   *Emotion and Meaning in Music.* Chicago: University of Chicago Press.

Moerman, Michael
1965   Ethnic identification in a complex civilization: Who are the Lue? *American Anthropologist 67:* 1215–1226.

Nelli, Humbert S.
1970   *The Italians in Chicago 1880–1930: A Study in Ethnic Mobility.* New York: Oxford University Press.

Parsons, Talcott
1959   The school class as a social system. *Harvard Educational Review 29*(4): 297–318.
1968   (1937)*The Structure of Social Action (Vol. 2).* New York: The Free Press.

Pelto, P., and G. Pelto
1977   *Anthropological Research: The Structure of Inquiry.* New York: Harcourt-Brace.

Philips, Susan
1975   The invisible culture: Communication in classroom and community on the Warm Springs reservation. (Unpublished dissertation), University of Pennsylvania.
1972   Participant structures and communicative competence: Warm Springs children in community and classroom. In C. Cazden, D. Hymes, and V. John (eds.), *Functions of Language in the Classroom.* New York: Teachers College Press.

Pike, K.
1967   *Language in Relation to a Unified Theory of the Structure of Human Behavior.* The Hague: Mouton.

Rogers, Carl
1951   *Client-Centered Therapy.* Boston: Houghton-Mifflin.

Sacks, Harvey
1972   On police assessment of moral character. In D. Sudnow (ed.), *Studies in Social Interaction.* New York: The Free Press.

Sacks, Harvey, Emanuel Schegloff, and Gail Jefferson.
1974   A simplest systematics for the organization of turn-taking for conversation. *Language 50:* 696–735.

Sapir, Edward
  1949   (1931) Communication. *Encyclopedia of the Social Sciences* (Vol. 4, p. 78),
          New York: Macmillan. Reprinted in D. G. Mandelbaum (ed.), *Selected Writings
          of Edward Sapir in Language, Culture and Personality.* Berkeley: University
          of California Press, p. 104.
  1925   Sound patterns in language. *Language 1:* 37–51.
Scheflen, A. E.
  1973   *Communicational Structure: Analysis of a Psychotherapy Transaction.* (For-
          merly *Stream and Structure in Psychotherapy*). Bloomington: University of
          Indiana Press.
Scollon, Ronald, and Suzanne Scollon
  1980   Face in interethnic communication. In J. Richards and R. Schmidt (eds.), *Com-
          municative Competence.* London: Longmans.
  1979   Literacy as interethnic communication: An Athabaskan case. *Sociolinguistics
          Working Papers No. 59,* Austin, Tex.: Southwest Educational Development
          Laboratory.
Sherzer, Joel
  1977   The ethnography of speaking: A critical appraisal. *Georgetown University
          Round Table on Languages and Linguistics 1977.* Washington, D.C.: George-
          town University Press.
Shultz, Jeffrey, J.
  1975   *The Search for Comembership: An Analysis of Conversations among Strangers.*
          Unpublished dissertation, Harvard Graduate School of Education.
Stern, Daniel
  1977   *The First Relationship: Infant and Mother.* Cambridge: Harvard University
          Press.
Stern, Daniel, and John Gibbon
  1979   Temporal expectancies of social behaviors in mother–infant play. In E. Thomas
          (ed.), *Origins of the Infant's Social Responsiveness.* Hillsdale, N. J.: Lawrence
          Erlbaum.
Sudnow, David
  1980   *Talk's Body: A Meditation between Two Keyboards.* Harmondsworth, Middle-
          sex: Penguin.
  1978   *Ways of the Hand: The Organization of Improvised Conduct.* Cambridge, Mass.:
          Harvard University Press.
Toennies, Ferdinand
  1957   (1887) *Community and Society.* Charles P. Loomis (trans., ed.) E. Lansing:
          Michigan State University Press.
Trow, Martin
  1966   The second transformation of American secondary education, in R. Bendix and
          S. M. Lipsit (eds.), *Class, Status, and Power.* New York: Free Press.
Van Ness, Howard
  1977   Social control and social organization in an Alaskan Athabaskan classroom: A
          microethnography of "getting ready" for reading. Qualifying Paper, Harvard
          Graduate School of Education.
Wallace, Anthony F. C.
  1970   *Culture and Personality* (2nd ed.). New York: Random House.
Waller, W.
  1932   *The Sociology of Teaching.* New York: John Wiley.
Weber, Max
  1978   (1922) *Wirtschaft und Gesellschaft* (Vol. I, pp. 1–14) (Tübingen, 1922) Trans-

lated as "The Nature of Social Activity" pp. 7–32 in W. G. Runciman (ed.)
Weber: Selections in Translation. Cambridge: Cambridge University Press.

Yngve, Victor H.

1970   On getting a word in edgewise. *Papers From the Sixth Regional Meeting,
Chicago Linguistic Society*, pp. 567–577. Chicago: Chicago Linguistic Society.

Zorbaugh, Harvey

1928   *The Gold Coast and the slum*. Chicago: University of Chicago Press.

Subject Index

Printed in the United Kingdom
by Lightning Source UK Ltd.
99743UKS00001B/94-102